Praise for *The Leap* WITHDRAWN

"It's high time we got clearer on what enlightenment is and isn't. *The Leap* is readable, important, and long overdue. It offers a thorough portrait of this long-mysterious state with care and love."

— Dr. Robert K.C. Forman, author of
Enlightenment Ain't What It's Cracked Up to Be
and *Mysticism, Mind, Consciousness*

"In *The Leap*, Steve Taylor takes a radically new approach to spiritual awakening, suggesting that the experience is more common than one might suspect, is not bound to any religious or spiritual tradition, and may be playing an essential role in human evolution. *The Leap* is filled with provocative statements, some of which you may agree with and some you may disagree with — but you can be sure that this is a book you will never forget. It establishes Steve Taylor as a major spiritual author and teacher, whose lucid and articulate writing will evoke wonder and wisdom among readers."

— Stanley Krippner, PhD, Alan Watts Professor of Psychology,
Saybrook University, and coauthor of
Personal Mythology and *Haunted by Combat*

"A wonderfully detailed demystification of awakening within and without traditions that is a pleasure to read and offers hope for our dangerous times."

— Claudio Naranjo, author of *Healing Civilization* and designer of the
SAT Programs for personal and professional development

"A wonderful synthesis of modern research and timeless wisdom that makes the mysterious process of spiritual awakening more comprehensible than ever before."

— Peter Russell, author of *From Science to God*

"This book is both insightful and inspiring. Building on the foundations of his previous books, Steve Taylor's expertise and profound understanding of awakened states shine through and culminate in his proposition of an evolutionary leap that awaits humankind. For anyone who is interested in or has experienced an awakening, this book is not to be missed, as Taylor eloquently conveys an in-depth understanding of this fascinating phenomenon. It's an excellent book that everyone should read."

— **Dr. Penny Sartori**, author of *The Wisdom of Near-Death Experiences*

THE
LEAP

• An Eckhart Tolle Edition •

THE LEAP

THE PSYCHOLOGY OF SPIRITUAL AWAKENING

STEVE TAYLOR

FOREWORD BY ECKHART TOLLE

New World Library
Novato, California

An Eckhart Tolle Edition
www.eckharttolle.com

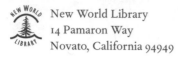

New World Library
14 Pamaron Way
Novato, California 94949

Text design by Tona Pearce Myers

Library of Congress Cataloging-in-Publication Data
Names: Taylor, Steve, [date]– author.
Title: The leap : the psychology of spiritual awakening / Steve Taylor.
Description: Eckhart Tolle Edition. | Novato, CA : New World Library, 2017. |
   Includes bibliographical references.
Identifiers: LCCN 2016044908 (print) | LCCN 2016051080 (ebook) |
ISBN 9781608684472 (alk. paper) | ISBN 9781608684489 (Ebook)
Subjects: LCSH: Psychology, Religious. | Spirituality—Psychology. | Religious
   awakening.
Classification: LCC BL53 .T39 2017 (print) | LCC BL53 (ebook) | DDC
   204/.2—dc23
LC record available at https://lccn.loc.gov/2016044908

First printing, February 2017
ISBN 978-1-60868-447-2
Ebook ISBN 978-1-60868-448-9
Printed in Canada on 100% postconsumer-waste recycled paper

New World Library is proud to be a Gold Certified Environmentally Responsible Publisher. Publisher certification awarded by Green Press Initiative.
www.greenpressinitiative.org

10   9   8   7   6   5   4   3   2

Contents

Foreword by Eckhart Tolle   ix

Introduction   1

1 Falling Asleep, Longing to Awaken   13

2 Wakefulness in Different Cultures   25

3 Natural Wakefulness: Awakened Artists   43

4 Natural Wakefulness: Confusion and Integration   61

5 Gradual Awakening in Spiritual Traditions   75

6 Gradual Awakening outside Spiritual Traditions   89

7 Sudden Awakening: Transformation through Turmoil   105

8 Sudden Awakening: *Kundalini* and Energetic Awakening   129

9 Other Types of Sudden Awakening: Is It Possible to Awaken through Psychedelics or Technology?   141

10 The Aftermath of Awakening: Spiritual Crisis   157

11 After the Storm: Lingering Traits and Questionable Teachers   175

12 What It Means to Be Awake: A New World and a New Self   183

13 What It Means to Be Awake: A New Mind and a New Life   199

14 The Natural Wakefulness of Children   219

15 Demythologizing Wakefulness   235

16 The Evolutionary Leap: A Collective Awakening   251

The Human Race Will Rise Again   269

Acknowledgments   271

Appendix: An Inventory of Spiritual/Secular Wakefulness   273

Notes   275

Bibliography   287

Resources   293

Index   295

About the Author   305

Foreword

You are a human being. These two words not only describe who you are as a member of a particular species but, if examined more deeply, also point to the twofold nature of your identity. *Human* is who you are on the level of form; that is to say, your body and mind. Those two aspects of your form identity make up your conditioned self. That self is conditioned by genetics and the environment, as well as other factors as yet unknown to science. *Being*, on the other hand, points to the essence of who you are as timeless, formless, and unconditioned consciousness. *Human* and *being*, form and essence, are ultimately not separate, in the same way that a wave or ripple on the surface of the ocean is not separate from the ocean or from any other wave or ripple, although it may appear to be so.

Being, or pure consciousness, emanates from the Universal Source of all life — God — as light emanates from the sun. Unlike the sun, however, the Source does not exist in space and time. It is unmanifested and therefore inconceivable, so there is nothing you can say about it. However, your consciousness emanates from the Source, so you can never be separate from it, just as a ray of sunlight cannot be separate from the sun but always remains connected with it. The Source emanation pervades the entire cosmos — which is to say, our dimension of space and time — and it is the intelligence underlying and guiding the evolution of what we perceive as the physical universe. So the universe, including human beings, was not just created in the distant past but is still in the process of being created. It's a work in progress, so to speak. You need to understand this basic premise to be able to appreciate and derive great benefit from reading this book. As Steve Taylor puts it, evolution is not just behind us, but in front of us as well.

Furthermore, and contrary to the creed of our mainstream culture, there is direction and purpose behind the evolutionary process, as he explains in this book. Where it is going, however, is beyond all imagination. What we *can* say is that the evolutionary impulse behind the process is the growth of consciousness. The universe wants to become more conscious, and the main life purpose for all human beings is to come into alignment with that universal purpose. Seen from a higher perspective, of course, all that exists is already in alignment with it, even if it seems to be opposed to that purpose, but it is aligned only unconsciously. Entering into conscious alignment with universal purpose is an amazing evolutionary leap.

However, what does it really mean for human beings at their current evolutionary stage to "become more conscious" or to "awaken"? If I had to put it in a nutshell, I would define it as "disidentification from thinking." When you realize that the voice in your head, your incessant compulsive thinking, is not who you are, then you have begun to awaken. A new dimension of consciousness has arisen, which we could call *awareness*, *presence*, or *wakefulness*. You haven't fallen below thought; you have risen above it. Now you can use thought instead of being used by it. Your sense of self shifts from identification with your mental positions and narratives to the alive presence within you, which is consciousness itself. You realize the *being* behind the *human*, so to speak. Something that transcends your conditioned personality begins to emerge. You realize your essential identity as unconditioned consciousness itself, and you can verify within yourself the truth of Jesus's words: "You are the light of the world."

Although this book provides plentiful conceptual clarification regarding wakefulness, as well as many highly interesting firsthand accounts by people who have experienced that shift in consciousness, you cannot truly understand the meaning of awakening except through awakening, which means going beyond discursive thinking and concepts. The concepts, however, can be helpful if used rightly, as pointers toward realization rather than as ultimate explanations or mental constructs that you need to believe in. In any case, this book will be of real benefit to readers who are either already undergoing the awakening process or who have reached a point of readiness, perhaps as a result of experiencing a deep crisis, a loss, or some kind of psychological turmoil in their lives. This book can greatly assist those readers in understanding what is happening to them and coping with the confusion or disorientation that often accompanies the initial stages of that shift in consciousness. Others may discover that they have already had awakening experiences without realizing it or that they have been going through a gradual awakening for some time without recognizing it for what it is.

The fact that enormous collective challenges almost certainly lie ahead for humanity — most of them self-created by the unawakened, egoic state of consciousness that still has the majority of humans in its grip — should not be interpreted as an indication that a more widespread awakening is not going to occur. The opposite is probably the case: the crises we are experiencing, and the greater turmoil to come, may act as a catalyst for a collective shift in consciousness. As Steve Taylor puts it: "The evolutionary leap was already under way before these problems became so serious, but perhaps it has become — and is becoming — more powerful as a result of them."

Challenges are the lifeblood of all evolution. Every life-form, from plants to animals to humans, evolves as a response to the challenges it encounters. Your comfort zone is not the most likely place where you are going to find spiritual awakening, although the ego may tell you otherwise. If you look to people, places, things, or circumstances for fulfillment or happiness, you will be disappointed again and again. Don't tell the world, "Make me happy!" You would be placing an impossible demand on it and condemning yourself to perpetual frustration. Instead, allow the world to make you conscious. You may find that every challenge, every obstacle that life seems to put in your path, is an opportunity for awakening, for becoming present, or for deepening the state of presence. Many challenges you encounter, whether of a personal or collective nature, will have been created by human unconsciousness, either your own or that of other people. Every seeming obstacle to your happiness or fulfillment is a potential portal into presence! Just modify your response to it and see what happens. Your life is not determined by what happens to you, but by how you respond to what happens. Most importantly, don't add to the collective unconsciousness, which manifests particularly in the media and politics, through your reactivity. Bring the light of consciousness to every encounter, every problem, and every Facebook post!

Life always gives you what you need, and right now it has given you this book to use as a guide or companion through challenging times. It contains a great deal of precious wisdom, expressed in the straightforward, clear, and down-to-earth language that Steve Taylor is so good at. I have a feeling that, by way of a miracle, it may even reach one or two people in the media and in politics!

— Eckhart Tolle, bestselling author of
The Power of Now and *A New Earth*

Introduction

I used to think that spiritual awakening was out of the ordinary — an extremely rare state that is practically impossible to attain, unless you're prepared to become a hermit and spend decades meditating for hours a day in solitude and silence. I thought that probably only a small number of human beings in history had ever become awakened, that is, attained an ongoing state of inner peace and wholeness with a sense of connection or unity with the world around them, and a selfless desire to love and support their fellow human beings. I certainly hadn't met anyone like that, and I didn't expect to — at least not in this lifetime. It goes without saying that I didn't consider myself to be awakened either.

I associated spiritual awakening with Eastern traditions, such as Buddhism and Hinduism. The term *enlightenment* conjured images of monks with shaved heads and red robes, or gurus with long beards surrounded by flowers and prostrating devotees. I assumed that if there were any spiritual awakened people alive, most of them were in India, or perhaps Tibet or China. After all, that is where the greatest and purest spiritual traditions and the world's most profound spiritual texts such as the Upanishads and the Dao De Jing came from.

In comparison, my own Western European culture seemed like a spiritual desert. I liked reading about Christian mystics, and it was clear that some of them had been spiritually awakened (or at least had had glimpses of awakening), but the Christian religion itself seemed too laden with beliefs and concepts to serve as a framework for spiritual awakening. The happiness paradigm of my culture meant doing well at school and college, getting a good job with good prospects, buying a nice house where I could

entertain myself by watching television and surround myself with possessions and comforts. Life was all about achievement and entertainment, material goods and fun. Surely if I wanted to find enlightenment or awakened
individuals, I had to go to the East.

I was wrong. This book describes how I came to learn that spiritual
awakening is far from uncommon. It describes how I came to learn that it
doesn't just happen to Eastern sages but to seemingly ordinary people in all
walks of life. It describes how, after a number of encounters with ordinary
awakened people, I began to study spiritual awakening as a psychologist.

My study began with the dissertation for my master's degree, then my
PhD, and then my research as an academic. I began to seek out people who
had undergone a shift into a higher — a more expansive and harmonious
— state of being. Initially, for my master's dissertation, I sought out people
who had undergone this shift following intense trauma and turmoil in their
lives. I was surprised how easy it was to find cases, and many more people contacted me to share similar experiences once my initial research was
published. Then I decided to broaden my research and investigate cases of
spiritual awakening that weren't specifically linked to turmoil and trauma.
I investigated other types of awakening — people who had undergone a
gradual awakening through years or decades of spiritual investigations or
practice, and a small number of people who simply seemed to be naturally
awakened; that is, people who have been awake for as long as they can
remember, without making any special effort or undergoing any transformative experience.

The vast majority of people I interviewed aren't spiritual teachers and
don't see themselves as part of any particular spiritual tradition or religion.
These people have conventional jobs and no backgrounds in spiritual traditions or practices. (As a result, in many cases, they were initially confused
by what happened to them.) Partly because of this, I began to detach the
concept of awakening from religious and even spiritual traditions. I began
to see it as a particular state of mind and being that could be interpreted in
terms of spiritual traditions but didn't necessarily belong to them.

Throughout history, the shift into wakefulness has often happened to
people who were part of religious or spiritual traditions, and so it was usually interpreted in terms of those traditions. If it happened to a Buddhist

monk, the shift was described as *bodhi*, or "enlightenment"; if it happened to a Hindu, it might be termed *moksha* (freedom) or *sahaja samadhi* (permanent or ongoing oneness); if it happened to a Sufi, it might be described as *baqa*, or "abiding in God"; if it happened to a Christian, it might be termed *deification*, or union with God. However, the shift into wakefulness can also occur — and most often does, according to my research — outside these traditions and so doesn't have to be interpreted in religious or spiritual terms.

Different spiritual traditions explain and interpret this shift in different ways, emphasizing different aspects. It's as if they offer different views of the same landscape, magnifying, filtering, and selecting certain features. But when the shift occurs outside spiritual traditions — that is, in people who don't have a spiritual background and so don't have a ready framework within which to interpret it — it's as if we're given a view of the landscape itself, in a more naked and unconstructed state.

Through my research as a psychologist I've attempted to identify the characteristics of this shift, the different ways in which it can occur, and the reasons why it occurs. What are the triggers or causes of awakening? Why does it occur to some people and not others? What actually happens inside a person's being or psyche when they experience awakening? In what way do awakened or wakeful people experience the world differently than others? How are their relationships, values, and goals different? How does wakefulness relate to our species as a whole and to the overall evolution of consciousness?

These are some of the main topics I'll be discussing throughout this book. There's a great deal of confusion about enlightenment — partly because it has been interpreted in so many different ways by different teachers in different traditions — and I'd like to dispel some of this. Terms such as *spiritual awakening* and *enlightenment* often have different meanings to different people. If you ask a hundred different spiritual teachers how they define *wakefulness* or *enlightenment*, you will probably get a hundred different answers. Many people have an impulse to wake up but, because of this general confusion, they aren't completely sure where they're heading or where they should go. I hope to clear up some of this confusion by clearly identifying the characteristics of wakefulness and by establishing exactly what it means to live in the state.

My Approach in This Book

This book stems from other important avenues of study, besides my research as a psychologist. I've been studying the world's spiritual traditions and practices since the age of nineteen. I've gained a thorough, wide-ranging knowledge of their different interpretations and approaches, how they understand and interpret the state of wakefulness, and the practices and paths they recommend to cultivate it. I don't adhere to any particular tradition myself, although I've always felt a strong affinity with Indian traditions such as Vedanta, Yoga, and Tantra, and also with Chinese Daoism. At the same time, I have a deep respect for the Buddhist, Christian, Jewish, and Sufi spiritual traditions.

Another important avenue is my own personal experience of wakefulness, which impelled me to investigate the state and without which none of my research would make any sense. Although this book isn't autobiographical, it describes how, in the process of discovering that the state of wakefulness is much more common than I had realized, I also discovered that it is in the closest place of all — my own being. After believing that awakening only happened to a small number of people in remote parts of the world, I came to realize that it had actually happened to *me*.

I don't try to explain away this state as the result of unusual brain activity. As a psychologist, I've never been particularly interested in studying the brain and examining the type of neuronal activity associated with particular experiences. Some scientists have suggested that spiritual experiences can be linked to increased or reduced activity in certain parts of the brain, but to me, this isn't particularly relevant. It's like studying the map of a country rather than exploring the country itself.

The assumption that spiritual experiences are *generated* by certain types of brain activity is highly dubious. For a start, the assumption that the brain is the source of *any* of our conscious experience is problematic. In the language of the philosophy of consciousness, this is the "hard problem" of explaining how the soggy lump of matter that we call the brain can give rise to the amazing richness and variety of our subjective experience. (One philosopher suggests this is the equivalent of turning water into wine.[1])

In fact, it's just as valid to reverse this causal link and suggest that, if there are any particular brain-states associated with awakening experiences, these states can be *produced* by the experiences themselves rather than the other way around. If you're walking in the countryside and a bear jumps out in front of you, you will experience a surge in adrenaline and increased activity in the parts of the brain associated with fear and stress. Your experience of seeing the bear will correlate with a certain neurological state. But this neurological state doesn't *produce* the image of the bear. Wakeful states exist in themselves as experiences and can't be reduced to — or explained away in terms of   neurological activity.

In a similar way, I don't think it's possible to explain wakefulness away as self-delusion. Some people, including some self-appointed spiritual teachers or gurus, undoubtedly delude themselves into thinking that they're awakened. But this certainly isn't the case for the majority of people I encountered. I was deeply impressed by the insight and authenticity with which they described their new identities and experiences. Rather than escaping from reality into delusion, they have entered an intensified and expanded reality. They are living in a higher-functioning state, with a more authentic purpose, more authentic relationships, and an increased sense of connection. It is clear from the major changes they have made to their lives — and from the incomprehension they have attracted from the people around them — that they aren't just thinking themselves into believing that they're spiritually awakened. The difficulties some of them faced after awakening, including a sense of confusion, also indicate this. After all, if they wanted to escape into a self-delusory state of well-being, they would surely have excluded these difficulties from their experience.

At the same time, we should be alert to the possibility that some claims of wakefulness may not be genuine, whether this is due to self-delusion, narcissism, or a more straightforward desire to exploit vulnerable followers in order to gain wealth and power. In fact, one of the aims of my research — and of this book — is to establish the characteristics of the wakeful state so clearly that there's a means of distinguishing between fake and genuine wakefulness. Because spiritual teachers are unregulated, there has always been a problem with deluded or exploitative people setting up themselves as gurus and wreaking havoc among vulnerable followers. But if we have a clear idea of what it actually *means* to be awake, then it should be easier to identify fraudulent or deluded teachers.

A Sequel

The Leap is a kind of sequel, although an unusual one in that it's a sequel to two of my previous books rather than just one.

One of my previous books, *Waking from Sleep*, is a study of *temporary* awakening experiences or higher states of consciousness. I had always experienced these myself, and for several years I collected reports of them. In *Waking from Sleep* I analyze these experiences, looking at the characteristics, situations, and activities that generated them, and the underlying psychological and ontological processes that took place when they occurred. (Here I use the term *ontological* to refer to our being, in the same way that the term *psychological* refers to the mind.) I put forward a theory that the experiences are linked to an intensification and stilling of life-energy. This book attempts something similar but for states of *permanent* wakefulness.

However, *The Leap* is also, as its name suggests, a sequel to my earlier book, *The Fall*, which focuses on anthropology, archeology, and history. It suggests that the original state of human beings was one of natural wakefulness, in which people experienced the sacredness and aliveness of the world around them and felt a strong connection with nature and the whole cosmos. According to *The Fall*, earlier human beings experienced no sense of separateness from the world and could sense a powerful spirit-force pervading everything, including their own being. However, beginning about six thousand years ago, a "Fall" occurred. This was a shift of being, the development of a new kind of human self, with an intensified sense of individuality and a new sense of separateness. For the first time, human beings experienced themselves as separate from nature, from their own communities, and even from their own bodies. For the first time, they experienced themselves as individual entities living within their own mental space, with the rest of reality "out there," on the other side.

On an external cultural level, this shift expressed itself in many devastating ways. It caused a massive upsurge in brutality, conflict, and oppression. It gave rise to hierarchal societies and constant warfare between different groups. It led to the oppression of women and a new, repressive, guilt-ridden attitude toward sex. On an internal ontological level, it meant a loss of the natural spirituality that earlier peoples experienced (and that was retained by some of the world's indigenous peoples — some of whom retain it even now). Our ancestors lost a sense of nature's sacredness and aliveness, a sense of connection to the cosmos, and the awareness of the spirit-force pervading everything. The world became despiritualized and we became separate from it. We "fell" out of a natural state of harmony into a state of anxiety and discord.

Spiritual awakening is, in some ways, a reversal of this process. It means undoing the pathology of separateness and duality and regaining the sense of connection and harmony that earlier peoples experienced. However, at the same time, spiritual awakening entails a "leap" into a new state of being. Despite its disastrous effects, the new sense of individuality that our ancestors developed in the Fall brought some benefits: a new intellectual acuity that led to technological advances and a more rational understanding of the world. When we undergo a leap into spiritual wakefulness, we retain these benefits. We attain what might be called a trans-Fall state, which integrates the spiritual awareness of pre-Fall peoples with the intellectual-logical ability of the "fallen" era.

The term *Leap* has both an individual and a collective meaning. On an individual level, it refers to the shift out of an ordinary state of being into the more expansive higher-functioning state of wakefulness. And just as the Fall refers to a collective psychological shift that some groups of human beings began to undergo thousands of years ago, the Leap, on a collective level, refers to a movement toward wakefulness that I believe is occurring throughout the world, and involves the whole human race. The Leap is also a process of collective spiritual awakening.

The Structure of This Book

The structure of this book loosely follows the stages of awakening itself. We begin by examining the ordinary state of being that we wake up *out of*. We'll see that almost every culture in history has been aware of the possibility of waking up out of this limited state into a more expansive and intense awareness. We also examine the different ways in which different cultures have conceived of wakefulness.

Then we look at the process of awakening. I suggest that there are three different ways in which a person can wake up permanently. There are a small number of people who seem to have been born awake, whose awakened state unfolds naturally and easily without any special effort or particular event. Then there are those who wake up gradually over a long period of time, through a commitment to spiritual practice such as meditation and yoga, or through following spiritual paths, traditions, or lifestyles. And finally — and this is the largest group — there are those who wake up suddenly and dramatically, often following intense psychological turmoil. Because it is the most common form, we spend quite a bit of time examining sudden and dramatic awakening, and looking at several examples from my research.

Then we examine the aftermath of awakening and the difficulties that can sometimes occur. Particularly when it occurs suddenly and dramatically, awakening may involve a phase of spiritual crisis. In its most benign form, this may simply be a period of confusion. At the same time as feeling an intense sense of well-being and inner peace or fullness, the newly awakened person may be slightly puzzled by their new state, without a framework to make sense of it. In most cases, they will naturally gravitate toward spiritual traditions and practices, and come to understand the nature of their transformation. But in more extreme cases, sudden awakening may be very disruptive and cause psychological problems that could be mistaken for psychosis. There may even be physical problems, including unexplained pains and an inability to sleep. If the newly awakened person doesn't understand what is happening, and if they aren't supported through the process, there's a danger that they could be diagnosed with psychosis or schizophrenia. In fact, I believe that a good number of people who are labeled as mentally ill and put on high doses of psychotropic drugs may actually have undergone (or be undergoing) spiritual awakening.

Then we examine the characteristics of the wakeful state, based on my research, and how it differs from our normal sleep state. For me, these differences are mainly psychological and experiential. In many ways, awakened individuals experience a higher-functioning state that makes life more fulfilling, exhilarating, and meaningful than it may appear in a normal state of being. As a result of this internal shift, they often make major changes to their lives. They begin new careers, hobbies, and relationships. They feel a strong impulse to make positive contributions to the world, to live in meaningful and purposeful ways, rather than simply trying to satisfy their own desires, enjoy themselves, or pass the time.

After discussing the characteristics of wakefulness, we compare the characteristics of the awakened state with some of the characteristics of childhood. Does wakefulness imply a return — at least in some senses — to childhood? Is this perhaps what Jesus meant when he said that we must "become like little children" in order to "enter into the kingdom of heaven"?[2]

In the final section of the book, we turn to the collective aspect of awakening. Here I suggest that the best way to understand the Leap is in evolutionary terms. We're speaking of an *evolutionary* leap. We examine the evidence that this collective Leap is already under way and suggest that what we know as wakefulness could be the next phase in the evolution of consciousness on our planet. Wakefulness is higher than the present normal human state in the same way that the normal state is higher than the consciousness of other animals, including primates. In other words, awakened people may be prematurely experiencing a state that is latent in many other people — and in the whole human race collectively — and that will become more common as time goes by, and will one day become the norm. As long as we don't destroy the life-support systems of our planet and make ourselves extinct as a species, wakefulness may eventually become human beings' normal state.

At a time when the world is suffering massive challenges, it is essential that this collective Leap unfolds as quickly as possible. Our own conscious efforts to awaken are important to intensify the shift that is already under way. Our own personal evolution will contribute to the evolution of our whole species.

A Note on Terminology

Before sitting down to write this book, I thought long and hard about what term I should use to describe the state that is its subject. I initially considered *enlightenment*, but I've never been particularly comfortable with this term, partly because it's an inaccurate translation of the original Buddhist term *bodhi*. Nineteenth-century translators of Buddhist texts translated *bodhi* as "enlightenment," but it derives from the Pali verb *budh*, which means "to awaken," so the literal meaning of *bodhi* is closer to "awakening." Also, there's a tendency to think of enlightenment in completely positive terms, as a state of perfect bliss and ease in which all difficulties and faults drop away. This didn't seem wholly appropriate in view of some of the difficulties that many of my interviewees experienced.

I therefore decided to continue with the waking terminology that I adopted in *Waking from Sleep*, where I used terms like *awakening experiences* and *sleep*. In the present book, I use *awakening* to describe the shift from a normal to a higher state of being and the term *wakefulness* to describe the higher state itself. For me, the term *wakefulness* isn't as positively loaded as *enlightenment*. *Wakefulness* implies a wider, deeper, and more open awareness, which might not necessarily be a straightforward, trouble-free state.

Although I sometimes use the term *spiritual awakening* (even in the title of this book), I prefer the simple term *awakening*. As I've said, wakefulness, for me, is primarily a state of being, which often occurs outside the context of spiritual or religious traditions. I also suspect that the term *spiritual* encourages people to esotericize the state, to think of it as extraordinary and otherworldly, when I see it as natural and normal.

I initially toyed with more psychologically valid terms such as *higher-functioning state*, *state of expanded being*, or *state of optimum being*. But those sounded a little too clinical. In any case, the primary function of words is to describe concepts and pass on meaning from one person to another. Sometimes it's better to use terms that are familiar rather than inventing new ones. The terms *awakening* and *wakefulness* aren't perfect, nor could they ever be. After all, the state to which they refer transcends language. Ordinary language was designed to describe ordinary states of awareness, not a state in which subject/object duality fades away and the past and the future have no meaning or else become one with the present. Words are only signposts. And if you have already experienced the wakeful state yourself — even if only temporarily — then you know the reality to which they are pointing.

1. Falling Asleep, Longing to Awaken

When we use terms such as *wakefulness* and *awakening* it's important to understand what we're waking up *from*. In other words, it's important to understand the "normal" state of being that we transcend when we wake up.

As my terminology suggests, what we wake up from is essentially a state of *sleep* — a state of constricted, limited awareness, and of discord and suffering. This state is so familiar to us that we assume it's natural and normal, and we take it for granted. But, in fact, this state is aberrational, even pathological. It's a kind of madness that we confuse with sanity simply because we experience *real* sanity so rarely.

Here I'll discuss the main characteristics of this state of sleep. I won't go into extensive detail, as this is an area I've already covered in my previous books. For the sake of clarification, I'll divide the characteristics into four different categories. In chapters 12 and 13 I'll look at the characteristics of wakefulness using the same categories.

Bear in mind that there are variations in these characteristics. There are different degrees of sleep, just as there are different degrees of wakefulness. Some people are more asleep than others, just as some people are more awake than others.

Affective Characteristics of Sleep

The affective characteristics refer to the inner experience of being asleep, how it feels to live in a sleep state. The main aspect of this experience is our sense of *separation and disconnection*.

Separation and Disconnection

As I suggest in *The Fall* and *Waking from Sleep*, prehistoric humans — and later, the people who became known to us as indigenous peoples — experienced the world in a very different way than most of us in the modern world. One of the main differences is that they appear to have had very little sense of separation from the world. They felt closely connected to nature, to their land, and to the whole of the earth, to the extent that they didn't see themselves as individuals in the same way that we do. Their sense of identity extended into their land and their whole community. This is part of the reason why indigenous peoples have been so horrified by European people's rapacious attitude toward nature, their treatment of it as nothing more than a supply of riches and resources to be ransacked. Indigenous peoples feel a strong empathic connection to nature, that it's part of their own being, and so recoil from hurting the earth in the same way they recoil from harming themselves.

The collective psychological shift that our ancestors underwent thousands of years ago — the point when human beings began to "fall" asleep — occurred when they lost this sense of connection. A new, highly individualized sense of self developed. People began to experience themselves as egos enclosed within their own mental space, looking out at the world. For the first time, they experienced themselves as separate from the natural world — not beings who were living *in* nature, as a part of it, but beings who were somehow *outside* nature.

This new separate self brought a sense of ego-isolation, of apartness and aloneness. There was a new duality; our ancestors were "in here" with the rest of reality "out there." There was also a *fragmentedness*, as if human beings were fragments broken off the whole, with a feeling of loss and incompleteness. Other people were also "out there." As human beings, we became less connected to one another, with a weakened sense of empathy and community. Our own needs and desires as individuals began to take precedence over the welfare of the whole group.

This sense of separateness even extended to the body. Rather than see the body as an integrated part of our being, we saw the self — our own ego — as an entity trapped inside a body that was somehow *other* to us; the body was a vehicle that was carrying us but wasn't actually part of us.

At the same time, we became disconnected from *our own being* — from our essence or spirit. Our sense of identity became constricted to a very narrow focus — our own ego. In the same way that a city can become so large and prominent that it seems to be a separate entity from the rest of the land that it's a part of — and in the same way that the inhabitants of the city can lose touch with the rest of the land and see themselves *just* as city dwellers — we lost contact with the expansive radiance and spaciousness of our whole being.

Thought-Chatter

One of the strangest characteristics of our sleep state is the associational chatter — the endless stream of images, memories, anticipations, reflections, and snippets of information — that usually runs through our minds when we don't occupy our attention with external things. Again, we largely take this for granted, so it's difficult for us to understand how bizarre it really is. Why *should* we experience this random and involuntary thought-chatter whenever we turn our attention into our own minds? It seems to be a quirk of our strongly developed sense of ego, perhaps one that occurs when our ability to self-reflect combines with our abilities to recollect the past, anticipate the future, and imagine different scenarios. It seems also to be related to our sense of ego-isolation and the *constrictedness* of our sense of self, almost as if our thoughts become restless and agitated in response to the atmosphere of anxiety and lack of space.

Abstraction

Because of our ego-isolation and the thought-chatter that almost constantly runs through our minds, we spend much of our time in a state of *abstraction*. Rather than live in the world, we live in our minds. We perceive the world dimly, through the mist of our thought-chatter and filters of pre-existing concepts. Rather than live in a state of mindfulness, genuinely *experiencing* the reality of our sensations and perceptions, we live in a state of *elsewhereness* (as I refer to it in my book *Back to Sanity*).

In *Back to Sanity* I suggest that there are three different modes of attention that we experience as we live our lives: abstraction, absorption, and awareness (the "three As"). *Abstraction* is when we immerse our attention in our thoughts. *Absorption* is when we immerse our attention in external objects such as activities or entertainment. *Awareness* is when we give our attention fully to our experience, our surroundings, and the perceptions and sensations we're having in the present moment.

When I teach courses and workshops (either at my university or independently), I often ask participants to estimate how much time they spend in each of these modes in a typical day. People tell me, almost without fail, that they spend the least amount of time in a state of awareness. Typically, people estimate that they spend most time in a state of absorption (an average of around 60 percent), with their attention immersed in tasks, chores, hobbies, or distractions. They spend the second greatest amount of time in a state of abstraction (around 30 percent), and only around 10 percent of the time in a state of awareness.

Anxiety and Discontent

The internal mental atmosphere of the sleep state is a negative one. It's a dark, dank, and oppressive place, the mental equivalent of a small room with no windows and hardly any light.

The constant chatter of our minds creates a sense of disturbance and restlessness inside us, and the frequently negative tone of our thought-chatter generates negative emotions and an overall negative mood. Meanwhile, our ego-separateness creates a sense of lack, of "something missing," as well as a sense of isolation. Finally, there's a sense of narrowness, with our sense of self confined to the tiny space of our own ego, disconnected from the wide-open space of our whole being and its quality of radiance.

In our sleep state there's also a sense of *fear*. Our separateness creates a sense of vulnerability and insecurity, of being threatened by the world and by other people. This insecurity is exacerbated by our chattering thoughts, which anticipate the future and create fear-based scenarios that we imagine repeatedly. There's also usually an underlying fear of death, which we may not even be conscious of. Death threatens us by seeming to represent the end of everything we are, and everything we achieve or accumulate. It generates a sense of absurdity and meaninglessness, and so we do our best not to think about our own mortality.

A Perceptual Characteristic: Deintensified Perception

Another major characteristic of prehistoric and indigenous peoples' experience of the world was their intense perception of their surroundings. They seem to have had a sense that natural things were alive and sentient, and pervaded with a spiritual force. Different peoples with no connection to each other had different names for this spiritual force. In the Americas, the Hopi called it *maasauu*, the Lakota called it *wakan-tanka*, and the Pawnee called it *tirawa*. The Ainu of Japan called it *ramut* (translated as "spirit-energy"), while indigenous peoples in parts of New Guinea called it *imunu* (translated as "universal soul"). In Africa, the Nuer called it *kwoth* and the Mbuti called it *pepo*. These concepts are strikingly similar to the universal spirit-force that spiritual and mystical traditions speak of — for example, the concept of *brahman* in the Indian Upanishads. This spiritual force was also part of the reason for indigenous peoples' respectful attitude toward nature and their dismay at European peoples' exploitative attitude toward it. In addition to feeling a sense of kinship with the natural world, they felt it was spiritually *alive* and therefore sacred.

How did we lose this intense perception of nature and this awareness of a spirit-force in the world? How did the natural world become less real to us, more mundane and less sacred and beautiful?

This is partly because we live so much inside ourselves, in a state of abstraction. Our experience of the world is therefore less direct and immediate. But this loss of vividness is also related to energy. Our powerful sense of ego — and our constant thought-chatter — uses up a massive amount of energy, and as a result there's little energy available for us to use through *perception*. It may even be that, when the Fall occurred, our perception became automatized as a kind of energy-conserving measure so that the powerful new ego could have more energy at its disposal. Our attention was switched off to the world around us so that we didn't have to "waste" any energy in perceiving it.

As a result, the world became an inanimate place to us. We no longer sensed the aliveness of rivers, rocks, and the earth itself. We no longer sensed the sentience of trees and other plants, nor the consciousness of insects and other animals. The world became full of *objects*, which we were free to use and abuse for our own devices. We lost the awareness of a spirit-force pervading the world and all the things in it.

Rather than see all things as infused with this force and therefore all interconnected, we began to perceive separateness. The world became made up of distinct material objects with empty space stretching between them. As a result, we also lost the meaning and harmony that many indigenous peoples perceive in the world, and the sense of being at home in it. For us, the world became a neutral and even hostile place, and life became an empty space between birth and death for us to try to fill with enjoyment and any sense of meaning we could create through our own efforts.

Conceptual Characteristics

The sleep state is characterized not only by a certain kind of perception but also by a type of *con*ception — that is, a certain outlook on the world, and sense of our identity and our place within it.

Egocentric Outlook

In conceptual terms, one of the main characteristics of sleep is a *narrowness* of outlook. In sleep, people tend to be immersed in a narrow personal world of problems and concerns. They aren't particularly interested in other people's problems, or in social or global issues. Environmental problems, for instance, are too abstract and vague for them to make sense of. They aren't particularly concerned about global inequality or poverty, or even about inequality or poverty (or oppression or exploitation) within their own countries. Generally, because of their narrow vision, they only become concerned about these issues when they have a direct effect on them — for example, once disruption to weather systems brings regular floods in their towns or when they (or members of their family) are exploited or oppressed. Otherwise, these issues are too *wide* for them to comprehend, and their personal needs and desires usually take precedence over them.

Group Identity

In sleep, people have a strong need for identity and belonging. They feel a powerful impulse to belong to groups and to identify themselves as members of those groups in terms of religion, ethnicity, nationality, and any other label they can find. They like to define themselves as Christians or Muslims, Croats or Serbs, English or Scottish or Welsh, Republicans or Democrats or Socialists — even Manchester United or Los Angeles Lakers fans. Accordingly, they see themselves as distinct and different from those who belong to other groups, and are liable to fall into conflict with those groups whose interests may conflict with theirs. They feel the urge to help expand the power and influence of their group — for example, to convert people to their religion — and feel a sense of pride when their group prospers, such as when their nation expands its territory or when their sports team wins a trophy.

This need for identity and belonging is largely because of the sense of vulnerability and fragility generated by our separateness. We feel alone within our own mental space, with an overwhelmingly vast and complex world "out there," on the other side. We feel threatened and so need some support, to feel part of something bigger than ourselves, to provide shelter and protection.

As we'll see later, in wakefulness there's a completely different perspective. Awakened individuals have little or no sense of group identity. They see distinctions of religion or ethnicity or nationality as superficial and meaningless. They see themselves purely as human beings, without any external identities, who are no different from anyone else. As a result, they don't put members of their own group before others, but rather treat all people equally. They don't feel any pride in their nationality or ethnicity; they feel just as connected to "foreigners" as they do to their own "people."

Behavioral Characteristics

Because the sleep state brings so much discord and discontent, the effort to *escape* from their psychological suffering dominates many people's lives.

There are two major ways that people try to alleviate their unease. First, they try to simply *divert* themselves from their inner discord by immersing their attention in external things. This partly explains the massive popularity of television over the past half century or so — it's a simple and effective way to direct our attention outside ourselves and so escape our inner discord. Second, people try to overcome their basic sense of separateness and lack by *adding* things to themselves. They try to make themselves more significant by accumulating possessions and wealth, collecting achievements, or increasing their success, status, or power.

The sense of vulnerability and fragility I mentioned above also has a major impact on our behavior. Along with creating the need to join groups and take on different identities, it creates a strong need for *acceptance*. It makes us keen to *fit in*, to do what we feel is expected of us rather than follow our deeper impulses. As a result, we're in danger of living inauthentically, of suppressing our true selves for the sake of acceptance.

This sense of vulnerability also generates a strong sensitivity to *slights* or insults. Because we feel fundamentally insecure, it's easy for us to feel disrespected, to feel wounded by other people's behavior toward us, even if they don't intend to offend us. These emotional wounds often fester inside us for a long time, giving rise to resentment, creating grudges, and often leading to conflict between individuals and groups.

⌘

So this is our normal state of sleep: a state of separation and discord, in which we feel trapped inside our own mental space and subjected to the random chatter of thoughts and associations, and in which we're preoccupied with our personal concerns and dominated by a desire to escape our discord through diversion and accumulation.

Temporary Wakefulness

This state of sleep holds a great deal of power over us. Apart from during childhood, some people never experience any other way of being. They spend every moment of their lives asleep, without ever realizing that they're asleep. Consequently, they don't realize that it's possible to wake up. They're like prisoners who don't realize they're in prison, and so never think about escaping.

Very occasionally, however, most of us *do* experience brief moments of wakefulness, when the limitations to our normal awareness fall away and we glimpse a more intense reality. In *Waking from Sleep*, I examine accidental and temporary experiences of wakefulness. I define an *awakening experience* as "an experience of clarity, revelation, and joy in which we become aware of a deeper (or higher) level of reality, perceive a sense of harmony and meaning, and transcend our normal sense of separateness from the world."[1]

Awakening experiences occur when we temporarily transcend our normal state of being — or, more strictly speaking, our normal self-system. The structure of our normal self-system — with its strong sense of ego, firm boundaries, and automatic perception — dissolves away, like a tent swept away in a wind. This can happen in times of inner relaxation and stillness, when our normal thought-chatter fades away and there's a higher level of energy inside us, infusing our perceptions and enabling us to perceive the world more vividly. This is why awakening experiences are often generated by contact with nature, meditation, watching or listening to arts performances, and other sedate, mind-quieting activities.

Alternatively, our normal self-system may be temporarily swept away as a result of intense stress and psychological turmoil. In fact, my research shows that intense psychological turmoil — perhaps caused by loss, failure, divorce, or bereavement — is the most common trigger of awakening experiences (with contact with nature, meditation, and watching or listening to arts performances following closely behind). Turmoil and stress can be like an earthquake, breaking down the structure of the normal self and allowing a more expansive and intense state of being to unfold.

Different intensities of awakening experiences and different characteristics emerge at different intensities. A low-intensity awakening experience may be an experience of heightened awareness in which your surroundings become more real, alive, and beautiful. A medium-intensity awakening experience may include a powerful sense of connection, a feeling that you're no longer separate from your surroundings. You might feel a strong sense of compassion or love toward other human beings (and other living beings), sensing that you're not separate from them either. You might have an awareness that all things are pervaded with — or are manifestations of — a radiant spiritual energy so that all are essentially one. In a high-intensity awakening experience, the whole material world may seem to dissolve into an ocean of pure consciousness or blissful radiance, which you feel is the essence of the universe. You might sense that this is the essence of your own being, too, so that in a sense you *are* the universe.

The more intense awakening experiences are, the less common they are. Probably most of us have had low-intensity awakening experiences, and probably only a small number of us have had high-intensity ones.

However, awakening experiences are, by definition, only temporary. They might last a few seconds, a few hours, even a few days, but at some point the normal self-system reemerges and reestablishes itself, and we return to our normal state of being. It's almost as if our normal self-system exists as a kind of psychic mold or template, which is always able to reform. Or to use another metaphor, it's as if a tree has been blown down but its roots are still intact so that it can grow again.

But in permanent wakefulness the structure *doesn't* reform. Our normal self-system dissolves away permanently — not only the structure but also the mold or template so that it isn't able to reform. The tree is completely uprooted. In permanent wakefulness a new, higher-functioning self-system takes over, with a more expansive and intense awareness. The shift is so fundamental that the person may feel that they have been reborn, that they are a different person living in the same body.

In many ways the permanently wakeful state is a stable, ongoing variant of the temporary awakening experience, with the same fundamental characteristics. Perhaps the only major difference is that permanent wakefulness includes conceptual and behavioral aspects — such as a loss of group identity, a strong tendency to altruism, and a lack of interest in materialism or status seeking — that aren't so apparent in temporary awakening, simply because these characteristics don't have the opportunity to express themselves on a temporary basis.

I would therefore loosely define *permanent wakefulness* as a higher-functioning state in which a person's vision of and relationship to the world are transformed, along with their subjective experience, their sense of identity, and their conceptual outlook. This shift brings a sense of well-being, clarity, and connection. The person develops a more intense awareness of the phenomenal world, and a broad, global outlook, with an all-embracing sense of empathy with the whole human race and a much-reduced need for group identity.

You might doubt that it's actually possible to live in this state. Wouldn't permanent wakefulness make it impossible for us to focus on the practicalities of everyday life? How would we concentrate on earning a living, cooking our food, paying our bills, and so on, while living in a state of ecstasy and oneness?

It's important to remember that people who live in this state can *control* their experience. They don't helplessly swim in an ocean of blissful oneness all the time — they can still concentrate on practical tasks when they need to. They can still make decisions and plans, and organize their lives. But their sense of well-being, connection, and wholeness is always there as an undercurrent, in the background, which they can tune into at any moment.

The wakeful state is higher functioning in a variety of ways. Along with having a richer perception of the world and a more intense awareness, awakened individuals don't feel a sense of incompleteness or disconnectedness. Their minds aren't constantly assailed by buzzing, chattering thoughts that create a sense of discord and anxiety. They feel a fundamental sense of groundedness and wholeness, and a lack of self-centeredness. They're no longer preoccupied with their own concerns and desires; they feel a high degree of compassion and a strong capacity for altruism and self-sacrifice. And as my definition mentions, they have a wide sense of perspective and a decreased need for group identity or belonging, which means that they can extend compassion equally to all members of the human race (and other species) beyond all differences of culture and ethnicity.

As with temporary awakening experiences, there are different varieties and degrees of permanent wakefulness. Some people's wakefulness may be fairly low level; the characteristics of the state aren't particularly intense for them. For example, they may still experience some disruptive involuntary thought-chatter and occasionally find themselves identifying with it; and they may occasionally find themselves getting caught up in self-centered desires or ambitions. At the same time, they may experience a constant richness of perception, and a constant sense of participation in and connection to the world, rather than a sense of separation. They may also have little sense of group identity and a wide sense of perspective, in which social or global issues seem as important as their own personal issues. A person who experiences wakefulness to a high degree, however, may have little or no involuntary thought-chatter, and may experience a sense of *unity* with the world around them rather than simply connection. Again, as with awakening experiences, the more intense and the deeper the state of wakefulness is, the less common it is.

Over the next few chapters we'll see that the shift into permanent wakefulness can occur both gradually and suddenly. In gradual wakefulness, there are many steps along the journey between sleep and wakefulness, and many different shades between the two states. We could say that, at different points, a person may be slightly awakened, moderately awakened, or highly awakened. Sudden awakening is slightly different in that there's a dramatic shift from a state of sleep to a state of wakefulness without moving through the intermediate ground. But even here, there are different gradations of wakefulness. People can shift into higher or lower intensities of wakefulness.

You could think of the journey from ordinary consciousness to wakefulness as a path that leads up the side of a mountain (although it would be accurate to think in terms of many different paths up the mountain rather than just one). In gradual wakefulness, there's a slow and steady journey up the path, which passes all points along the way. But in sudden wakefulness, a person shifts dramatically to a point much further along the path, as if they have been teleported there. Even so, there's still a variety of different points that they can shift up to, in the same way that a helicopter might lift someone up to different heights of a mountain.

2. Wakefulness in Different Cultures

When the state of sleep originally developed — at the time of the Fall — most people accepted it as normal. They felt a sense of unease and frustration, but weren't aware of its source, and did their best to alleviate or escape from their psychological suffering.

However, a small number of people didn't accept their sleep state. Among cultures that underwent the Fall, there were a small number of people who rebelled against sleep. These people had a strong sense that it was aberrational and that their vision of the world was unnaturally constricted. They sensed that it was possible to experience a more expansive and intense state of being in which the world became sacred and spiritual again. In other words, unlike the vast majority of people, they sensed that it was possible for them to wake up, both temporarily and permanently. They experienced accidental moments of awakening, and began to realize that there were certain activities or practices that were likely to generate awakening experiences, such as fasting, sleep deprivation, meditation, or ingesting psychedelic plants or substances. These small groups of people also began to realize that wakefulness could be cultivated as a permanent state, and developed systems of self-development, featuring spiritual practices and lifestyle guidelines, to do this. They developed what we now know as spiritual traditions. Across Asia, they developed the traditions of Daoism, Buddhism, Vedanta, and many others. Across the Middle East and Europe, they developed the teachings of Sufism, Kabbalah, and mystical Christianity.

In the same way that a landscape can be seen from different vantage points, and every onlooker may emphasize certain features over others, all of these groups conceived of the wakeful state in a slightly different way. Because of the varying traditions and worldviews of their cultures, they all developed slightly different interpretations of what it means to be awake, and how to cultivate the state.

In this chapter, I'll summarize how the world's main spiritual traditions conceive of wakefulness and draw out the common themes behind their interpretations. One of the aims of this book is to look at wakefulness as a psychological state, outside the context of spiritual or religious traditions. But here we'll see how the state appears when it *is* interpreted in spiritual and religious terms. By drawing out the common themes, we'll be able to see the most important features of the fundamental psychological and ontological landscape that lies behind the different interpretations.

Wakefulness in Indian Traditions

Of all cultures in the post-Fall world, ancient India developed the deepest understanding of the state of wakefulness and the most sophisticated systems of self-development in order to attain the state. In the Hindu tradition (leaving aside Buddhism for the moment), this understanding is expressed through texts such as the Upanishads and the Bhagavad Gita, and in traditions such as Yoga and Tantra. In common with other traditions, Yoga philosophers made a clear distinction between temporary experiences of awakening and wakefulness as a permanent state. In its temporary form, awakening could occur as *savikalpa* or *nirvikalpa samadhi*. *Samadhi* literally means "ecstasy," and *savikalpa samadhi* literally means "ecstasy tied to a particular form." This means seeing the world as the manifestation of spirit, and realizing that we're part of its oneness and therefore one with everything in the world. However, in *nirvikalpa samadhi* the world of form disappears all together. It dissolves into an ocean of pure spirit, which one feels is the ultimate reality of the universe. (This is equivalent to the high-intensity awakening experiences I described in the previous chapter.) One has the same sense of oneness as *savikalpa samadhi* but without the concept of self. A person doesn't just become one with the world, they actually *become* it.

However, it's also possible to live in a permanent, ongoing state of *samadhi*, called *sahaja samadhi*. In this state, *samadhi* becomes integrated into everyday life. You can live a completely normal human existence — working, eating, and interacting with other people, even thinking when necessary — and may appear to be a completely ordinary person. But inside, you have no sense of separateness, and are free of fear and desire. There's a continual sense of inner stillness, peace, and wholeness. As the Upanishads express it, the individual self — *atman* — becomes one with the spirit-force that pervades the universe, *brahman*. You become aware that your essential nature — and the essential nature of all reality — is *satchitananda* (being-consciousness-bliss). Bliss or joy is the nature of *brahman*, so union with *brahman* means experiencing this bliss.

The main focus of Hindu spirituality, therefore, is *union*, which is one possible translation of the term *yoga*. Wakefulness in this tradition is about transcending the duality between subject and object, between the individual and the world. It's about realizing that, at the essence of your being, you are one with the whole universe. At the essence of your being is a blissful spiritual energy, a pure radiant consciousness, that is indestructible and eternal. This energy is also the essence of everything else that exists, and of the whole universe itself. When you experience this, you move beyond sorrow and beyond death.

Buddhist Concepts of Wakefulness

Buddhism grew out of Hindu spirituality but doesn't have the same emphasis on union. Rather, Buddhism emphasizes cultivating selflessness and equanimity. In Theravada Buddhism, the earliest Buddhist tradition, it's difficult to define wakefulness accurately because of the Buddha's reluctance to discuss metaphysical or philosophical issues. (In one text, the Buddha uses the analogy of a man who has been wounded with a poisoned arrow but refuses to let anyone remove it until he finds out where the arrow came from, who shot it, what caste he is a member of, and so on. In other words, the paramount thing is to pull out the arrow, that is, to relieve human suffering; the philosophical or metaphysical issues are a distraction.) *Nirvana* literally means a "blowing out" of the flame of life, a state in which you no longer exist as an individual and are free from the craving that keeps you tied to the wheel of rebirth. *Nirvana* can be interpreted as a simple state of extinction, in which you become free of suffering in the simple sense that you no longer have to be reborn into a world where suffering is the nature of things. Or it can be interpreted in more mystical terms, as a state in which you don't literally cease to exist but only cease to exist as a separate entity; the *separate self* becomes extinct as you become one with the whole cosmos.

However, in one text, the "Snake-Simile Discourse," the Buddha goes into detail about the process of awakening. He describes four different levels of wakefulness, which involve decreasing self-centeredness and desire and increasing detachment and equanimity. You become increasingly free from desire and aversion, until at the highest level of wakefulness — that of the *arahant*, or "fully realized being" — you reach a state of complete mental ease and equanimity, and lose any trace of ego. You live in a state of pure being, without the past or the future, and don't generate any new karma so that you will not be reborn. At this point, you are incapable of behaving improperly. Whereas the unawakened person has to make a conscious effort to be moral and virtuous (through the practice of *sila*), the fully awakened person is in a state of effortless morality.

In other forms of Buddhism, wakefulness is described more directly. In the later Mahayana tradition, it's described in terms similar to *samadhi*, as a recognition of the "suchness" (or basic reality) of things and an awareness of their underlying oneness. Suchness is sometimes associated with the concept of the *dharmakaya*, which has similarities with *brahman*. As with *brahman*, the whole world emerges from the *dharmakaya* and all things are one in it. According to the famous Japanese Buddhist teacher D. T. Suzuki, enlightenment means the realization of the *dharmakaya* within oneself and the experience of its "all-embracing love and all-knowing intelligence."[1]

The Mahayana tradition (and Zen, which is the form Mahayana Buddhism took in China and Japan) views wakefulness as a natural state that is always present, like gold within ore. In other words, awakening is a process of uncovering our true nature. Buddha nature is latent in all beings. It's an active principle with a transformative power so that awakening is at least partly a process of allowing this transformative power to manifest itself.

Wakefulness in Daoism

It's one of the strange synchronicities of history that many of the world's earliest (and still most profound, even today) spiritual and philosophical traditions emerged at roughly the same time, apparently independently of each other. At roughly the same time as Indian figures such as the Buddha and Patanjali (who wrote or compiled the basic teachings of Yoga in the Yoga Sutras) developed their teachings, further west, in ancient Greece, figures such as Heraclitus and Plato were developing the foundations of modern Western philosophy. And during the same period, to the east of India, Chinese sages were developing similarly profound teachings, making their own attempts to conceptualize the wakeful state and develop practices to cultivate it.

In ancient China, the concept of an all-pervading spiritual principle was called the Dao. The Dao (sometimes spelled with a *T*, as the Tao) is usually translated as "the way" or "the principle." It's the fundamental essence of the universe, a spiritual force that gives rise to all things and that flows through all things; it maintains the balance and order of the universe. As such, it clearly has similarities with *brahman* and the *dharmakaya*.

In Daoism, the spiritual-philosophical tradition that developed around the concept of the Dao, the term *ming* is closest to wakefulness. The ancient Daoist sage Chuang-tzu uses this term to describe a state in which you no longer experience duality and separation, and realize your true nature as the Dao and so become one with it. You "empty yourself out" until you are no longer an individual; you experience oneness. (Again, there are clear parallels with Hinduism here, with its emphasis on union and the transcendence of our apparent separation from the world.) As Chuang-tzu advocates, "Be empty: that is all. The perfect man's use of his mind is like a mirror."[2] In the state of *ming*, your mind is completely still as well as empty. And in this state, your life becomes the spontaneous expression of the Dao. You give up your own will and live in a state of "actionless activity" (*wu wei*). You still live an active life but don't act deliberately or with conscious intent. You simply allow the Dao to act through you.

As in Buddhism, the Daoist concept of wakefulness emphasizes equanimity. When you attain union with the Dao, neither positive nor negative events affect you. You have a peaceful, stable self-sufficiency inside you that nothing can disturb. You also lose the fear of death, because the distinction between life and death no longer has any meaning, as with other distinctions such as "I" and "you," and "I" and "the world."

In a more general sense, the great Daoist text, the Dao De Jing (or Tao Te Ching) — my own personal favorite of all spiritual texts, along with the Upanishads — describes wakefulness in terms of recapturing the spontaneity, openness, and unself-consciousness of childhood. In a strikingly similar way to Jesus advising us to "become like little children,"[3] the Dao De Jing advises us to "return to the state of the infant," and says that the person who "has in himself abundantly the attributes (of the Dao) is like an infant."[4]

Wakefulness in Monotheistic Religions

The concept of wakefulness is central to Daoist, Buddhist, and Hindu spirituality but it's less overt in the Abrahamic religions — Judaism, Christianity, and Islam.

In *The Fall* I suggest that the development of monotheistic religions represented a movement into further ego-separateness. When I began to read anthropological texts as part of my research for *The Fall*, I was surprised to learn that most of the world's primal or indigenous peoples aren't theistic in the sense we understand it. (According to the statistics of the social anthropologist Gerhard Lenski, for example, only 4 percent of contemporary hunter-gatherer groups have a concept of a "creator god concerned with the moral conduct of humans."[5]) "Unfallen" peoples don't believe in gods who oversee the world and control its events. Instead, they have concepts of a spirit-force or energy that pervades the world, and of individual spirits that interact with natural phenomena. Like gods, spirits can control natural events — they can cause illness, make rain, change the direction of the wind. However, they aren't conceived as anthropomorphic entities like gods but rather as abstract forces or powers, almost like vapors.

The concept of gods as personal, anthropomorphic beings was a result of the intensified sense of ego. On the one hand, it was a clear sign of how despiritualized the world had become. The natural world was no longer sacred, as it had been to primal peoples. Now sacredness was confined to specific places such as churches or temples, and to specific people such as priests. Now the "divine" was otherworldly, apart from the world rather than within it. At the same time, the concept of gods was a reaction to the aloneness and unease that human beings now experienced. The belief in gods who oversaw the world and controlled all its events was a psychological response to insecurity and separation. It made the world seem a more benign and orderly place, and gave people a sense of protection and security. In addition, believing that gods were always present, watching over them, helped to alleviate people's sense of ego-isolation or aloneness.

The concept of an afterlife associated with these theistic beliefs also performed an important psychological function. Particularly in monotheistic religions (not so much in polytheistic religions such as those of ancient Greece or Rome), the afterlife is conceived as an idyllic place, an eternal paradise in which we can satisfy all our desires and live in perfect bliss and peace, free from the suffering that blights our lives on earth. This concept of the afterlife acted as a consolation for the suffering that filled human life after the Fall — not only psychological suffering but also the social suffering of constant warfare, oppression, and brutality.

In this sense, there was nothing transcendent about monotheistic religions. They were a defensive reaction against the intensified sense of ego and its psychological and social effects. And this is still true. Conventional Christianity, Islam, and Judaism are conceptual rather than transformative; that is, they are based on beliefs and conventions of behavior rather than self-transformation.

However, within these cultures there were people who sensed the possibility of transcending their sleep state. These people — known as mystics — radically reinterpreted some of their religions' teachings in light of their experiences of wakefulness. They took religions based on consolation and radically reenvisioned them as transformational systems.

In this sense, wakefulness as it's expressed in monotheistic religions like Judaism, Christianity, and Islam takes people *beyond* those religions. When people wake up, they lose the sense of being identified with — and the need to belong to — a particular religious tradition. They begin to feel an all-embracing empathy and compassion that takes them beyond the divisions of religious or ethnic groups. As a result, such awakened individuals, even when they are affiliated with one particular religion, are usually ecumenical and open to other faiths. They see all religious and spiritual traditions simply as different paths to the same destination, or different views of the same landscape. Unlike conventionally religious people, they don't see their tradition's beliefs as "the truth" and try to defend them against opposing views.

Partly because of this, awakened individuals throughout history have had an uneasy relationship with the religious traditions they were affiliated with. Conventional religious leaders struggled to make sense of mystics' awakened interpretations of religious teachings and often viewed them as blasphemous. Whereas conventionally religious people conceive of God as a personal being who oversees the world from another dimension of reality, religious mystics see God as an immensely powerful and radiant energy that pervades the whole world. And most radically, religious mystics don't see this God as separate from themselves. God is the essence of their own being so that, in a sense, they are also God.

Such insights as these inevitably led to conflict with religious authorities and accusations of heresy. For example, the ninth-century Sufi mystic Mansur Al-Hallaj was prone to falling into a trance in which he would declare "I am the truth." He also wrote spiritual poetry describing his oneness with God, including lines such as:

> Thy Spirit is mingled in my spirit, even as wine is mingled with
> pure water.
> When anything touches Thee, it touches me too, in every case
> Thou art I.[6]

As a result, he was imprisoned for eleven years and finally executed. In the Christian tradition, the great fourteenth-century mystic Meister Eckhart may well have also been imprisoned and executed, if he hadn't died of natural causes before his trial for heresy began.

Wakefulness in the Jewish Tradition

In Judaism, the main mystical tradition is Kabbalah. As with Hindu and Daoist spirituality, the ultimate aim of Kabbalah is union with the divine, or *En Sof* (literally, "without end"). In the Zohar, the major work of Kabbalah, this state of union is called *devekut* — literally translated as "cleaving to the divine" — and described as a state of mental stillness and emptiness, ecstasy and awe. It's a place of no thought, in which we transcend our normal sense of ego and become aware of the harmony and unity of the cosmos, and also our own unity with it.

According to the Zohar, the universe and everything in it is pervaded with translucent light (in fact, the term *Zohar* literally means "splendor" or "brilliance"). This radiance is the fundamental reality of the world, but our normal, limited awareness — that is, our sleep state — denies us access to it. In order to experience it, we have to expand and intensify our awareness; we need to wake up. Kabbalistic texts recommend a variety of meditative exercises to do this, including prayer, chanting, visualizing symbols, contemplating the letters of the Hebrew alphabet, and contemplating and visualizing the wonders of the universe. They also recommend cultivating an attitude of indiscriminate joy, which creates an opening for the divine to flow through us (as opposed to sadness and depression, which close us off to the divine).[7]

The depiction of wakefulness in Kabbalah includes a strong altruistic element that isn't so much a part of Hindu, Daoist, or Christian traditions (although it occurs in Buddhism in the concept of the bodhisattva — the enlightened being who decides to return to the world rather than step off the wheel of *samsara*, in order to help other people become enlightened). The ultimate aim of Kabbalah isn't so much individual but *collective* transformation. When a person becomes awakened, their experience effects the whole of humanity, in the same way that when a light is turned on it illuminates the space all around it. Every person's awakening promotes *tikkun olam*, the "healing of the world." In the Zohar, the aim of prayer isn't merely to bring the adept closer to union with God but also to generate joy and peace in the world, which are "brought down" to the world and spread to all those who are open to it.

A different form of Jewish mysticism emerged in the Hasidic tradition, which originated in sixteenth-century Poland. According to Hasidism, God is present in everything, including the human soul (where God is "the soul of the soul"). In our normal sleep state, we're alienated from the divinity inside us; we live in a state of forgetfulness and separation. However, we can awaken to this divine presence through intense devotion, prayer, and meditation. These spiritual practices can enable us to transcend time and space and become absorbed into God so that we become one with the universe.

Wakefulness in the Christian Tradition

Evelyn Underhill, the great scholar of mysticism, identified five stages of awakening in the teachings of Christian mystics. The first stage is awakening of the self, when the mystic experiences heightened awareness and is aware of a divine energy pervading the world. These glimpses of wakefulness make the mystic painfully aware of the limits of their normal consciousness and encourage them to go through a second stage, purgation, where they try to transcend these limits by purifying themselves, living a life of renunciation and self-denial. This leads to the third stage, illumination, where heightened awareness returns but is more stable and intense, with a vision of all-pervading divine presence and an inner joy or ecstasy.[8]

For some mystics this is the end point of their development, but for others, according to Underhill, illumination is followed by a fourth stage, the "dark night of the soul." In this stage of desolation and despair the mystic feels abandoned by the divine, as if, in Meister Eckhart's words, "there were a wall erected between Him and us."[9] They feel spiritually arid and full of self-loathing. However, this dark night is actually a phase of further purgation, in which the soul empties itself out completely so that it can experience union with the divine.

If the mystic emerges from the dark night, they reach the final stage of the mystical path, that of union or deification. Here the mystic doesn't just *see* God in the world — as in the awakening or illumination stages — but becomes one with God. The soul becomes one with the ground of reality (or the "Godhead," as Meister Eckhart calls it) and with the entire cosmos. There's no longer a separate "I." The mystic's identity now includes the whole world.

The concept of union with God is as central to the Christian mystical tradition as it is to Kabbalah and Hasidism. A thirteenth-century Christian mystical text called *On Cleaving to God* even uses the same terminology as the Zohar. According to this text, we, through loving God, can "pour ourselves" into his being and become absorbed into it. In other words, our love of God can transform us into God. Meister Eckhart also describes how love allows us to "enter into" God and then enables us to "know Him as He is."[10] The sixteenth-century Spanish mystic John of the Cross writes similarly of a state of "spiritual marriage" with God in which we live in a "dark silence" that is at the same time "filled with light and heavenly music."[11]

It's worth emphasizing that these Christian (and Jewish) mystics aren't describing temporary *experiences* of oneness (although, of course, they describe these, too). Here they are talking about wakefulness as an ongoing, stable state of being. Again, they are describing a state akin to the Hindu concept of *sahaja samadhi*, in which a person lives in constant union with the divine throughout their everyday life. Evelyn Underhill gives the examples of fifteenth-century Catherine of Genoa and sixteenth-century Teresa of Avila, both of whom lived in "unbroken consciousness" of the divine at the same time as living highly active and productive lives in everyday society. The seventeenth-century French mystic Marie de l'Incarnation gives an excellent description of this state of permanent contemplation (or *sahaja samadhi*): "My soul has dwelt in her centre, which is God.... One can read, write, work, do what one will, and nevertheless this fundamental occupation always abides and the soul never ceases to be united with God."[12]

Wakefulness in Sufism

The goal of Sufism, the mystical tradition of Islam, is also union with God, not just as a temporary experience but as a permanent state. *Fana*, usually translated as "passing away," is the Sufi term for a temporary awakening experience in which a person's identity fades away and dissolves into union with the world, and nothing remains except divine radiance and oneness. In this way, *fana* is similar to the Hindu concept of *nirvikalpa samadhi*. And in the same sense that *sahaja samadhi* is seen as a permanent, ongoing state of *samadhi*, in Sufism *baqa* (or "abiding in God") is a more stable and ongoing variant of *fana*. The person doesn't cease to exist but their individuality is absorbed into God, giving them a permanent sense of his being pervading both the world and their own being.

In *baqa* the mystic no longer has a will of their own but lives in and through God in a state of ecstasy. The person no longer has a sense of planning their own life or making things happen. In this way, there's a strong similarity with the state of actionless activity (*wu wei*) that arises when we live in harmony with the Dao. Life unfolds naturally and spontaneously by virtue of divine power. As in Buddhism, there's a complete lack of desire and ambition, and a complete indifference to praise or disrespect.

Sufism emphasizes altruism and collective awakening, as do the Jewish mystical traditions. This differs from Theravada Buddhism, in which awakening effectively means leaving the world behind — becoming free of karma so you don't have to be born again. In Sufism, as in Kabbalah, the awakened person has a responsibility to share their wakefulness with others, to manifest it in the world of time and space. Their awakening contributes to the awakening of the whole human race.

The Core Characteristics of Wakefulness according to the Traditions

It's truly remarkable that so many people in different cultures at different times in history had the same insight: it was possible for them to transcend their normal state of being, which was limited and constricted, and cultivate a more expansive and intensive state. It's remarkable that so many different systems and paths developed independently as methods of transcending our normal state of sleep. It's almost as if, three or four thousand years after the Fall something was stirring within the collective human psyche — an impulse to awaken. (In *The Fall*, I refer to this as the First Wave.)

The similarities between different spiritual traditions' conceptions of the state of wakefulness (and the process of awakening) are so strong that it seems that they're all speaking about the same fundamental state but interpreting and framing it in slightly different ways. Drawing on the analogy I used earlier, they are looking at the same landscape from different vantage points. For example, it seems clear that the all-pervading spiritual force — God or the ground of reality — described by Jewish, Christian, and Sufi mystics is essentially the same universal spiritual force that Daoists refer to as the Dao and Hindu mystics as *brahman*. (The Jewish concept of *En Sof* is practically identical to the Hindu concept of *brahman*.) This all-pervading spiritual force is also essentially the same as the concept of spirit-force developed in indigenous cultures, as described in the previous chapter.

There are slight differences in the way spiritual traditions conceive of this force. For example, the Dao is conceived in dynamic terms, as a flowing force that we need to align our lives with. *Brahman* is more static and neutral — we aim to experience union with it rather than harmonize our lives with it. But the overall similarity is much more striking than the divergence. Across different traditions, this force is described as pervading all things and the spaces between all things. It underlies the whole phenomenal world in such a way that the phenomenal world may appear to arise from it, as a manifestation of it. It unifies all things, folds them all into its oneness. In addition, this spiritual force is frequently depicted as having qualities of radiance and bliss (as in the Vedantic concept of *satchitananda*, or being-consciousness-bliss). In the Upanishads and the Bhagavad Gita, *brahman* is often compared to the sun. For example, the Gita states, "If the light of a thousand suns suddenly arose in the sky, that splendour might be compared to the radiance of the Supreme Spirit."[13] We've also seen that the term *Zohar* can be translated as "splendor" or "brilliance." And the Zohar itself describes the universe as pervaded with translucent light. Brilliant radiance is a quality of the awakened person's inner self, too — this is the "inner light" of mystical Christianity or the "light of the *atman*" in Hinduism. This makes complete sense, of course, since the spiritual essence of the universe is also the essence of our own being.

(Interestingly, awakened people may also *emit* light. There may be an atmosphere of radiance around them that can be sensed and absorbed by other people. Many reports of encounters with awakened people describe this radiance. For example, when the English author and poet Edward Carpenter visited the spiritually awakened poet Walt Whitman, he was immediately aware of a "certain radiant power in him, a large benign effluence and inclusiveness, as of the sun."[14] Similarly, when the British spiritual author Paul Brunton visited the Indian sage Ramana Maharshi he described his awareness of a "spreading ripple of telepathic radiation from this mysterious and imperturbable man."[15])

Just as traditions conceive of an all-pervading spiritual force in slightly different ways, it's easy to see their different concepts of wakefulness

— *sahaja samadhi*, enlightenment, *ming*, *devekut*, union with the divine, *baqa* — as slightly different interpretations of the same essential state of being. If we compare their descriptions of the characteristics of wakefulness, we see the same themes emerging again and again, although with different degrees of emphasis. The same themes emerging across different traditions suggests that they are the main characteristics of wakefulness *itself*, as it exists before interpretation. Using the landscape analogy again, if the same features reoccur in every description of a lake from a different viewpoint, we can assume that they genuinely exist as inherent features of that lake. If just one person said that a mountain was purple, we may be doubtful, but if all the viewers said it was purple then we may be inclined to believe them.

So what are the core characteristics of the wakeful state according to the spiritual traditions we've looked at?

Perhaps the strongest theme is *union*. Wakefulness is a state in which we move beyond separateness and into connection and union. Most importantly, wakefulness means connecting with the spiritual essence of the universe — whether we call it *brahman*, the Dao, or God — and with the deepest part of ourselves. The universal essence is also the essence of our own being.

The biggest obstacle to this connection (both to the spiritual essence of the universe and to our own being) is our powerful sense of ego, with all its desires, ambitions, and attachments. The ego's strong boundaries enclose us within our own mental space; it separates us from the world. Therefore, we must weaken this self, soften its solid boundaries, so that we can transcend separateness and connect with spirit. (The traditions describe this process as self-annihilation and self-naughting.) Our senses of gravity and identity have to shift away from our narrow personal self and become part of a wider and deeper expanse of being.

A second characteristic of wakefulness highlighted by all the traditions we've examined is *inner stillness*, or *inner emptiness*. Awakened individuals don't have busy, chattering minds and aren't assailed by turbulent emotions and desires. They are peaceful inside; their consciousness is pure and calm, like a lake.

In fact, all traditions agree that developing inner stillness is an essential part of the process of awakening. In other words, if you want to wake up, you have to learn to slow down and calm your mind, and transcend the layers of thought and emotion that cloud your consciousness. Regular meditation is important for this reason, among others. By meditating you may come to realize that you're not your thoughts and make contact with deeper, more spacious layers of your being beyond thought. Meister Eckhart describes "the storm of inward thought" that normally plagues our minds, and writes that "if God is to speak his word in the soul, she must be at rest and at peace."[16] Similarly, the Maitri Upanishad describes how, "When the mind is silent...it can enter into a world which is far beyond the mind: the highest End."[17]

A third characteristic of the wakeful state across all traditions is *self-sufficiency*. Awakened individuals have little or no concern for world success, possession, or personal ambition and are unaffected by praise, blame, or humiliation; they have no need for other people's approval. They don't need to *add* anything to themselves such as success, status, or wealth because they already feel whole. The Buddhist Heart Sutra clearly summarizes this: "In their indifference to personal attainment, and their lack of desire for self-justification, enlightened men and women can never be humiliated or upset by others."[18] The Bhagavad Gita describes the awakened person as being "the same in pleasure and pain; to whom gold or stones or earth are one, and what is pleasing or displeasing leaves him in peace."[19]

However, this lack of concern for other people's opinions of them doesn't mean that awakened individuals have no concern for other people. On the contrary, their lack of self-interest and their increased sense of connection leads to a fourth characteristic of the wakeful state across spiritual traditions: *a high degree of compassion and altruism*. At the same time as connecting with the spiritual essence of the world and with their own essence, awakened individuals connect strongly with other human beings. They have a strong capacity for empathy, an ability to *feel with* other people. They can sense other people's suffering, frustration, and pain, which gives rise to an altruistic impulse to alleviate their suffering or aid their development. Partly because their own ambitions and desires are no longer important to them, they feel a strong impulse to *serve* others, and to practice kindness and generosity. This spirit of altruism is clearly expressed by the seventh-century Buddhist monk Shantideva, who writes: "I wish to remove the suffering of every living being, enabling all to move towards enlightenment.... My concern for the welfare of others gains me greater merit than any act of worship."[20]

Ultimately, this compassionate attitude stems from an awareness that spirit is present in everyone so that, in a sense, we *are* everyone else. Therefore, when other people suffer, we suffer ourselves. As the sixteenth-century Jewish mystic Moses Cordovero states, "Whoever sins injures not only himself but also that part of himself which belongs to another." In this way, it's important to love others because "the other is really oneself."[21]

A fifth common theme of wakefulness among spiritual traditions (related to the first theme of union) is the *relinquishing of personal agency*. In other words, awakening means losing the sense that you are directing your own life and following your own ambitions or plans. Instead, your life becomes the expression of something greater than you, of a force that is flowing through you. This is the Daoist idea of *wu wei* — actionless activity — when we realize that the Dao is our nature and everything we do is the natural expression of it. In monotheistic spiritual traditions, the mystic gives up their own personal will so that they can live through God — or so that God can live through them. In Kabbalah, for instance, a person's individual will has to be "raised" until it becomes one with *En Sof*, the divine principle that both pervades and transcends the world. When we align our personal will with God's will, we become agents of that divine will. A powerful, transformational energy begins to flow through us with which we can help heal the world.

Let me end by briefly highlighting two other clear — and in some ways obvious — themes. The first of these is that wakefulness brings a more intense and complete awareness of reality. The world as we perceive it in ordinary consciousness is only a limited, shadow reality. As the Greek philosopher Plato expressed it, we're sitting in a cave, staring at the shadows on the wall in front of us, while the real world passes behind us. In reality, the world isn't mundane and meaningless but radiant with meaning and harmony. In reality, there's oneness rather than separation. In Indian Vedantic terms, the illusion of *maya* (deception) is uncovered, revealing a world of unity in place of an illusory world of duality and separateness. Or in the words of the eleventh-century Sufi mystic Al-Ghazali, this is a state "whose relation to your waking consciousness is analogous to the relation of the latter to dreaming. In comparison with this state your waking consciousness would be like dreaming!"[22]

Finally, and perhaps most obviously, wakefulness is seen across traditions as *a state of intense well-being*. Every tradition agrees that to wake up means to transcend anxiety and fear and attain a sense of great serenity and bliss. In Buddhism, *bodhi* entails a cessation of suffering. In Daoism, *ming* means living with spontaneous ease. In Indian Vedanta, bliss is one of the qualities of consciousness itself, as in *satchitananda* (being-consciousness-bliss). The essence of *brahman* is joy: "*Brahman* is joy: for from joy all beings have come, by joy they all live, and unto joy they all return."[23] So self-realization is literally an awakening into bliss. Similarly, in Jewish spirituality, *devekut* is a state of joy and exaltation, as is the Sufi state of *baqa*.

The Perennial Psychology

It's fascinating that there are such close similarities between spiritual traditions — especially when the religions associated with them create so much division and conflict between them. It's tempting to suggest that the mystics of Judaism, Islam, Christianity, Buddhism, and Hinduism have much more in common with each other than they do with the mainstream followers of their religions. (A Christian monk I'm friendly with once told me that he felt much more comfortable talking to Buddhist monks than he did talking to born-again Christians.) Mystics from all traditions have the common aim of cultivating wakefulness, while the common aim of all mainstream religions is to offer consolation and psychological support. To use a medical analogy, while mystics try to heal themselves (that is, to transcend sleep), conventionally religious people simply try to manage the symptoms.

Near-death experiences are a good analogy to show the similarities between different traditions. It's common for people who "die" for a short time in medical emergencies (most frequently a heart attack or cardiac arrest) to experience a continuation of consciousness, even though their bodies and brains show no sign of activity. Researchers have found a number of core characteristics of near-death experience, including a sense of leaving one's body, traveling through darkness toward a place of light, meeting "wise" beings or deceased relatives, and so on. However, the experience is often interpreted in slightly different ways by people in different cultures. For example, when a Hindu person has a near-death experience they may believe that they've encountered Krishna, but when a Christian has the experience they may believe that they've experienced heaven and the presence of Jesus.

The same seems to be true of the wakeful state. The core state of wakefulness is interpreted in slightly different ways by people from different spiritual or religious traditions. The phrase *perennial philosophy* is sometimes used to refer to the common core of the world's religious and spiritual traditions, but perhaps it would be accurate (as the philosopher Ken Wilber suggests) to use the term *perennial psychology*. After all, the wakeful state isn't so much a way of thinking about the world (as the term *philosophy* suggests) but a way of *experiencing* it. It's a particular state of being that human beings in all cultures have experienced and which, in theory, is possible for *all* human beings to experience.[24]

By looking at the main themes of this state across different spiritual traditions we've hopefully gone some way to uncovering the essential psychological landscape of the state. It will be interesting to test these themes against the characteristics of the experiences of secular wakefulness, which we're going to look at in the following chapters, to make sure that we're dealing with the same essential experience.

Now, however, we're going to turn to the process of awakening and investigate how it occurs.

3. Natural Wakefulness:
Awakened Artists

There are three different ways in which wakefulness can occur. First, it may occur naturally. A person may simply be awake as their normal condition. Second, wakefulness can develop gradually over a long period of time, usually as a result of regular spiritual practice or adherence to a particular spiritual path. (For example, a Buddhist or Christian monk may gradually awaken as a result of following a lifestyle of self-discipline, meditation, silence, and solitude. A person who doesn't follow a particular spiritual path but regularly practices meditation and yoga — perhaps twice a day — may also gradually awaken.) And third, wakefulness may occur suddenly and dramatically, usually in response to intense psychological turmoil.

In the following two chapters, we're going to look at the first of these three ways: natural wakefulness. Before this, however, I'd like to clarify exactly what *happens* when a person becomes awakened. That is, I'd like to look in more detail at the steps involved in the process of shifting from a normal state to a wakeful state.

The Wakeful Self-System

One term that is important to understand in relation to the process of awakening is *self-system*. The self-system is largely equivalent to the term *mind*. It is everything that creates and constitutes who we think we are. It includes our sense of identity, with all the memories, beliefs, concepts, attitudes, and psychological attachments that inform it. The self-system also performs psychological functions such as concentration, information processing, cognition, and so on.

This self-system is an aspect of our being, but not our whole being. The self-system exists *within* the open space of our whole spirit or essence, which is an influx of the essential spiritual reality of the universe. Our spirit is, in Indian Upanishadic terms, the *atman*, the individual spiritual self, that stems from *brahman*, the all-pervading spiritual energy. It has a radiant, blissful nature that we experience in moments of stillness, when our self-system becomes inactive and its boundaries soften.

Normally, though, our self-system has strong boundaries. It separates itself from the rest of our being (and the rest of the cosmos outside us), like a city surrounded by walls that sees itself as an autonomous, self-sufficient settlement. The most prominent aspect of our normal self-system is the ego. The ego is the center of our identity and our individuality, the organizing center of the self. It generates a constant stream of thoughts and associations. Because it's so powerful and active, it uses up most of the energy of our self-system — and even of our whole being.

All of the characteristics of the sleep state that we examined in chapter 1 are produced by this self-system, with its strong boundaries and incessant thought-chatter: the sense of separation and lack; inner discord and discontent; automatized perception; a narrow, egocentric outlook; materialistic and self-seeking values; and so on.

The wakeful state also has a kind of self-system, but a very different one than the sleep state. It's more subtle and unobtrusive, and its boundaries are much softer (and may not even exist) so that it isn't separate from the whole of our being. Revisiting the city analogy, it's more like an eco-town that is so well integrated into the landscape as a whole that it's difficult to tell where it ends and the countryside begins. As a result, this self-system is always filled with the energy of our expanded being. This radiant spiritual energy — with its natural quality of well-being — pervades our being like fresh country air, so that there's always a sense of energetic well-being.

This self-system still has an organizing center with a sense of identity but, again, this is much less obtrusive, much softer, and less active than in the self-system of sleep. It doesn't continually chatter away to itself and doesn't use up nearly as much energy. Again using the analogy of a city, you could compare the ego of our normal self-system to an emperor who lives in the center of the city, with a giant palace and government buildings.

The ego-emperor is half-mad and continually jabbers away to himself; he selfishly uses up most of his people's wealth and resources. The wakeful self-system doesn't have an emperor but rather a simple administrator or executor who simply does what has to be done without claiming any authority.

So awakening can be seen as a shift from our normal self-system into a wakeful self-system that is so subtle and labile that we might not even sense that it's there at all. (This is why wakefulness is sometimes — mistakenly, I believe — seen as a state of complete no-self.)

The three different ways in which wakefulness occurs can be interpreted in terms of this shift from one self-system to another. Wakefulness that occurs gradually, through adherence to spiritual practices and paths, involves gradually reshaping our self-system until the strong boundaries and the powerful ego of our normal self-system have faded away. But sometimes, as we'll see, the shift from one self-system to the other can happen suddenly and dramatically. The old self-system may suddenly collapse — usually as the result of intense psychological turmoil — and a new one may emerge to replace it, like a butterfly emerging from a chrysalis.

Finally, a small proportion of people may not need to undergo a shift, either gradual or permanent, because the wakeful self-system is normal and natural to them. We'll now examine some of these people.

Natural Wakefulness

Sleep is the normal state for most human beings. Although as young children we naturally have some of the characteristics of the wakeful state (a topic that we'll investigate in more detail later), by the time most of us reach adulthood our state of being has become more constricted and our perception has become less intense. If we intuit that we're asleep and feel an impulse to wake up — that is, to expand and intensify our awareness — we have to work at it. We have to follow practices and a lifestyle that facilitate awakening by undoing some of the psychological structures and processes that generate our sleep state. However, a very small number of people don't need to try to wake up because they never fell asleep.

Those who are spontaneously awake are perhaps the smallest group of awakened people. Their wakefulness isn't caused by an event or any practice, it simply *is*. Like other people, they undergo a process of psychological development as they move from childhood to adulthood, but their process is different. They develop the different kind of self-system I've just described, one without a sense of individuality and separateness, and with very soft and fluid boundaries, if any at all. As a result, they experience interconnection with the rest of the world and other beings. Although they still have thoughts, their thought processes are less chaotic and random. Their minds are quieter than other people's, and they aren't as immersed in or identified with their thoughts. They sense that their true identity is a strong and stable witness who stands apart from the thinking mind and from the negative and positive events of everyday life. In the words of Walt Whitman, "Apart from the pulling and hauling stands what I am...Both in and out of the game, and watching and wondering at it."[1]

Naturally wakeful people don't seem to develop the automatic, familiarized perception that most of us experience as we become adults. This is because their weaker ego-center consumes much less energy. As a result, their perception doesn't have to become automatic as a way of conserving energy. Naturally wakeful people retain the vivid and fresh perception of children. To them the world never loses its powerful is-ness and beauty, and life itself never loses its sense of strangeness and wonder.

It's not quite true, though, to say that naturally wakeful people *remain* as children. They usually develop the same mature psychological abilities as other adults: to think logically and abstractly, control their attention, control and override narcissistic or unreasonable desires, organize, plan and make decisions, and so on. But while most people develop these abilities and lose the connectedness and heightened awareness of childhood, spontaneously wakeful people develop the abilities and *retain* the wakeful characteristics of childhood.

Awakened Artists

Many naturally wakeful people don't become known in a spiritual context. They usually don't establish themselves as spiritual teachers. They may investigate different teachings as a way of making sense of their own experiences and later, once they understand their own wakefulness, feel a particular kinship with different teachings and traditions that resonate most deeply with their own experiences. However, they usually don't follow specific spiritual paths or become affiliated with particular traditions. Some of them may not even be aware of spiritual traditions at all, at least initially.

This lack of affiliation with spiritual traditions might seem strange, until you consider that the main purpose of spiritual paths is to facilitate spiritual awakening. If someone is already awakened, the path is unnecessary. In the raft parable, the Buddha compares his own teachings to a raft that helps a person cross a lake. Once the person has reached the other shore, the Buddha asks, would they continue to carry the raft over their head while they walked? Obviously not — they would put it down and leave it on the lake shore. In other words, once the person has awakened, the Buddha's teachings are no longer necessary. So in the same sense, a naturally wakeful person has no need for spiritual practices that are intended to awaken them.

People who are spontaneously awake are more likely to become creative artists than spiritual teachers. Spiritual wakefulness and creativity, particularly poetry and painting, are closely connected. The wakeful state seems to lend itself to poetic or visual expression. As I've suggested elsewhere (in the afterword to my book of poems, *The Meaning*), it's as if poetry is the out-breath of spiritual experience. That is, the impulse that awakened people feel to express their insights or describe their experiences often takes on a poetic form — not necessarily poetry itself but a poetic type of writing. Normal prose seems to be too mundane and restrictive to describe the wakeful state. After all, everyday language is based on duality between subject and object, and different tenses of time — all of which become unimportant (and even illusory) in the wakeful state. But poetic writing isn't constrained by these limits. It's more flexible and allusive and so can convey insights and experiences beyond normal consciousness. This is why so many of the world's great spiritual texts such as the Upanishads, Bhagavad Gita, and Dao De Jing are written in a poetic form.

I'll begin by discussing two examples of naturally wakeful people from the field of literature.

Walt Whitman

To my knowledge, the first ever psychological study of the wakeful state was conducted by Canadian psychiatrist Richard M. Bucke and published as *Cosmic Consciousness: A Study in the Evolution of the Human Mind* in 1901. Bucke gathered thirty-six examples of people he believed had attained "cosmic consciousness," including historical figures, such as the Buddha, Moses, Jesus, Dante, and eighteenth-century Swedish philosopher Emanuel Swedenborg, and a number of contemporaries, some of whom he knew personally. The main characteristics of cosmic consciousness as identified by Bucke are joyfulness; a revelation of the meaning, purpose, and aliveness of the universe; a sense of immortality; a loss of fear of death; and an absence of the concept of sin. Bucke also highlights the importance of light. Cosmic consciousness may feature an experience of being "immersed in a flame or rose-coloured cloud, or perhaps rather a sense that the mind is itself filled with such a cloud or haze."[2]

Bucke suggests that there are different degrees of cosmic consciousness, similar to the Buddha's different levels of enlightenment and Evelyn Underhill's different stages of the Christian mystical path (and also to my suggestion that there are different degrees of wakefulness). One cosmically conscious person may not be "lifted so very much above ordinary humanity," while another may be so far beyond ordinary consciousness that they are effectively "a God."[3] Bucke also recognizes that awakening to cosmic consciousness may initially bring some confusion. Some people may find it difficult to understand their new state and wonder if they have become deluded or even insane. However, Bucke notes that this period of doubt is only temporary. People quickly become convinced by the revelatory quality of their experience. They recognize that they are aware of a more intense and expansive reality than before, one that is *more real* rather than a distortion of reality.

Interestingly, Bucke adds a few other characteristics that aren't mentioned by spiritual traditions. For example, he believes age is a factor, that the onset of cosmic consciousness occurs between the ages of thirty and forty. He also believes — controversially and falsely — that cosmic consciousness is more likely to happen to men than women. He also mentions that cosmic consciousness brings "added charm to the personality — so that men and women become strongly attracted to the person," and also that it brings "a change in the appearance" or "transfiguration."[4]

Bucke's interest in cosmic consciousness was inspired by two factors. First, he had a powerful temporary awakening experience when he was thirty-five years old. He had spent the evening reading poetry with friends and was on his way home in a horse-drawn cab when he experienced, in his words, "a sense of exultation, of immense joyousness, accompanied or immediately followed by an intellectual illumination quite impossible to describe," and he became aware that "the Cosmos is not dead matter but a living presence; that the soul of man is immortal."[5]

Second, Bucke was inspired by the American poet Walt Whitman — initially by his poetry and then by his personal encounters with Whitman. Bucke not only included Whitman in his book as an example of cosmic consciousness but also regarded him as the "highest instance of Cosmic Consciousness" (above the Buddha, Moses, and Jesus). In Bucke's view, Whitman was able to integrate his mystical consciousness into his ordinary personality without allowing it to take over and "tyrannize over the rest."[6] This meant that he could live in a completely ordinary way, interacting with ordinary people in everyday life, rather than become otherworldly and detached, and live as a monk or hermit.

Although the details of his early life are sketchy, there are no signs that Whitman became awakened at a specific point in time. No events stand out as possible triggers of an awakening. As we'll see, sudden awakening is often triggered by a period of intense psychological turmoil, but there's no evidence that Whitman went through such turmoil in his early life. Whitman's wakefulness was not generated by prolonged and regular spiritual practice either or by following a particular spiritual tradition. Eastern spiritual traditions and practices were little known in the United States during Whitman's early years — he was born in 1819. In his later years, Whitman developed some familiarity with Indian philosophy but not any deep or detailed knowledge. (For example, when his contemporary Henry David Thoreau first read Whitman's *Leaves of Grass*, he was deeply impressed and said it was "wonderfully like the orientals." Thoreau asked Whitman if he had read oriental works, and he replied, "No, tell me about them."[7])

Rather, Whitman's wakefulness seems to have been completely organic and spontaneous, a state that was wholly natural to him.

Whitman lived in a state of heightened awareness. To him, the world was a fantastically real, beautiful, and fascinating place. As Bucke writes of him: "His favourite occupation seemed to be strolling or sauntering about outdoors by himself, looking at the grass, the trees, the flowers, the vistas of light, the varying aspects of the sky, and listening to the birds, the crickets, the tree frogs, and all the hundreds of natural sounds. It was evident that these things gave him a pleasure far beyond what they give to ordinary people."[8]

With this heightened awareness, Whitman sensed the sacred aliveness of the world and the radiance and harmony of a spirit-force pervading every object and creature. The whole world was divine, including his own being and body. As he writes in "Song of Myself":

Divine am I inside and out, and I make holy whatever I touch....

.   .   .   .

I see something of God each hour of the twenty-four, and
    each moment then,
In the faces of the men and women I see God, and in my own
    face in the glass.[9]

As well as bring an intense sense of the is-ness of things, the heightened awareness of the wakeful state brings an intense sense of now-ness. Our present-tense experience — our awareness of our surroundings, perceptions, and sensations — becomes so powerful that we give complete attention to it. The past and future become completely unimportant as we realize that there's *only* now, that life can only ever take place in the present moment. As a result, the whole concept of time becomes meaningless. Life is no longer a road with directions forward and backward; instead, it becomes a spacious panorama without movement or sequence. In Whitman's words, "The past and present wilt — I have filled them, emptied them."[10] And here he describes his intense experience of now-ness:

I have heard what the talkers were talking, the talk of the begin-
    ning and the end,
But I do not talk of beginning or end.

There was never any more inception than there is now,
Nor any more youth or age than there is now;
And will never be any more perfection than there is now,
Nor any more heaven or hell than there is now.[11]

Whitman's awareness of a spirit-force pervading everything meant that to him there were no separate or independent phenomena. To him, all things were part of a greater unity. In his poem "On the Beach at Night, Alone," for example, he describes his awareness that all things are part of a "vast similitude." All suns, planets, human beings, animals, plants, all of the future and the past, and all of space are essentially one and the same:

This vast similitude spans them, and always has spann'd,
and shall forever span them, and compactly hold them, and
    enclose them.[12]

Whitman sensed himself as a part of this "vast similitude," too. He felt such a strong connection between himself and other people that he shared his being with them; he felt that he actually *was* them. He writes, "I am of old and young, of the foolish as much as the wise," and "all the men ever born are my brothers...and the women my sisters and lovers."[13]

Interestingly, as well as being recognized by Bucke as an example of cosmic consciousness, Whitman is highlighted by the psychologist Abraham Maslow as an example of what he calls the "self-actualized person." (Maslow offers Mahatma Gandhi, twentieth-century author Aldous Huxley, and the early psychologist William James as other examples.) Maslow uses the concept of self-actualization with roughly the same meaning as wakefulness. He describes self-actualized individuals as being largely free of negative thoughts or feelings and less materialistic and self-centered (and therefore more altruistic) than other people. Maslow suggests that they have a greater than normal need for peace and solitude, a sense of duty or mission beyond their own personal ambitions, and a strong sense of the interconnectedness of phenomena (including themselves). One of their most pronounced characteristics, according to Maslow, is a powerful sense of appreciation and gratitude. As Maslow writes, self-actualized people "have the wonderful capacity to appreciate again and again, freshly and naively, the basic goods of life, with awe, pleasure, wonder and even ecstasy, however stale these experiences may have become to others."[14]

This was certainly true of Walt Whitman. When we hear the word *miracle* we usually think in terms of extraordinary feats such as healing incurable diseases or turning water into wine. But in the wakeful state, we don't need to look outside the normal realm of things for miracles. Miracles are everywhere around us. The everyday world becomes strange and miraculous. As Whitman writes,

> Who makes much of a miracle?
> As for me I know nothing but miracles.

It's wonderful that he should be immortal, he writes, but "my eyesight is equally wonderful, and how I was conceived in my mother's womb is equally wonderful." But as far as he's concerned, nothing is more miraculous than he himself: "Seeing, hearing, feeling, are miracles, and each part and tag of me is a miracle."[15]

Whitman's joyous celebration of life by no means meant ignoring death. On the contrary, the subject of death crops up again and again throughout his poems, right from the first pages of "Song of Myself" (where he says that it is "just as lucky to die" as it is to be born). Whitman sensed very powerfully that rather than be the end of our existence, death is actually a kind of liberation, a transition to a fuller and more blissful state. Like his fellow poet William Wordsworth sensing "intimations of immortality," Whitman heard "whispers of heavenly death" everywhere around him. In a moving short poem, "To One Shortly to Die," Whitman describes visiting a friend on his deathbed. The bed is surrounded by weeping relatives, but as Whitman rests his hand on his friend he senses that he is preparing to leave his body and beginning to transcend his pain. It's not a time for sadness but for joy:

> Strong thoughts fill you and confidence, you smile,
> You forget you are sick, as I forget you are sick.
> You do not see the medicines, you do not mind the weeping
>   friends, I am with you,
> I exclude others from you, there is nothing to be commiserated,
> I do not commiserate, I congratulate you.[16]

When I read Whitman's poetry, I find so many beautiful and profound descriptions of the wakeful state that I'm tempted to agree with Richard M. Bucke and see the "great, gray poet" as an example of a very high intensity of wakefulness that very few other human beings have ever attained. In Whitman the characteristics of the wakeful state are expressed intensely and purely. When I read "Song of Myself," for example, I don't interpret it as poetry in the conventional sense but as a great spiritual text written in poetic form. To me this poem in particular stands along with the Upanishads and the Dao De Jing as one of the most profound and powerful spiritual texts in human history. In fact, as much as I admire those two ancient texts, Whitman's work is even more powerful because of the way it embraces the whole of human life and shows the spirit-force pouring through the minutiae of the everyday world. The Upanishads tell us that all is spirit, that we're one with the universe and that the soul is deathless, but Whitman *shows* it. *Brahman* shines through the countless ordinary people — craftsmen, soldiers, sailors, even prostitutes — Whitman describes meeting. He portrays a giant canvas of human life — including sex, friendship, business, and even warfare and illness — filled with a powerful underlying divinity and sacredness.

Certainly, though, the overriding impression we receive from Whitman's poetry is very similar to the Upanishads, since they're both so full of dazzling spiritual radiance and so deeply pervaded with joy. Like the authors of the Upanishads, Whitman tells us clearly that, far from being absurd and meaningless (as it sometimes might appear from the standpoint of our sleep state), life is miraculous and wonderful; the whole universe is imbued with sentient bliss and harmony, even if we might not be able to explain or understand it fully. As he writes toward the end of "Song of Myself":

> Do you see, O my brothers and sisters?
> It is not chaos or death — it is form, union, plan — it is eternal
>   life — it is Happiness.[17]

D. H. Lawrence

The British author D. H. Lawrence — who was born in 1885, while Whitman was still alive — was a great admirer of Walt Whitman, calling him "the greatest and the first and the only American teacher."[18] He recognized Whitman as a kindred spirit, someone who shared the same intensified vision of the world as he did. I discussed Lawrence's wakefulness briefly in my book *Out of the Darkness*, but this is a good place to explore it in a little more detail.

In some ways, Lawrence is a clearer example of natural wakefulness than Whitman because his life is so well documented. He wasn't widely read — or widely respected by literary critics or other authors — during his lifetime, but Lawrence's reputation grew during the 1950s and 1960s. He became one of the most popular authors of the twentieth century and was the subject of countless biographies and critical studies. As with Whitman's, Lawrence's wakefulness wasn't triggered by a particular event and didn't develop gradually due to adherence to spiritual practice or a tradition. Lawrence became aware of Eastern philosophies later in life and felt particularly attracted to Hindu spirituality. For example, he admired a book he read on Kashmiri Shaivism (an Indian Tantric tradition) as "true psychology" that made Western psychology seem "shallow and groping."[19] However, he certainly wasn't aware of Eastern spirituality when his natural wakefulness began to express itself in early adulthood.

Lawrence began to publish poems, stories, and novels in his early twenties. From the start, his work was characterized by his heightened awareness and his strong sense of connection to the natural world, including animals. Many of Lawrence's friends were amazed by his alertness and sensitivity; they described him almost as if he was a different type of human being. One close friend, the literary critic John Middleton Murry, describes Lawrence as possessing a kind of "sixth sense." Another, the author Aldous Huxley, describes him as a person who was somehow "of another order, more sensitive, more highly conscious, more capable of feeling than even the most gifted of common men...he inhabited a different universe from that of common men — a brighter and intenser world."[20]

Lawrence died at the age of forty-four but was amazingly prolific in his short life. He wrote forty-five books in a wide variety of genres — fiction, travel, psychology, philosophy, and literary criticism. He was also a painter and produced hundreds of canvases. (Unfortunately, the only exhibition of his paintings he held in his lifetime, in London in 1929, was shut down by police because of its allegedly obscene content.) Of course, he's most famous for his novels, including two of the most beautiful novels in English literature, *The Rainbow* and *Women in Love*. However, Lawrence's wakeful experience of the world expresses itself most clearly in his poems.

In his poetry, Lawrence frequently uses the word *god*, but his concept of God has little to do with the personal father-figure God of conventional religion. His god is *brahman*, the spirit-force that pervades the universe. To him the world is divine, shining brilliantly with spirit. "All the time I see the gods," he writes in his poem "Name the Gods," describing how a man mowing a field of wheat represents to him "the swaying body of God."[21] In another poem, he writes:

> There is no god
> apart from poppies and the flying fish,
> men singing songs and women brushing their hair in the sun.
> The lovely things are god that has come to pass.[22]

Lawrence senses this spirit-force everywhere around him and inside him, too — it's "the presence which makes the air so still and lovely to me" and which "softly touches the sides of my breast and touches me over the heart."[23] He knows that the only true fulfillment is to feel our oneness with this divine force. As he writes in one of his most beautiful poems, "Pax":

> All that matters is to be at one with the living God
> to be a creature in the house of the God of Life.
>
> Like a cat asleep on a chair
> at peace, in peace
> and at one with the master of the house, with the mistress,
> at home, at home in the house of the living,
> sleeping on the hearth, and yawning before the fire.[24]

Lawrence saw the world as pervaded with the spirit-force so to him there was no such thing as inanimate matter. All things — even rocks, clouds, and stars — were gloriously alive and sentient. Like Whitman, Lawrence was free of the sense of separateness that is such a strong feature of our sleep state. This meant that he was able to enter into the being of other creatures (including human beings) and experience the world as they did. This is one of the most exhilarating qualities of his writing — his ability to convincingly depict the inner life not only of human beings but also of animals. At times his sense of connection and empathy was so powerful that it was almost as if Lawrence actually *became* other beings. As Huxley writes, "He seemed to know, by personal experience, what it was like to be a tree or a daisy or a breaking wave or even the mysterious moon itself."[25]

Natural wakefulness, and wakefulness in general, isn't static. That is, a person's wakefulness doesn't simply emerge and then remain in the same form for the rest of their life. Wakefulness evolves. It may deepen and intensify. Different aspects of the state may unfold, and different characteristics may become more or less prominent. It's not the end of a journey but a *different* journey. It's like shifting onto a different road — moving from the low road to the high road, you might say. It's a different road with a different landscape but it's still a type of journey involving movement and progression.

D.H. Lawrence was always naturally awake but his wakefulness intensified, particularly during the last few years of his life. In *Out of the Darkness*, I suggest that his close encounters with death caused this intensification. Lawrence suffered from ill health almost from birth and came very close to death at least three times as an adult. First, he caught pneumonia at the age of twenty-six. Second, he caught Spanish flu in 1919 in the epidemic that killed millions of people after the First World War. Third, he caught malaria, typhoid, and then pneumonia in 1925 when he was living in Mexico. By this time, he was seriously ill with tuberculosis, which killed him five years later. However, it was during this final period of his life, when he was slowly dying, that his wakefulness became most intense, as described in the profound spiritual poems he wrote during this time (published after his death as *Last Poems*).

In some of the most moving of these poems, Lawrence describes facing the prospect of his own death with serene acceptance. He isn't afraid because, like Whitman, he intuits that death is a transition rather than an end point, the beginning of a new journey. In his poem "Gladness of Death" he describes death as a "great adventure" that is full of "an after-gladness, a strange joy."[26]

Other Awakened Artists

The nineteenth-century nature writer Richard Jefferies is one lesser-known author who was naturally wakeful to a high degree. His autobiography, *The Story of My Heart*, is an amazing description of how the world appears in an intensely wakeful state. Jefferies describes how he was "no more than eighteen when an inner and esoteric meaning began to come to me from all the visible universe, and indefinable aspirations filled me."[27] Everything around him seemed to "burn" with this meaning, and — as with Lawrence and Whitman — the world was a strange and miraculous place to him:

> As I write these words...I feel that the whole air, the sunshine out yonder lighting up the ploughed earth, the distant sky, the circumambient ether, and that far space, is full of soul-secrets, soul-life, things outside the experience of all ages. The fact of my own existence as I write, as I exist at this second, is so marvellous, so miracle-like...that I unhesitatingly conclude that I am always on the margin of life illimitable, and that there are higher conditions than existence.[28]

The English poet William Wordsworth was also naturally awake. Wordsworth's intense sensitivity to the beauty and the is-ness of the natural world made him the archetypal Romantic poet and the most influential poet of the nineteenth century. He spent most of his life in one of the most beautiful parts of England, the Lake District, and his poems are full of detailed descriptions of the sublime, awe-inspiring landscapes of the region. Many of Wordsworth's passages describe his awareness of the spirit-force pervading the natural world, some of which come very close to descriptions of the all-pervading presence of *brahman* in the Upanishads (which Wordsworth almost certainly never read). For example, in one of his most beautiful and profound poems, "Lines Written a Few Miles above Tintern Abbey," he writes:

> And I have felt
> A presence that disturbs me with the joy
> Of elevated thoughts; a sense sublime
> Of something far more deeply interfused,

Whose dwelling is the light of setting suns,
And the round ocean and the living air,
And the blue sky, and in the mind of man:
A motion and a spirit; that impels
All thinking things, all objects of all thought,
And rolls through all things.[29]

In another of his most beautiful poems, "Intimations of Immortality," which I compared above to Whitman's "Whispers of Heavenly Death," Wordsworth describes how children's fresh, intense perception enables them to see a world "apparell'd in celestial light" with "the glory and freshness of a dream." However, as we become adults we move away from the "heaven" of our infancy. "Shades of the prison-house begin to close" and the glorious vision of childhood fades "into the light of common day."[30] This is a good example of how natural wakefulness fades into sleep as we grow older. However, Wordsworth himself didn't seem to undergo this process of falling asleep. Even at age seventy-five he was still able to write a poem like "So Fair, So Sweet, Withal So Sensitive," where the beauty of a mountain-daisy amazes him and enables him to "converse with Nature in pure sympathy."[31]

Although we know very little about his life, the poet and painter William Blake, Wordsworth's near contemporary, also seems to have been naturally awake. In his poems Blake writes of being able to see "heaven in a wild flower" and "eternity in an hour,"[32] and was so sensitive to the is-ness of things that, as a friend of his reported, he would spend hours staring in wonder at knots in a piece of wood. This was probably also true of Percy Shelley, another nineteenth-century English poet, whose poems display a similar heightened awareness to Wordsworth's and the same awareness of the spirit-force pervading the world. In his famous poem "Hymn to Intellectual Beauty," Shelley describes this spirit-force as "the awful shadow of some unseen Power" that "floats though unseen among us."[33]

There are many other possible examples of awakened poets and authors; in fact, it would probably be possible to fill a whole book with them. (Perhaps I will one day!) In American literature alone, figures such as Ralph Waldo Emerson, Henry David Thoreau, Emily Dickinson, E. E. Cummings, Henry Miller, and Robinson Jeffers were clearly familiar with the wakeful state. European literature also offers many clear examples of awakened artists, such as the German poet Rainer Maria Rilke, the great German novelist Hermann Hesse, and the French Romantic poet Alphonse de Lamartine.

There are also many painters who seem to have experienced wakefulness as a natural state. The Romantic tradition was expressed as strongly through visual art as it was through poetry. European painters such as John Constable, William Turner, Caspar David Friedrich, and the American painters Thomas Cole and George Inness clearly perceived the natural world with a heightened intensity, free from the functional automatic perception of the sleep state, and felt strongly connected to it. Just as Wordsworth and Whitman had the literary skill to convey their spiritual vision and insights through poetry, these artists had the technical ability to convey their sense of wonder and transcendence through their paintings. As for poetry, there was a strong association between wakefulness and visual art, which continued through the nineteenth century with impressionists such as Claude Monet, Camille Pissarro, Pierre-Auguste Renoir, and Vincent van Gogh, whose paintings shimmer with intense isness and beauty. Arguably, most of the great artists until the beginning of the twentieth century expressed an awakened perspective to some degree, until naturalism and impressionism became unfashionable and abstract and conceptual art took over.

Of course, some of these poets and painters may only have known awakening on a temporary rather than a permanent basis. Perhaps some of them simply had regular awakening experiences rather than wakefulness as an ongoing state. (This could well be true of figures such as Shelley and van Gogh, for example.) Nevertheless, these examples do show that wakefulness can occur naturally, without the support of spiritual practices or paths. After all, most of the people I've discussed in this chapter knew little or nothing about Eastern spiritual traditions — or even Western mystical traditions — and would certainly not have thought of themselves as enlightened or awakened. They illustrate that wakefulness can express itself in many different ways and is primarily a psychological or ontological state that belongs to human nature itself rather than to any particular tradition or teaching.

4. Natural Wakefulness: Confusion and Integration

For Walt Whitman and D. H. Lawrence, wakefulness seems to have been fairly uncomplicated. They simply were naturally awake, and their wakefulness emerged and expressed itself without apparent difficulties. However, in this chapter we'll look at examples of natural wakefulness where there were difficulties, mainly due to lack of self-understanding and self-acceptance.

When wakefulness occurs in the context of spiritual or religious traditions, a person has a readily available framework (together with the guidance of others who have experienced wakefulness) to help them understand their state. Without such support, naturally wakeful people may experience some confusion and doubt. They may feel threatened by their spiritual impulses and try to repress them. It may take them several years to understand and accept their innate wakefulness fully.

Naturally awakened people who live in cultures that don't support a spiritual understanding of the world are in particular danger of this difficulty. The values of their culture may clash with their awakened impulses. We all absorb cultural influences as we grow up, and it may take several years for naturally wakeful people to work off their cultural conditioning so that they can begin to live authentically. They may feel a powerful impulse to live a different kind of life — to turn away from materialism and hedonism, to simplify their lives and spend more time in solitude, for example — but it may be a number of years before they feel confident and autonomous enough to follow the impulse. Until then, they may feel an intense sense of frustration because their innate wakefulness can't express itself.

Peace Pilgrim

The American wanderer and social activist who called herself Peace Pilgrim, one of the most remarkable and unusual awakened people of the twentieth century, was such a case. Peace Pilgrim was born Mildred Norman in 1908. After a fairly normal childhood — distinguished only by her precocious intelligence and unusual inquisitiveness — she began to ponder deep existential questions as a teenager. At the age of sixteen, she began to wonder about the nature of God and concluded that God wasn't a being but everything that was "beyond human understanding." She "touched God" as a force whose qualities were love, kindness, and truth. As she describes it: "It came to me that God is a creative force, a motivating power, an over-all intelligence, an ever-present, all pervading spirit — which binds everything in the universe together and gives life to everything. That brought God close. I could not be where God is not."[1]

Looking back in later life, Peace Pilgrim recognized a number of signs of "being prepared for her pilgrimage." In high school there was peer pressure to smoke cigarettes and drink alcohol, but she abstained from both. Her friends ridiculed and rejected her, but she justified herself by telling them, when a group of them were gathered together, "Life is a series of choices, and nobody can stop you from making your choices, but I have a right to make my own choices, too. And I have chosen freedom."[2] Another sign of Peace Pilgrim's future path was her harmonious relationships. Whenever there was any discord between her and others, or when anyone showed animosity toward her, she never felt resentment and always acted quickly to heal the relationship.

In other ways, however, Peace Pilgrim lived a fairly normal life until her thirties. She married at the age of twenty-five and initially abided by conventional American values, living a materialistic lifestyle. "I had been led to believe that money and possessions would insure me a life of happiness and peace of mind," she said. "So that was the path I pursued."[3] However, she soon began to realize that the materialistic lifestyle was meaningless and not the life meant for her. At the same time, she was confused because she had no idea what kind of life *was* meant for her.

Her lifestyle frustrated her more and more. In particular, she felt uncomfortable "about having so much while my brothers and sisters were starving."[4] She was filled with a deep yearning for a more meaningful path. One evening when she was thirty, she walked all night through the woods in desperation and finally came to a clearing, where she prayed. As she recalls: "I felt a complete willingness, without any reservations, to give my life — to dedicate my life — to service. 'Please use me!' I prayed to God. And a great peace came over me.... And so I went into the second phase of my life. I began to give what I could, and I entered a new and wonderful world."[5]

In one article I've read about Peace Pilgrim, this experience is interpreted as a moment of transformation in which her new spiritual self was born.[6] However, the experience wasn't related to any particular event or trigger (unlike most cases of sudden awakening) and wasn't generated by spiritual practice. The wakefulness that emerged had seemingly been present inside her. This was the point when she accepted her innate wakefulness after years of repressing it because it conflicted with the values of her culture. The confusion and frustration caused by this repression eventually became so intense — as the inner pressure of her innate wakefulness's drive to express itself grew stronger — that she had no choice but to surrender.

From this point, Peace Pilgrim lived a new, authentic life. She was aware of a powerful spiritual force inside her, which she sensed inside others as well, so that she felt an intense connection to everyone and a strong impulse to serve the human race as a whole. She lived a life of service, working with elderly people and people with mental health problems. She then served as a volunteer with peace organizations, such as the Women's International League for Peace and Freedom. (Her peace activism led to divorce from her husband, who fought in the Second World War.) She also drastically simplified her life: she became a vegetarian, lived on a low income, and freed herself from most of her possessions. She formulated a set of personal spiritual principles to live by, including purification of the body (through diet and exercise), purification of thought (refraining from negative thoughts), relinquishing attachments to material goods, relinquishing feelings of separateness, and relinquishing negative feelings or reactions.

Peace Pilgrim's innate wakefulness was nurtured and deepened by this lifestyle. In one of her pamphlets, *Steps Toward Inner Peace*, she describes another powerful experience that occurred while she was out walking one morning:

> All of a sudden I felt very uplifted, more uplifted than I had ever been. I remember I knew *timelessness* and *spacelessness* and *lightness*....Every flower, every bush, every tree, seemed to wear a halo. There was a light emanation around everything and flecks of gold fell like slanted rain through the air....I knew before that all human beings are one. But now I knew also a oneness with the rest of creation....And, most wonderful of all, a oneness with that which permeates all and binds all together and gives life to all. A oneness with that which many would call God.
>
> I have never really felt separate since.[7]

Soon after this experience, on January 1, 1953, Peace Pilgrim began her pilgrimage. After leading the Rose Parade in California (an annual New Year celebration), she kept walking. She continued to walk across the country, eventually arriving at the United Nations building in New York the following December. And from this point on, Peace Pilgrim never really stopped walking. With no possessions except a toothbrush, one set of clothes, a comb, and a pencil, she crisscrossed the United States seven times on foot, as well as walked in Canada and Mexico. Wearing a tunic with the words "Peace Pilgrim" on the front and "25,000 miles on foot for peace" on the back, she found that she could rely on strangers to approach her, and to give her food and a bed for the night (although she often slept outdoors). In effect, she lived as a wandering monk supported by laypeople. She walked an average of twenty-five miles a day, often stopping for speaking engagements or interviews along the way, particularly as she became more well known.

Throughout the rest of her life — another twenty-eight years — Peace Pilgrim experienced a constant sense of unshakeable inner peace and oneness, a constant sense of communion with the divine. As she writes, "There is a feeling of always being surrounded by all the good things, like love and peace and joy. It seems like a protective surrounding, and there is an unshakeableness within, which takes you through any situations you need to face.... There is a calmness and a serenity and unhurriedness — no more striking or straining."[8]

We saw in chapter 2 that the all-pervading spiritual force described by different spiritual traditions — and the spiritual essence of our individual being — is often described in terms of brilliant light, so it's interesting that Peace Pilgrim spoke of a "divine light" that she could share. She describes how, when she was with other people, she would feel her own divine nature connecting with theirs, and felt as if she were "lifting them" and "bringing God's light to them." She writes, "I try to envision them bathed in God's light and finally I do see them standing and reaching out their arms bathed in golden light. At that point I leave them in God's hands."[9] There are interesting parallels here with the Kabbalistic idea of *tikkun olam*, the healing of the world. In a very real sense, Peace Pilgrim was bringing her own enlightenment into the world to share it with others.

In 1981, at the age of seventy-two, Peace Pilgrim died in a car crash while being driven to a meeting. This might seem tragic, but it would not have appeared that way to Peace Pilgrim. Like Whitman and Lawrence, she saw death as a "glorious transition to freer living" and "life's last great adventure."[10]

Peace Pilgrim is similar to the awakened artists we looked at in the previous chapter in that her life was defined by what her wakefulness enabled her to *do* rather than her wakefulness itself. Her life was defined by her altruism and her sense of mission, which stemmed from her ability to empathize with other human beings and her overarching sense of justice and morality. She is a good example of spiritual activism to refute the notion that spiritual development means becoming narcissistic, passive, and detached from the world.

Gavin

In my own research, I haven't come across many examples of natural wakefulness, which is why I believe that it's the most uncommon type of wakefulness. But here I'll describe one of the cases I did come across.

Gavin Whyte is in his early thirties and the author of several works of fiction and nonfiction on spiritual themes. As a child, he was fascinated by the paranormal — he loved to read nonfiction about psychic phenomena rather than comics and storybooks — and started to write his own ghost stories. He always sensed that, in his words, "there was more to life than what we can see with the physical eyes." He also loved to spend time alone. His schoolteachers noticed that he had a quality of stillness and attentiveness. Unlike other children, he looked at them intently when they spoke to him.

In his teenage years, Gavin's parents began to think he was strange because he didn't seem to get upset when bad things happened. Once, at about the age of fourteen, the family was in a restaurant when a waitress spilled a drink in Gavin's lap. While everyone else was making a fuss, he just calmly took a napkin and started to wipe his trousers, causing his father to exclaim, "My God, did you see how he reacted?" A similar thing happened when he learned to drive at the age of seventeen, and his first car was stolen soon afterward. Gavin's father was devastated, but Gavin didn't see any reason to be upset. "I think my reaction made my dad even more angry than the crime itself," Gavin said. "But I couldn't see what all the fuss was about. It had been stolen and that was that."

His father was also worried about the amount of time Gavin spent alone. As Gavin told me:

> I used to lay on my bed in silence, much to my dad's confusion.
> I can remember turning off my bedroom light, lighting a candle,
> and just staring at it for ages. I used to lie on my bed doing nothing.
> I used to gaze up at the sky and let my mind wander. I had a strong
> impulse just to stare, to look and observe. I would take the family
> dogs out for walks and spend the time looking at the stars, trees,
> and flowers. I most definitely felt like the black sheep in the family.

Gavin had always loved Bruce Lee films and started to practice kung fu. This led him to dip into Eastern philosophies such as Zen Buddhism and Daoism. As a result, he had a framework to make sense of his meditative impulses and his desire for solitude, and didn't allow his family's confusion to affect him.

However, at the age of nineteen he went through a spell of frustration and depression. He was a musician and spent hours and hours recording songs in his bedroom. He was determined to become a successful pop musician; he continually sent off samples of his songs but didn't receive any positive feedback. He was "overly ambitious," he recognizes now, and his lack of success frustrated him so that he began to see himself as a failure. He was working at a supermarket and hated every minute of the job, feeling that he should have been a successful musician instead. His innate wakefulness was obscured by egoic tendencies. But one evening he had a powerful transformational experience that freed him from egoism and dissolved away his frustration so that his natural wakefulness was able to express itself more fully:

> I was out walking the dogs, about 12 o'clock in the afternoon. It was a beautiful day. I let the dogs off the lead and let them run around, and I found myself staring at a tree. I was glued to it.... The tree became the most beautiful thing I had ever seen — ever. It shone new colors. But not only that — I became one with the tree to such an extent that I no longer existed. All that was left existing was everything! I saw the oneness of life. My identity, along with all of its insecurities, ambitions, goals, and fears, melted away like ice in the desert. To this, all I could do was laugh.

Since this experience Gavin has felt a strong, ongoing sense of inner contentment and gratitude, and a continual sense of awe at the world, which he expresses through his writing. Sometimes egoic tendencies rise up, but he finds it easy to reconnect to the strong undercurrent of wakefulness that is always inside him. For example, when he feels that his mind has become too busy with thought-chatter, "I turn my attention to my breath or the movement of my body or the aliveness of the moment and watch thought-chatter quieten into the background. Then observation and the input of the other senses seem to absorb more energy than inner noise."

My Own Natural Wakefulness

This is a good place to refer to my own experience of wakefulness, since I see myself as another example of natural wakefulness.

I want to be careful here. In my own encounters with spiritual teachers and gurus, one of my guiding principles has been, "If someone proclaims themselves as enlightened, then they probably aren't." Genuinely wakeful people tend to be humble. They might agree that they are enlightened if you press them on the matter, but they tend not to broadcast it. Although they may feel a sense of mission, an impulse to share their wisdom and aid the development of others, they often don't go out of their way to attract attention or followers. On the other hand, narcissistic or self-deluded spiritual "teachers" are often self-aggrandizing, loudly proclaiming themselves as avatars or saviors and trying to attract as much attention (and as many followers) as possible.

As a result, I'm reluctant to "come out" as an awakened person. I'm a self-effacing Englishman and reluctant to make any claims that may be construed as arrogant. So let me preface this discussion of my own wakefulness by reminding you that there are different varieties and degrees of wakefulness, and I certainly don't claim that my own wakefulness is of the highest or purest degree. However, it would be foolish not to include my own experience of natural wakefulness simply for modesty's sake.

When I do presentations or workshops — and especially when I talk about my research into the connection between psychological turmoil and spiritual awakening — people often ask me, "Have you been through a spiritual transformation yourself?" My answer is usually something along the lines of, "No, for me there wasn't a sudden moment of transformation. There has been an innate spiritual sensibility inside me for as long as I can remember, which just seemed to be there naturally. My spiritual development was all about understanding this part of myself, accepting it, and allowing it to express itself fully."

When I was a teenager, my natural wakefulness caused me some difficulties because I couldn't make sense of it. It didn't fit into the culture I was born into. The two main aspects of my upbringing were soccer and television. Encouraged by my father, who was a devoted Manchester United fan, I spent all my time either playing or watching soccer or watching television. There was no religion in my upbringing — my parents didn't think of themselves as atheists but had no interest in religion. (Although you could say that soccer was my father's religion!) Culture wasn't prominent in my upbringing either — no music, very few books, and no intellectual or cultural interests. We rarely — if ever — went to the cinema or theater.

I don't have any complaints — I had a great time playing soccer with my dad and my friends in the street or at the park. My parents were attentive and loving and gave me a secure emotional foundation, for which I'm very grateful.

The problems came when, around the age of sixteen, I changed from the normal soccer-obsessed kid I'd always been to a much more introverted, self-conscious, and serious person who no longer felt that I belonged to my environment. I felt that I became this different person within the space of a few months.

I had been taught that the most important things in life were to have a good time and to "get on." My father especially had taught me the importance of being popular and sociable, and having an entertaining personality. I'd also been taught the importance of trying to earn money so that you could have a nice car and buy other nice things. But I had no interest in any of these areas. I went to pubs and drank beer and tried to be sociable, but I didn't enjoy it and never felt comfortable. I preferred to spend my time alone, reading or listening to music, or walking the streets. I was attracted to nature and quietness, but there was very little nature in my city. In the evenings, when it was dark, I'd often go back to my school, climb over the gates, and wander around the school fields simply because it was the only quiet and natural place near to me where I knew I wasn't likely to encounter other people. The open space of the fields and the open space of the sky and the quietness around me filled me with a sense of calmness and wholeness. The clouds looked so real and alive that they seemed to be sentient, and the black spaces between them amazed me with their deep richness. The sky was very important to me because it was the only untouched open natural space I had access to.

I felt exhilarated by these states of well-being and wonder, but I also thought there was something wrong with me. I didn't understand why I couldn't function the way I was supposed to. I was very quiet; I'd sit in groups of people in a pub or youth club but find it impossible to say anything. As a result, people began to think I was "weird." My parents were worried about me; they saw me as a "loner" who borrowed "strange books" about philosophy and psychology from the library.

Luckily I did quite well at school. I passed exams that enabled me to go to university so that I didn't have to face the challenge of choosing a job or career immediately after school. I thought I'd meet like-minded people at university, but I was mostly disappointed. There was an even stronger emphasis on drinking and socializing than in my home environment, and I had an even stronger sense of alienation. But at least I was studying literature, which meant that I had a lot of free time. In my second year, I saw an advertisement for a talk on Transcendental Meditation (TM) — I wasn't sure exactly what meditation was, but I felt attracted to it. After the talk, I signed up for TM classes and was given my own mantra. I experienced the healing and calming effects of meditation straight away, although I didn't have the self-discipline to practice it regularly.

At university I started a daily routine that I'd follow for many years afterward. I'd stay up very late, usually until around four or five o'clock in the morning, and get up around lunchtime (or later) the next day. I loved going on walks when the streets were deserted and everyone else was asleep; I enjoyed the stillness and spaciousness. I felt a strong connection with trees and felt that in some way the trees came to life when the rest of the city was asleep. I could sense their sentience and felt that they were communicating with each other as well as with me. In my second year at university I lived on the outskirts of town, close to the countryside, and spent a lot of time walking or cycling through the fields, lanes, and villages, absorbing the healing influence of nature.

Around this time (as I describe in *Waking from Sleep*) I went through a process of purgation and renunciation. I stopped going to my lectures at university, isolated myself from other people, and tried to live as simply as possible. I cut myself off from all the things I depended on for identity or security. I inflicted discomfort — and sometimes pain — on myself, sleeping on a hard floor and taking cold baths. Although I wasn't aware of it at the time, I was living like an ascetic monk. The whole process was instinctive, without any conscious aim, but in retrospect I can see that I was trying to develop self-discipline, to strengthen my willpower. At the same time, I was trying to pare down my life to its essence so that I could free myself from the environmental influences I'd absorbed and uncover my true self.

During this time, I still felt confused and alienated. I had no idea who I really was or what I was meant to be doing. At times, I felt so desperate that

I thought about committing suicide. After I left university — with a poor degree, due to all the lectures I had missed — I had no desire to follow any particular career and no idea what my future might hold. For the next couple of years I drifted between periods on the dole (claiming unemployment benefits) and low-paid menial jobs. I had moments of intense well-being — even euphoria — but my underlying wakefulness was often overlaid with my depression, unease, and confusion.

However, around the age of twenty-two, I finally began to understand my natural wakefulness. I had already developed some self-understanding after reading Colin Wilson's classic study of alienation, *The Outsider*, which explained to me why I couldn't fit in to ordinary society and suggested that it was actually a *positive* thing to be different. The book gave me a framework to make some sense of my isolation and alienation, although its emphasis was more existential than spiritual. But then I stumbled upon *Mysticism: A Study and Anthology* by F. C. Happold, which contained short excerpts from spiritual texts and the writings of Christian and Eastern mystics. Most of the passages resonated deeply with me. I recognized my own experiences in them. Out of all the passages, the excerpt from the Upanishads touched me most. Soon afterward, when I read the Upanishads as a whole, I felt a tremendous sense of homecoming and reassurance. I saw my own vision of the world in them, particularly in the passages that describe the presence of *brahman* in all things. I knew that I could see *brahman* in the world, too, particularly in the sky. After that, I read Walt Whitman's "Song of Myself," D. H. Lawrence's *Selected Poems*, and many other spiritual books. Just as importantly, I discovered the spiritual music of Van Morrison and his albums *Inarticulate Speech of the Heart* and *No Guru, No Method, No Teacher*. This music was borne out of — and depicted — exactly the same spiritual sensibility I was experiencing, and was a powerful inspiration to me. It opened up a landscape of spiritual experience that was deeply familiar, in which I could feel completely at home.

Now everything began to make sense. I was building an intellectual framework to make sense of my wakefulness. My confusion was dissipating, replaced by a sense of orientation and direction. I felt like I had arrived home and began to trust and accept my wakefulness, which began to stabilize and intensify as a result. It was a wonderful period — I felt ecstatic, uplifted, in touch with my own essence, and in communion with the world. I could sense beauty and wonder everywhere around me and the presence of spirit-force (or *brahman*) pervading the world. Just a couple of years after contemplating suicide, I felt incredibly grateful to be alive. I still had no idea where I was going in my life but it didn't seem to matter. All that mattered was to be alive in the glorious present. I finally understood and accepted myself.

It wasn't all easy sailing from this point, though. After about three years of ecstatic wakefulness, new challenges emerged. Music was one of my passions and at the age of twenty-four I was invited to join a friend's band — as bass guitarist — and moved abroad. There I began to disconnect from the framework I'd built up. I started to follow a typical musician's hedonistic lifestyle, smoking and drinking too much; I was surrounded by other people who did the same. I knew that this lifestyle wasn't congruent with my real self, and the dissonance caused frustration. I was also in a difficult relationship with my girlfriend and struggled with the demands of everyday life (such as earning enough money to live). After struggling for so long to connect with the core of my own being, I became disconnected, and felt frustrated and depressed again.

I now see this period of my life as a time of integration. Although I may have been well developed spiritually, I was undeveloped in other areas of my life. I had poor emotional and social skills, and a lack of self-confidence and self-efficacy. It might not have mattered so much if I was a monk, but the modern world is a complex and demanding place and I knew I needed to learn to function in it. My being was imbalanced, which meant my wakefulness wasn't fully integrated and could be easily destabilized.

However, as I matured and developed in these areas my being became much more integrated and my wakefulness become more stable and deep-rooted. My frustration and depression faded away permanently. Around the age of thirty, I stopped smoking, became a vegetarian, began to meditate regularly, and learned yoga. I harmonized my lifestyle with my inner self, as Peace Pilgrim did after her powerful experience in the woods at the age of thirty.[11] I was back home again, but this time home felt a little different. Obviously my wakefulness was essentially the same, but it had a slightly different tone. My earlier wakefulness had been more of a high-arousal state, exhilarating and dynamic, but this time around it was closer to a low-arousal state — calmer, more contained, less volatile. It was akin to the serene type of awakening experience that comes after a deep meditation or time spent in beautiful natural surroundings, not the ecstatic type of awakening experience that is sometimes generated by sex or dancing, which I had experienced before.

I've remained in this stable state of wakefulness ever since. Some characteristics have intensified, new aspects have unfolded, and new insights and revelations have emerged. But after a long process of self-understanding and integration, my natural wakefulness has essentially manifested itself fully.

Understanding Natural Wakefulness

The above examples illustrate the importance of possessing an intellectual framework to make sense of one's wakefulness. Without this, wakefulness can easily be overridden by confusion and frustration.

However, it's interesting that the examples of natural wakefulness in the previous chapter — such as Walt Whitman and D. H. Lawrence — don't appear to have had these difficulties, at least so far as we can tell. To some extent, it may depend on the culture a person is born into, and how incongruous or acceptable wakefulness appears in relation to its values and conventions. Wakefulness is particularly incongruous in urban, industrialized, competitive, and consumerist cultures, such as the modern Britain I was born into or the prewar America in which Peace Pilgrim grew up. Both Whitman and Lawrence were born into largely preindustrial societies, when modern competitive capitalism was at an early stage. As a result, perhaps there wasn't as much cultural resistance to their wakefulness.

Wakefulness is encouraged and supported in some cultures that have strong spiritual traditions, such as in India or Thailand. In these cultures, naturally wakeful people presumably have fewer problems understanding and integrating their wakefulness. (This issue of whether wakefulness is supported or pathologized will be important later, in chapter 10, when we examine the spiritual crisis that sometimes occurs after sudden awakening.)

Speaking more generally, however, how should we understand natural wakefulness? Why do a small minority of people appear to be born naturally awake? Or more precisely, why do a small number of people seem to naturally have a different kind of self-system, with a more connected and expansive sense of identity and without the automatized perception of our normal state?

The best way to think of naturally wakeful people is to see them as rare "evolutionary throw-forwards." I don't want to say too much about evolution at this point because I'm going to discuss the connection between wakefulness and evolution in detail in the last chapter of this book. However, evolution is partly a process by which living beings become progressively more conscious and alive, whereby they develop a more intricate and expansive awareness. In these terms, naturally wakeful people can be seen as the early representatives of a state of more expansive awareness that will one day become normal to all human beings. They're early manifestations of the *evolutionary* leap that our species may be undergoing, and a sign that it's occurring.

In the next chapter we'll look at what could be interpreted as another sign of this evolutionary leap: the *impulse* to awaken that leads many people to investigate spiritual practices and paths, and which also leads to the second of three ways in which wakefulness can occur.

5. Gradual Awakening
in Spiritual Traditions

The second way wakefulness can occur — after natural wakefulness — is gradually and incrementally over a long period of development. Sometimes this happens accidentally, but in most cases gradual awakening is undertaken consciously and occurs by following spiritual practices and paths.

Most people accept their normal vision of the world as reality and their normal state of psychological discord as inevitable. But for those who realize that they are asleep — who instinctively sense that their awareness is limited, that their psychological discord can be healed, and that there's a more authentic identity beneath the normal superficial self — the impulse to wake up usually becomes the main motivating force of their lives. These people aren't particularly interested in taking up a profession and becoming successful or wealthy, or in accumulating possessions like cars or furniture. They aren't particularly concerned about their appearance or trying to impress other people with their status or charm. Rather than seeking pleasures and comforts, they devote their lives to something much more important: following their impulse for self-transformation. They become what are sometimes called seekers, but what we will call "awakeners."

For some people, this impulse to awaken is completely innate and was always inside them. For others, it emerges after temporary awakening experiences. A person might have an experience of heightened awareness, oneness, and deep serenity while walking in the countryside, while making love, or after taking a psychedelic substance such as LSD. They become suddenly aware that *there is more*, that their normal vision of the world is limited and their normal state of being is just *one* state of being. They feel that the state of being they experience in these moments is somehow truer and more authentic than their normal one. After experiencing heightened awareness, they may begin to investigate spiritual paths and practices as a way of regaining access to this dimension in a more stable and ongoing way. Although I'm generally cautious about using psychedelic substances as a method of awakening, they can provide what Ken Wilber calls a "peek experience" (as opposed to a *peak* experience), a glimpse of an unsuspected transcendental dimension that brings about a change in their conception of reality and a shift in values. (I'll discuss the question of whether psychedelics can lead to permanent, ongoing wakefulness in chapter 9.)

This impulse to wake up can cause frustration if it doesn't find an outlet. As with people who are naturally wakeful, awakeners might wonder if there's something wrong with them, why they don't feel satisfied with the pleasures and goals that most people strive for. They might feel that they are "outsiders" who can't fit in to ordinary life. (Colin Wilson's *The Outsider* is all about people in this phase.) But awakeners can usually find an outlet for their impulse to wake up without difficulty, due to widespread public knowledge of spiritual practices and paths. Awakeners are instinctively drawn to spirituality, even if they might not be aware of why they feel attracted to it. They may only be aware of the impulse to quiet their minds, to find inner peace, or to overcome self-centeredness, although, at a deeper level, these are expressions of their instinct to awaken. (Of course, there are other reasons why people follow spiritual teachings or practices besides a straightforward impulse for awakening. Some people adopt spirituality as a kind of religion and use it to satisfy their psychological needs for belonging, identity, and consolation. For example, followers of guru-centered spiritual traditions sometimes see the guru in quasi-divine terms, projecting notions of perfection and omnipotence onto them and using their worship and faith as a way of escaping from their own psychological issues.)

For some people, gradual wakefulness may come from following a formal spiritual tradition, such as Buddhism, Sufism, or Kabbalah. Or with even more commitment, a person may experience gradual wakefulness by becoming a monk and living the monastic lifestyle of ascetic self-discipline, renunciation, prayer, and meditation. Or more informally, a person may experience gradual wakefulness without following a specific spiritual path but through living a spiritual lifestyle of their own choice. They may practice regular meditation, altruism, and service, and spend a good deal of time in solitude and quiet. These practices and lifestyles may have the effect of gradually transforming their being, moving them slowly from a state of sleep into wakefulness.

Paths and Practices of Gradual Awakening

Before looking into cases of gradual awakening from my own research, we'll return our attention to the spiritual traditions we looked at in chapter 2. In that chapter we looked at how they conceive of the state of wakefulness; in this section we'll look at how they suggest we should go about *reaching* this state. That is, we'll look at the different paths, practices, and lifestyle guidelines they recommend to bring about gradual wakefulness.

Of course, spiritual practices like meditation can induce temporary awakening experiences, which is part of their value. But even more valuable is their long-term, cumulative effect. As well as allowing us to step outside the narrow, claustrophobic room of our normal state of being for short periods, they can enable us to gradually *dismantle* the room so that we can become permanently free.[1]

Spiritual paths and spiritual practices represent an amazing discovery: the state of being that we develop as we become adults isn't firm and fixed. We have the freedom and capacity to *change* our state of being. To borrow Plato's cave metaphor, we aren't doomed to spend our whole lives staring at the shadows on the wall of the cave; we're free to gradually turn ourselves around, to face the light. This isn't easy — the intense effort and self-discipline required to achieve this transformation are beyond most people. But it can be done. The psychological structures that generate our normal experience can be permanently altered. The psychic mold that causes normal psychological structures to quickly reform after awakening experiences can be dismantled.

Millions of people discover their capacity to self-transform in every generation, but it was originally made thousands of years ago, after human beings underwent the psychological transformation that I call the Fall. The people who first made this discovery formed the spiritual traditions we looked at in chapter 2. Through experimentation they developed specific practices and techniques to gradually transform their state of being. They also developed general lifestyle guidelines to facilitate this change. In some cases, these practices and guidelines grew into highly detailed systems of self-development, which served as very effective paths of wakefulness.

As I mentioned in chapter 2, ancient India developed the deepest and most sophisticated understanding of wakefulness. And ancient Indian sages and philosophers designed a wide variety of spiritual practices and paths to facilitate awakening.

The Buddha's Eightfold Path was one of the first — if not *the* first — attempts to clearly and carefully delineate a system of cultivating wakefulness. The Buddha actually referred to his path as one of "gradual training." In one of the earliest Buddhist texts, the Udana, he uses the metaphor of an ocean shelf that gradually slopes down to a sudden precipice: "So also in this Dhamma and Discipline there is a gradual training, a gradual course, a gradual progression, and there is no sudden penetration to final knowledge."[2]

The Eightfold Path sets out a wide variety of lifestyle guidelines, covering three main areas: wisdom, ethical conduct, and concentration. Wisdom includes "right view" or "right understanding," which means seeing the world as it is, without delusion and ignorance, and understanding the nature and origins of human suffering. (*Right view* has also been interpreted as a nondogmatic, detached way of seeing without any preexisting concept.) Wisdom also includes right intention or right thought, which means resolving to change, to rid yourself of negative qualities, and to commit to the spiritual path. The ethical aspect of the path includes right speech, right action, and right livelihood. The concentrative aspects of the path — right mindfulness and right concentration — open up the four *jhanas*, states of deepening absorption in which you progressively transcend desires, thoughts, and sensations and reach a final state of complete emptiness and pure awareness. In other words, the path leads to a state of wakefulness in which, in the Buddha's words, there is "purity of equanimity and mindfulness, neither pleasure nor pain. He sits, permeating the body with a pure, bright awareness, so that there is nothing of his entire body unpervaded by pure, bright awareness."[3]

Several centuries after the Buddha, around the second to third century CE, the Indian sage Patanjali developed (or at least first set in writing) a similar path to awakening. The Yoga Sutras, the text in which Patanjali describes his eight-limbed path, is typically seen as the most authoritative text on Yoga philosophy and practice. On the eight-limbed path, you begin by (1) regulating your behavior (for example, abstaining from violence and dishonesty, refraining from sensory pleasures and possessions) and (2) developing self-discipline. You then proceed through (3) yoga *asanas* (postures) and (4) breath control, and then into (5) sensory withdrawal, when you begin to practice mental *inwardness*, resting your attention in your own mental space. You then learn the (6) practice of complete mental focus, concentrating on an object or an activity so fully that your mind becomes quiet and still, then move on to (7) the practice of meditation, where you learn to empty your mind and yet at the same time remain highly alert and conscious. After successfully proceeding through these stages, you attain the final state of (8) *samadhi*, a permanent higher state of consciousness in which you transcend duality and experience the self as part of the spiritual essence of the universe.

Due to the clear similarities between Patanjali's eight-limbed path and the Buddha's Eightfold Path, most scholars believe that Patanjali was influenced by the Buddhist model. The basic ideas that Patanjali collected and codified were probably developed before Buddhism (and in turn had probably influenced the Buddha), but it seems clear that Patanjali adopted the framework of the Buddhist path in an attempt to create a similar model out of the teachings of Yoga. Despite this, there are some clear differences between the two paths. For example, the Buddhist path doesn't include yoga *asanas* or breathing exercises (although meditative breathing is a Buddhist practice). Most important, the eight aspects of the Buddhist path don't have the same linear orientation as the stages of the path of Yoga. The eight interconnected factors are worked on concurrently. (As such, the Buddhist Eightfold Path is an early version of the integral philosophy developed by the twentieth-century Indian philosopher Sri Aurobindo and more recently by Ken Wilber.)

Both Hinduism and Buddhism are broad traditions, of course, and other paths of awakening were developed within them. In Tantric — and some Yogic — schools, awakening is interpreted in terms of raising *kundalini*, the "coiled energy" at the lowest of our seven chakras. Once *kundalini* is aroused, it travels through an energy channel (the *sushumna*, which runs roughly parallel with the spine), all the way up to the highest chakra, the *sahasrara*, at the crown of the head. Here it manifests itself as wakefulness. If you can permanently settle or establish the energy at the seventh chakra, you will be in a permanent state of wakefulness in which you attain *nirvikalpa samadhi* in union with *brahman*. The instinctive energies associated with the lower chakras move upward and are transformed into a higher spiritual energy called *ojas*. According to the Yoga Kundalini Upanishad, at this point, with the rising of *kundalini*, "The Yogin is exclusively absorbed in the Atman....He takes his stand in his own Self" and "enjoys this highest state. He becomes devoted to the Atman and attains peace."[4]

Tantric and Yogic texts recommend methods that can be used to raise *kundalini*, including *asanas*, *mudras* (gestures), breath (*prana*) control, and forms of meditation. The Yoga Kundalini Upanishad states that two things are necessary to raise *kundalini*: the restraint of *prana* and a technique called *saraswati-chalana*, which involves sitting in the *padmasana* posture, manipulating your breath, and holding your ribs so that the *saraswati nadi* can be opened and *kundalini* can flow through. Another hatha yoga text, the *Khecarividya*, recommends a *mudra* called the *khecari*, in which the tongue is placed above the soft palate toward the nasal cavity.[5]

In the Buddhist tradition, the Sri Lankan scholar Buddhaghosa formulated a seven-stage path to awakening. This progressive process begins with purification of conduct and mind and ends with purification by knowledge and vision, which is equivalent to enlightenment. Later Buddhist traditions formulated their own systems. The Mahayana text the *Abhisamayalamkara*, for example, suggests a five-stage path toward enlightenment that includes renunciation, meditation, and the realization of emptiness, leading to a final stage of complete purification of being. Meanwhile, the Tibetan tradition of Dzogchen developed a detailed path to awakening that includes a massive range of preliminary practices such as contemplating death and impermanence, building a relationship with a spiritual teacher, and developing compassion. These preliminaries lead to the main practice of meditation, progressing through deeper layers of absorption to the recognition of your pure awareness and emptiness of being.

Outside Buddhism and Hinduism, the Chinese Daoists developed their own paths to awakening. They conceived awakening as an overall process of cultivation. As with the paths of Yoga and Buddhism, the foundation of this process is ethical action, or virtue (*de*, in Chinese). Other aspects include meditation, psycho-physical exercises (such as qigong), correct diet, and living in harmony with nature. More specifically, awakening is conceived through a process of inner alchemy (*neiden*). Similar to *kundalini* yoga, lower forms of energy are transmuted into higher forms through breathing and meditation exercises. First of all, sexual energy (*jing*) is transmuted into vital energy (*chi*), which is then transmuted into spiritual energy (*shen*). *Shen* then becomes purified, which is equivalent to a state of *ming*, or enlightenment, in which you return to nothingness and become one with the Dao.

In the Christian world, the most systematic paths of awakening were developed as a part of monastic traditions. Monks in every tradition — including Buddhist and Hindu — make awakening the main aim of their lives and sacrifice everything else for it. Their whole lives are organized and arranged to facilitate a process of awakening. This involves renunciation, voluntary poverty, celibacy, long periods of silence and solitude, and long periods of prayer and meditation.

In Jewish spirituality, there's no monastic tradition, as befits its emphasis on integrating spirituality into everyday life and its belief that the enlightenment of the individual will help heal the world. Nevertheless, as noted in chapter 2, Kabbalistic texts recommend a variety of techniques and lifestyle guidelines to promote gradual spiritual development and move toward union with God.

All of these paths have slight differences, but their aim is essentially the same: to transcend our normal constricted and separate state of being and develop a more expansive and intensified state. We can think of them as slightly different routes — some more detailed than others — that lead to the same destination, wakefulness.

Common Themes

So what do these different paths tell us about the way to wakefulness? What are the common principles that we can follow if we want to transform our state of being? I will mention five here, which I believe are the most significant.

Ethical Behavior

The first principle that all traditions agree on — particularly in the initial stages — is *regulating one's ethical behavior*. The first stage of Yoga, *yama*, can be translated as "restraint" and includes five moral obligations: nonharming, truthfulness, nonstealing, chastity, and greedlessness. Similarly, three aspects of Buddhism's Eightfold Path refer to ethical conduct: right speech, right action, and right livelihood.

Why should ethical behavior be so important in spiritual development? This is probably a combination of three factors: mental purity, self-discipline, and energy. We create disturbance inside us when we behave unethically. Ripples of unease and anxiety flow both inside and outside us. (From the Buddhist and Hindu perspectives, this also creates bad karma.) When we behave ethically we become pure and still inside, and prepare ourselves for the deeper stillness of spiritual development. Unethical types of behavior such as greed, exploitation, and untruthfulness are also fundamentally self-centered; they are based on furthering our own interests over other people's. So regulating our behavior means moving beyond self-centeredness, which again becomes more important as we move further along the spiritual path.

In a similar way, behaving ethically requires self-control and self-discipline, which are also essential for further development. Some traditions (such as Yoga) believe that regulating our behavior is important as a way of conserving our energy. Rather than expending energy through desires and emotions (such as greed or hatred), our energy concentrates inside us, and this surplus energy is used to fuel spiritual transformation.

Purgation or Purification

A second principle in gradual awakening agreed on by all traditions is *purgation* or *purification*. This follows naturally from the self-discipline we develop by controlling our moral behavior. Purgation is a process of inner strengthening or spiritual training by which we gain some control over our impulses and desires, particularly our instinctive attraction to comfort and pleasure. Through this process we develop stronger willpower, become more self-sufficient, and less dependent on external conditions for our well-being. Our intention and impulse to wake up begins to override other impulses. Again, this process can be seen in terms of energy: as we restrain our desires for comfort and pleasure, we build up our inner energy.

In some traditions, the process of purgation or purification expresses itself in ascetic practices, such as the *tapas* of Yoga, which can mean celibacy, fasting, prolonged standing, or exposure to heat or cold. In Christianity (and to a lesser extent in Islamic mysticism), these ascetic practices were often more extreme, even to the point of sadism. The fourteenth-century mystic Henry de Suso spent years wearing a hair shirt and an iron chain, and wore a cross on his back containing thirty inward-facing needles and nails. Other traditions such as Buddhism or Kabbalah put less emphasis on this process of self-denial and self-control. The Buddha lived as an ascetic prior to his awakening and was aware of the dangers of the lifestyle. He therefore advocated the "middle way" between pain and pleasure. Tantric traditions take an even more divergent approach. They see the body as the manifestation of the divine and make a conscious effort to integrate it into their paths of awakening.

These two principles of behavioral regulation and purification can be viewed as preparatory stages of the spiritual path before real awakening begins. Together they form a process of developing self-discipline and inner stillness and stability (and also an intensification of inner energy) so that we're ready to *enter into* ourselves and begin the real work of remolding our state of being. (In Patanjali's model, this is equivalent to the stage of sensory withdrawal or *pratyahara*, which comes before meditation.)

Letting Go of Psychological Attachments — Renunciation

A third principle agreed on by all traditions (or if you like, the first method of *real* inner transformation they agree on) is *becoming free of psychological attachments*. Dissolving psychological attachments often occurs in an involuntarily way and, as such, can be a powerful trigger both of gradual and sudden awakening. But in traditional spiritual paths, this is undertaken through a conscious process of renunciation.

Renunciation means being free of the encumbrances and worldly concerns that dominate most people's lives. It means practicing voluntary poverty and living without possessions, and being free of worldly ambitions for success, wealth, or power, and social roles that confer status and identity. In some traditions, it also means being celibate so that one can be free of the responsibilities of family life. (As we've seen, Jewish spiritual traditions take a very different view to this, as do Tantric traditions. In Tantra, sex is seen as a form of spiritual practice.) Renunciation is, of course, the core of the monastic way of life. Monks separate themselves from ordinary human society primarily as a way of ensuring that they remain free of psychological attachments.

Renunciation is important to the traditions partly because they believe that awakening has to be the primary thing in our lives. We have to give our whole selves to it and so can't afford to be distracted by business, ambitions, or possessions. Once again, we can see this in terms of energy. The less attached we are to external things, the more we build up our inner spiritual energy. And finally, one of the biggest dangers of psychological attachments — as we shall see — is that they strengthen our identity, build up our ego, and make us more separate and disconnected from the world and our own deeper selves. (Interestingly, both Peace Pilgrim and I went through a process of purification and renunciation, not as part of the process of awakening but as a way of stabilizing and integrating our natural wakefulness. This suggests that purification and renunciation are often a necessary part of wakefulness in whatever form it manifests itself.)

Service

The fourth common principle of different spiritual traditions' approach to awakening is *service*. Altruism and compassion are characteristics of the wakeful state, but they can also help generate wakefulness. In Buddhism, *metta* — translated as "benevolence," "good will," or "loving-kindness"

— is the first of one of four sublime states that can be cultivated as a means of attaining enlightenment. The second and third of the sublime states are also related to kindness and service — compassion and empathic joy. (The fourth sublime state is equanimity.) In the Buddhist practice of *metta bhavana*, meditation is used as a way of cultivating *metta*, spreading loving-kindness out in wider and wider circles to embrace more and more people and eventually all sentient beings. As the Metta Sutta states, "Even as a mother protects with her life her child, her only child, so with a boundless heart should one cherish all living beings; radiating kindness over the entire world."[6] Service is a similarly important part of the Jewish and Sufi paths to awakening. In Sufism, for example, consciously practicing service is an essential part of the process of becoming one with God. Practicing self-sacrifice and altruism opens us up to God because the nature of God is love. Our own nature becomes attuned to God's, and we become one with it.

Meditation

The fifth and final theme of traditional paths of awakening is the practice of meditation. Meditation is the *sine qua non* of spiritual practices, the essential aspect of every path of awakening from Buddhism and Yoga to Daoism, Sufism, and Kabbalah. Even in Christianity, meditation practice has a long history, particularly in the monastic traditions and the Eastern Orthodox church. As I point out in *Waking from Sleep*, meditation can be an effective means of generating temporary awakening experiences. However, its main purpose — and its main effect — is long term: to bring about a gradual shift in our psyche; to change our psychological structure and our psychological functioning in such a way that we gradually move away from our normal state of sleep to a state of wakefulness.

In spiritual traditions, meditation is seen as essential for a number of reasons. First of all, it stills the mind, quietening our distracting thought-chatter and giving us a sense of inner peace. This enables us to go inward, too. The surface thought-chatter of our minds acts as a kind of barrier, which prevents us from investigating the deeper levels of our being. But when meditation stills the mind, we're free to go into ourselves, into deeper and purer levels of consciousness. In addition, meditation brings increased self-control. Once we learn to quiet our thoughts we have an increased capacity for concentration and an increased ability to control our desires and regulate our behavior.

Some meditative practices emphasize the importance of *observing* one's thought processes rather than quieting them. This is the basis of Buddhist *vipassana* meditation, where the aim is simply to stand back from your thoughts, watching them arise and fade away without being carried away by them. In practice, though, this type of meditation usually also leads to quieting the mind because our thoughts are naturally quieter and slower when we don't latch onto them.

Vipassana meditation emphasizes another important aspect of meditation in general: the process of *disidentifying* with our thoughts. All forms of meditation help bring about a kind of identity shift, where we come to realize that our true identity isn't the ego self that does our thinking for us but the deeper, more authentic part of us that *observes* the thinking ego self. While this identity shift is taking place, we also experience an increased sense of connectedness with the world around us, other human beings, and other beings in general. The more we meditate, the weaker the ego aspect of the self-system seems to become.

The energetic aspect to meditation is important because it explains why meditation generates heightened awareness. The normal chattering of our ego uses up a great deal of mental energy. Likewise, it takes a lot of energy to maintain the ego as a structure, with its strong boundaries and sense of identity. So when thinking becomes quieter and the ego becomes weaker as a structure, a large amount of energy is suddenly freed. This energy naturally redirects itself into perception. There's a redistribution of psychic energy — in fact, the exact reversal of the redistribution that occurred with the Fall, when perception was switched off to the phenomenal world so that energy could be conserved for the functioning of the ego. Perception becomes intensified and enriched, leading to heightened awareness and a renewed awareness of the is-ness and sentience of the world. In the words of the psychiatrist Arthur Deikman, who conducted one of the first studies into the effects of meditation in 1963, meditation brings about a "deautomatization of perception" that leads to an increased sense of the vividness and beauty of everyday objects.[7] We temporarily switch into a different kind of self-system in which the ego aspect (or sense of "I") is much less powerful and dominant.

But this doesn't have to be temporary, of course. If we meditate regularly, we can generate a permanent and ongoing deautomatization of perception.

Beyond Traditions

In view of these powerful positive effects, it's not surprising that meditation has come to be used *outside* spiritual traditions. Forms of secular meditation have become popular in the West, from the Transcendental Meditation popularized by Maharishi Mahesh Yogi and the Beatles in the 1960s to the modern phenomenon of mindfulness meditation developed by Jon Kabat-Zinn and others. Of course, many people don't (at least consciously) practice meditation because they want to move toward wakefulness. They may meditate to relieve stress and anxiety, experience calmness and mental clarity, increase their energy levels, or deal with physical pain. Nevertheless, it's likely that regularly practicing meditation will generate some degree of awakening in a person, even if they don't realize it.

The awakening effects of meditation are no doubt *less* powerful without the support of other spiritual practices (such as service and letting go of psychological attachments), but recent research shows that secular, independent meditation of this kind can bring about significant changes to our state of being. Research into mindfulness, for example, shows that it can bring about exactly the permanent deautomatization of perception I've just mentioned — a state of ongoing, *spontaneous* mindfulness, when a person becomes naturally mindful without making a conscious effort to be. Studies find that the long-term effects of regular mindfulness practice include heightened awareness and increased attentiveness (as well as increased *control* of attention), together with less automatic cognitive processes and more spontaneous and present-centered behavior.[8]

In fact, all of the principles of awakening we've looked at can be applied — individually and collectively — outside spiritual traditions. Just as the state of wakefulness doesn't have to be interpreted in the context of spiritual traditions, the process of awakening can take place outside spiritual traditions (while following the same basic principles highlighted by the traditions). And it's these cases of gradual secular awakening that we're going to examine in the next chapter.

6. Gradual Awakening outside Spiritual Traditions

If someone feels the impulse to awaken, it's easy to understand why they might feel drawn to established spiritual traditions like Buddhism or Kabbalah. Spiritual traditions provide a clear framework, a tried and tested path of development. They offer guidance and encouragement from others who have followed — and are following — the same path. In the Hindu tradition, for example, the guru has an important role as a guide through the process of awakening. Following a spiritual tradition can be like traveling along a well-worn route to a destination, with a seasoned traveler to show you the way. The framework may help to ensure that the seeker doesn't go astray, doesn't misread signals, and doesn't fall prey to self-delusion or self-inflation.

However, paths to wakefulness can be difficult to disentangle from the religious traditions that they are allied to. If you feel an impulse to wake up, you could follow the Christian monastic path of awakening, but that may involve accepting certain beliefs and concepts that make you uncomfortable. You might find the Sufi path of awakening attractive but not feel comfortable with the Islamic background of the tradition. In the same way, Hinduism's cultural background may make Yogic paths of awakening seem alien to you. Buddhism has less religious or cultural baggage than any other tradition, which is presumably why it's the most popular path of awakening for secular Westerners in the modern world. It is primarily psychological and existential rather than metaphysical or mythological. Its highly structured and detailed approach — perhaps the *most* structured of any tradition — also makes it appealing.

Overall, though — probably because of the declining influence of conventional religion — more and more people are following paths of gradual awakening outside spiritual traditions. This approach can be problematic, like traveling to a destination without a clear plan or direction. It can involve a kind of "pick and mix" supermarket approach to spirituality often criticized by traditionalists. Less direct support and guidance from teachers and fewer ground rules to follow may lead to disorientation. Without a grounding in tradition, there may be a greater danger of delusion and ego-inflation.

On the other hand, trying out different practices or elements of different paths and finding the ones that are best suited to us can allow for a more intuitive and empirical approach to awakening. We don't have to give our allegiance to any particular philosophy or accept any particular beliefs. We can simply focus on the transformational practices themselves, without any conceptual baggage.

Most of the examples of gradual wakefulness I've investigated have been of this kind — two of which I briefly summarize below.

Daniel's Gradual Awakening

Daniel was born into a middle-class family in Switzerland and, like many people in Western societies, was brought up to believe that happiness comes from achievement and success. After studying at the most prestigious business school in Switzerland, he took a high-paying banking job. On top of his long work hours, he studied for qualifications in finance and also began to go climbing, mainly because he loved the sense of achievement when he reached the top of a mountain. But despite his success, Daniel had a sense that something was missing. As he said, "My life got all too planned, rational, goal-driven. Mostly, I would have this subtle feeling of being stuck in a tight corset.... I had trapped myself in fixed and narrow views about myself and the world I inhabited that shut me out of truly experiencing it."

His thirst for achievement led Daniel to attempt to climb Mount Aconcagua in Argentina, the highest mountain in the Americas. This led to an important realization, which he described as follows:

On the last day of the ascent my girlfriend couldn't join us as she had been diagnosed with symptoms of pulmonary edema. In the days before the final push to the summit it increasingly became clear that nobody of our group was physically up to the challenge and the incident with my girlfriend was just another proof of that. I had grown somehow uneasy and tight during these days but, again, just wouldn't allow myself to acknowledge my deficiencies. Leaving my girlfriend back in the tent while I struggled to reach the top, the utter uselessness and stupidity of climbing the mountain became clear to me. I didn't really like climbing in high altitude. There was no joy in it. It was just a pure ego thing for me. I felt incredibly guilty for having dragged my girlfriend to the end of the world for nothing but to satisfy my egoism. As I was thinking that way and my motivation and energy faded, something happened. I remember looking at the starry night sky and feeling that I had completely lost my way.... Then I did something I hadn't done for a long time: I just gave up. And when I allowed myself to give in, I let go and turned around a few hundred meters short of the top. I turned my back on my old ways and it felt good somehow. I left some of my old self on that mountain that night.

After this trip, Daniel became increasingly frustrated by his materialistic way of life and more and more conscious that it would not lead to well-being. The financial crisis at that time meant that he had a lot of free time, and his girlfriend introduced him to Buddhism. He began to meditate and knew straight away that it was right for him. He quickly began to sense an inner well-being that he knew was more stable and authentic than the short-lived thrill of achievement. As he said, "It was one of these things you get a taste of and instantly know that that's what you have to hold on to, whatever the cost."

Not long afterward, he took LSD and experienced a profound sense of connection with nature and other human beings. As he continued his meditation practice, he began to realize more and more that he didn't need to "do" anything or "be somebody" in order to be happy.

Six months later, he gave up his apartment, sold most of his possessions, resigned from his job, and traveled overland to India with his girlfriend, with plans to explore spirituality more deeply. Unfortunately, his relationship with his girlfriend unraveled, and they split up before reaching India. But he continued on and, once there, effectively underwent a process of renunciation in which he relinquished his psychological attachments. As he told me, "My previous life completely unwound: no more lover, no more high-paying job, no more nice apartment with lakeside view. I felt painfully stripped and bare. But I knew I was doing the right thing."

In India, he meditated regularly and had some powerful spiritual experiences. But his most important experience occurred when he became ill with the flu during a *vipassana* meditation retreat. At first he felt full of self-pity but then experienced a moment of acceptance of his predicament, which initiated a process of surrender that touched every area of his life:

> In the following weeks I was able to let go of a lot of grief, guilt, and shame from painful experiences in my life. I shed a lot of tears but it was tremendously healing. My vision of things became gradually much clearer, more lucid. There was a newfound joy in just looking at and experiencing things. Awe and wonder returned to my life.... About ten days before I left the retreat, while meditating on a koan (rationally unsolvable Buddhist riddle) I had a sudden big opening into realizing that the only thing there was and forever will be was this One "thing" we are all manifestations of. The accompanying "high" of realizing that all was okay lasted almost three days. There were waves of energy and I was giggling a lot. At other times there was a deep silence, where I could be sitting for an hour or more completely unwavering in the same spot, being filled with bliss.

After a few more weeks in India, Daniel felt that he should return to Europe to try to integrate and stabilize his wakefulness. He felt that he needed to face the conditioning and the thought patterns associated with his previous life and try to transcend them. The challenge led to a deepening of his awareness. He began to experience a transcendence of duality, of the sense that he was a separate and distinct "I" experiencing the world.

Now he began to identify himself with an "eternal witness" beyond experience. He described this experience and this present state in these terms:

> It [the witness] is the silent always-omnipresent container in which and through which things manifest. So, the body and the "me" is an illusion and "real" at the same time. As this realization is becoming more integrated in my everyday perception of reality I am noticing a shift from a main concern about "me" to a concern about "us," which is what I think spirituality is all about. If there is a meaning to life then it is to live, and to live means to love. To love, for me, means to care about "us" more than about "me." Hence, a self-centered life painfully lacks meaning and thus fulfillment.

It is now — at the time of writing — six years since Daniel gave up his high-paying banking job and his promising financial career. He now works as a teacher and lives in a small village in the Swiss mountains. He has a sense of living authentically rather than through the values of his culture, and a strong sense of spaciousness. At the same time, he feels that he is in a state of flux, that his development is still continuing and may never come to an end. As he told me, "The only constant may indeed be change. I intend to try to flow as gracefully and genuinely as possible with it."

Ed's Gradual Awakening

Ed is an elderly American who has experienced wakefulness as his stable, ongoing state for around twenty years. His gradual awakening began in his forties, at a time when he was trying to fulfill his ambition to become a successful author. He had received many rejections from agents and publishers but eventually managed to publish two novels and a memoir. However, all three books were failures, critically and commercially, and eventually he felt he had no choice but to accept that he wasn't going to make it as a writer. He was also studying part-time for a PhD in English and taught low-level courses at his university but never managed to establish a successful academic career either. This also contributed to his sense of failure. He later recognized that this period of failure was helpful to his spiritual development. As he told me, "It was as if the cosmos was saying, very gently, 'Relinquish attachment to outcomes, or else.' I was invited to become detached by outcomes."

After this, he started to go through a "very gradual and gentle" process of awakening. He started reading and contemplating, and meditating. His meditation was irregular at first, but then he found a form of Tantric meditation that appealed to him. He practiced this intensively for four years and went through a gradual process of healing. His frustration and anger faded away, and he began to feel a general sense of compassion and forgiveness toward himself and anyone who had hurt him earlier in his life. Then he began to disidentify with his ego and open up to a deeper, more spacious part of himself, which seemed to experience a natural state of contentment and an easy and natural connection to the rest of reality.

Now Ed lives what he calls "a very surrendered life." He said, "I have no further ambitions. At this point there is nowhere to go." He senses that he has no ego-identity, that the name *Ed* is a convenient fiction, and that the essence of his being is formless and nameless, a universal consciousness that is expressing itself through him. He has no fear of death, since "I don't identify consciousness with form." He lives in a part of the United States where people are highly patriotic and define themselves in terms of their religious and political affiliations, but he simply feels himself to be "a citizen of the cosmos."

He also experiences much less thought-chatter than before his awakening. When thoughts do arise, he doesn't identify with them. He sees them as "clouds drifting by" that he doesn't have to latch onto. He enjoys doing nothing in particular and spends most of his time looking after his wife (who has Parkinson's disease), fishing, walking his dogs, or just contemplating nature.

Spiritual Literature as a Spiritual Practice

Reading isn't usually thought of as a spiritual practice. Indeed, some spiritual teachers are dubious about the importance of books — as the Zen saying goes, "The finger that points at the moon is not the moon." In other words, you can't describe the indescribable; you can't confine or reduce spiritual experience to words, either spoken or written. In addition, if we rely on books too much, there's a danger of becoming too entangled in concepts and ideas, of becoming immersed in the map and losing sight of reality. There's also a danger of intellectual pride, of believing that you're special because you have access to complex, esoteric knowledge to which other people aren't privy.

All of this is true, but I believe that books can still be helpful, in two ways. First, they can be helpful on a basic informational level, to provide guidance and orientation. Spiritual awakening can be confusing. As we saw in chapter 4, people who are naturally awake may not be able to understand or accept their wakefulness. And when awakening happens suddenly and dramatically, people may also struggle to make sense of their new state. Books can provide awakened individuals with confirmation and self-understanding, and help them build an intellectual framework to make sense of their state. I know this from personal experience — books such as F. C. Happold's *Mysticism* and the Upanishads were essential for me, as mirrors in which I could see myself. They gave me a clear sense of who I am and so helped to alleviate my confusion and frustration.

Second, some books seem to belie the "finger at the moon" adage. Some books *can* actually be the moon, in the sense that they can actually *communicate* wakefulness. A reader may experience temporary wakefulness as they read certain passages or poems, or even move gradually toward *permanent* wakefulness through ongoing engagement with certain books or authors.

Some poets, such as Walt Whitman or the thirteenth-century Sufi mystic Rumi, certainly have this effect. In fact, poetry is an effective way of communicating wakefulness because it encourages stillness in the reader. You can't read poems like emails or newspaper reports — you have to slow down, be attentive and receptive. In this way reading poetry can be a form of meditation. (It's interesting to note that this kind of contemplative reading is recognized as a spiritual practice in Christian spirituality, where it's called *lectio divina*, or "divine reading.")

I've come across several cases of gradual awakening where reading was an important factor. Most of these were linked to the books of Eckhart Tolle, whose writings have an uncanny power to transmit awakening to the reader. One person described to me how she has been "gradually experiencing inner awakening over the last five years thanks to Eckhart Tolle." Another person, Barbara, described a gradual process of awakening that occurred as a result of psychological turmoil combined with reading spiritual literature — mainly the work of Eckhart Tolle. She described how devastated she was by the "totally unexpected loss of my thirty-two-year good marriage," until a stranger in a bookshop recommended Tolle's *Practicing the Power of Now*. She described the book's impact this way: "That night I read the book right through and had a most astonishing realization in every chapter of what my loss was about.... The book gave me a direction for going forward. I slept for the first time in weeks." After this she read Tolle's other books, a book by Byron Katie, then some of my own books. She began to accept the loss of her marriage and find a new appreciation and wonder in the present moment. Her outlook and attitude toward life changed completely. As she described her present state, "Five years after the apparent 'catastrophe' [the end of her marriage], I am accepting, content and curious and passionate.... I feel a tremendous sense of appreciation and awe. I feel incredibly fortunate."

Involuntary Gradual Awakening

Although the gradual awakenings of Daniel, Ed, and Barbara were largely propelled by spiritual practice, the dissolution of psychological attachments was an important aspect of them, too. For Daniel, this was largely a conscious process — letting go of his career, ambitions, possessions, apartment, relationship to his girlfriend, and so on. However, Ed was *forced* to let go of his attachments by professional failure. He had no choice but to give up his ambition to be a writer, and this initiated a process of further letting go or detachment. In a similar way, the end of Barbara's marriage (and the dissolution of her attachment to the relationship) was the trigger for her awakening process. (As I mentioned in the last chapter, the dissolution of psychological attachments is related to the practice of renunciation in many spiritual traditions. Renunciation can be seen as a kind of conscious dissolution of psychological attachments.)

Ed's and Barbara's stories highlight the fact that gradual awakening can sometimes be an *involuntary* process. This was only partly the case for them, but other cases I've collected show gradual awakening as primarily an involuntary process — that is, a process that occurred without any conscious volition and without any spiritual practices or paths.

This involuntary awakening can occur when, without realizing, people follow lifestyles or undergo experiences that happen to include the same transformational elements as spiritual practices and paths. For example, their lifestyles may have strong meditative aspects to them and/or strong aspects of service. My friend, the spiritual teacher Russel Williams, underwent a three-year period of unintentional spiritual training while working for a circus. He groomed, fed, and watered the horses, and learned to use their different harnesses. He came to feel a powerful sense of connection with them. He also spent a great deal of time observing the horses in order to understand them. Here he describes how this life of mindful awareness and service affected him:

> I grew to love the animals. . . . It was impossible not to, living with them twenty-four hours a day. I was determined that I was going to understand them wholly, for what they were, and realized that the only way to do that was through observing them. . . . So I set my mind to watching and observing every detail, every moment of the day, for days on end.
>
> After about three months, I noticed that I wasn't thinking anymore. My mind had gone quiet. I realized that knowing and thinking are two different things, and that you could know without thinking. I wasn't forming opinions or jumping to conclusions anymore. I began to do things spontaneously, to live in the moment. I had a strong feeling that I was finally going in the right direction, that this was my path, and I should keep going with this, carry on observing the animals so intently.
>
> It wasn't till much later that I realized that the exercise I'd given myself was mindfulness meditation. In effect, I was meditating about twenty hours a day, seven days a week for three years, completely absorbed in caring for the horses. It was a life of continual service, with no thought for myself.[1]

In theory, any job or hobby that involves a high degree of mindful awareness and service could function as a kind of spontaneous spiritual practice that leads to gradual awakening. Another person I interviewed described how, while working as a flight attendant in her mid-twenties, she underwent spiritual development even before she knew what the term *spiritual* meant. As she described from her later perspective: "My real spiritual development started then. We all worked for a common purpose. There was a real atmosphere of camaraderie. It was heaven. When I stepped onto the airplane and we waited for the passengers you had to be so intensely present. There was no time for little me, for ego to come in. It was the best spiritual practice. Just pure presence the whole time. It suited me very well, a wonderful devotional practice."

Psychological Attachments and Involuntary Gradual Awakening

In most cases though, the primary factor in most involuntary gradual awakening is the dissolution of psychological attachments (or involuntary renunciation).

I provided examples of this in my earlier book *Out of the Darkness*. Psychological attachments are the concepts that we depend on for our well-being and sense of identity. Typically, they include hopes, beliefs, achievements, possessions, and status. These might be gradually broken down as a result of a long period of illness (such as cancer), professional failure, negative events such as divorce or unemployment, or alcoholism. These attachments are the building blocks of a person's identity, so as the attachments dissolve, the person's identity also begins to dissolve, and a new identity gradually emerges to replace it.

In *Out of the Darkness*, I introduced Cheryl, who suffered from chronic fatigue syndrome, as an example of spiritual growth through involuntary renunciation. Originally Cheryl was a high-achieving career woman who lived a busy, stressful life. But this life began to unravel due to her health problems. She had to leave work and eventually became so ill that she rarely went out; she often spent the whole day in bed. Aside from her terrible physical problems, Cheryl found that the illness led to a loss of status and identity that was painful psychologically. However, this process of loss was also a process of spiritual growth. She found a new ability to live in the present, a new appreciation of life and the beauty of her surroundings, and a new sense of connection. As she told me, "Now everything seems real.... It seems to have developed over the past year or so, a heightened awareness and a great joy in everything. I appreciate things I used to take for granted."[2] She recognized that her ego was being broken down and had the sense that something else — a deeper kind of identity — was emerging in its place. As she put it, "What's left when these things are gone is what's behind the ego. It's an awareness that we're not individuated — that you and I are the same consciousness. I feel like I'm part of something greater than myself."[3]

I found a similar example in my PhD research. Kelly, a Canadian woman, suffered major trauma and stress as a result of her ten years in the Canadian military. She later recognized that her experience led to a "humbling or deconstructing of the ego" that was "the biggest single factor in my spiritual transformation." Toward the end of the ten years, she began to feel depressed and burned out. As she described it, "I thought I was crazy. I was in the bathroom at work five times a day, hiding so I could cry. I had no control over my emotions. I felt out of control.... I would start yelling and swearing (which I never do) about minor things and then have no reaction whatsoever to major things. Everything was backward. I didn't know what was happening."

After leaving the military, Kelly was diagnosed with posttraumatic stress disorder (PTSD) and major depression. She felt that she had completely lost her sense of identity:

> It was a complete loss of me as an intelligent person, me as a functioning person, me as a person except as a blob on the couch. I was suddenly none of the things I had always been: effective, efficient, controlled, perfectionistic, high-performing, extremely competent. It was awful. I felt so low. But it was also freeing. It was frightening but there was full surrender to whatever was going to happen — my body forced it. I didn't have a choice. There was just me, on the couch, doing nothing, because I literally couldn't do anything. I was forced to see my failure. And I had no idea who I was anymore.

After about a year of medical and psychological treatment Kelly became relatively functional again and sought alternative treatments to help her further. After a couple of years of deliberate healing and growth through various therapies and treatments, she began to experience glimpses of wakefulness. Once, she was out walking:

> [And I] just stopped on the sidewalk and relaxed and took in the sun. I opened my eyes and the world looked different. It was alive. It was infinite aliveness. Everything was bright. Even the space between everything. The colours were incredible and the flowers looked happy. I looked down and I realized I *was* the sidewalk.... I was amazed at what was there the whole time. It was the biggest, best joke. It took me 20 minutes to turn the street corner where I was walking because I was laughing so hard; I just kept stopping and seeing everything. And it didn't matter that people were staring at me because I was laughing wildly.... And then the next day everything went back to normal.

After other awakening experiences, Kelly began to experience a state of continual bliss and presence. At first this caused some difficulties — she was so present that words seemed superfluous, and she found it difficult to speak. It took time for her to relearn how to express herself using conventional ways of speaking. But since then there has been a process of integration in which Kelly's wakefulness has stabilized and deepened, and her intellectual functions have returned. She summarized her present state as follows:

> Now everything is a choice — how deep do I go into the vastness? If I want to have a disembodied peak experience of nothingness I just have to sit still and close my eyes. Or if I need to work on something then I simply have to choose to narrow my focus to the task. Sometimes the mind is loud and sometimes quiet but it's almost always running, unless I do the choosing of the deep nothing state where there is no form....
>
> The deep aliveness of space is so amazing it takes your words away. When you're present all the time every day seems full. A day seems to last for such a long time....

I used to shop and be addicted to home and garden television. I wanted to be an interior designer. I was obsessed with objects and creating peace in space. I was looking to possessions as a way to feel better but now I don't need to feel better. There is no attachment. I gave away all my books; I don't need things. I can have them, but I don't need them.

I used to be on guard, ready to defend myself against potential criticism or judgment, always self-conscious, wanting to be seen in the best possible way....I was always aware of myself, how I was being perceived. All of that stopped. I could just see people instead of focusing on what they thought of me. I was just listening, with so much less judgment, just allowing them to be themselves. That meant that some people fell away; they needed more engagement from me. I wasn't going in on their stories.

As an interesting — and poignant — postscript to Kelly's story, her own experiences led to an interest in spiritual teachings and traditions. She earned her PhD in transpersonal psychology and is now a university lecturer and researcher in psychology. We've now begun to do research together — in fact, we co-created the "Inventory of Spiritual/Secular Wakefulness" that appears as an appendix to this book.

Understanding Gradual Awakening

When people undergo gradual awakening, what is actually happening to them? How do spiritual practices and paths bring about changes to our state of being and help us move from our normal state of sleep to a state of wakefulness?

Gradual awakening is a process of transforming our self-system, slowly altering and remolding our normal psychological structures and psychological processes in such a way that we begin to transcend our normal sleep state.

The two most significant characteristics of our normal self-system are its highly individualized and separate sense of "I" (or ego) and its automatized perception. Meditation is the main way that we transcend the separateness of the ego. As a structure, the ego is largely maintained by thinking, so when thinking begins to fade (or even just when we become less identified with our thinking), the ego begins to fade. However, dissolving psychological attachments, the building blocks of the ego, can also be an important part of this process. As they dissolve away, the ego itself dissolves away, too. (We'll look at this process of dissolving psychological attachments, an important aspect of sudden awakening, in more detail in the next chapter.) Service and altruism contribute to this process because they have ego-transcending effects. They make us less ego-oriented, less concerned with our own personal needs and desires. They weaken the boundaries of our self-system by increasing our connectedness to other people.

As the ego aspect becomes weaker and softer, we experience a greater general sense of connection — to other human beings and living beings, to the natural world and the whole universe. We experience a greater sense of inner fullness and spaciousness now that our identity is no longer limited to the narrow confines of the ego. We experience a greater sense of well-being now that we're no longer so identified with our thoughts and no longer experience a sense of fragmentation and isolation within our own mental space.

There's an energetic aspect to this, particularly in relation to perception. Our inner energy becomes reorganized and redistributed. As the ego becomes weaker as a structure, and as its thought-chatter becomes less powerful, more energy is available for us to use perceptually. Our perceptions become energized and so no longer need to be automatic. We wake up to a brighter, more intense world. We perceive the sentience of the world again, with the spirit-force pervading it. This increased energy contributes to our sense of well-being, too. An abundant, rich, and dynamic life force, whose nature is one of effervescent joy, flows through us.

In essence, then, we slowly create a new self-system through spiritual practice (whether it's voluntary or involuntary). Our sense of "I" is much softer and less dominant, with much weaker boundaries, quieter thought processes, and intensified perception. Our self-system is reshaped into a new higher-functioning self that is free from the discord that afflicts the normal ego-centered separate self, and that can function more harmoniously, more authentically, and more beneficially for the world.

At the same time, it may not be completely accurate to say that we actually *create* a new self-system. The wakeful self-system already exists inside us as a potential. It seems to be a kind of mold that our self-system naturally forms into. We feel instinctively drawn to spiritual practice as a way of manifesting this new self-system. Spiritual practice seems to naturally allow the wakeful self-system to form in a very slow and incremental way. In a sense, it slowly *undoes* our normal self-system, erodes it away so that the latent wakeful self-system can supplant it. It's not strictly a matter of the new self-system *replacing* the old one but of the old one transforming into a new form.

The difference between natural wakefulness and gradual awakening is that, with the latter, the wakeful self-system has yet to emerge. It's like a seed, which has the impulse to grow but is still dormant and needs to be nurtured. Awakeners are drawn toward spiritual practices and paths as a way of nurturing this seed, whereas in natural wakefulness, it has already blossomed. The wakeful self-system has already emerged and established itself.

The idea that this self-system is somehow latent inside us connects to evolution; we'll investigate this in more detail in the last chapter of this book. Everyone who engages in spiritual practice is instinctively moving in *the same direction*. They aren't attempting to remold their self-system according to their own independent agenda. They're developing essentially the same characteristics; it's essentially the same type of new self-system that is forming inside them.

To me, this suggests that this self-system is latent inside the human race in general, that it has already established itself as a kind of psychological structure or mold. It's as if a road has already been laid and we're traveling along it, following a predetermined course. If this structure wasn't already established, we would all be moving in different directions, developing different characteristics and different varieties of self-systems.

You could make another analogy with sex and reproduction. People seem to be naturally drawn to spiritual practice as a method of forming this new self-system in the same way that human beings are drawn to sex in order to reproduce. Once a new human being has been conceived through sex, its development proceeds along predetermined lines, from conception to birth to adulthood. A man and a woman don't actually create a new human being from nothing. It already exists as a potential form; a blueprint for its development already exists. But a man and a woman facilitate its emergence and its development. In the same way, we use spiritual practice to facilitate the emergence of a new kind of self that already exists as a potential and whose path of development is already established.

7. Sudden Awakening:
Transformation through Turmoil

The most common way in which human beings shift into a permanent state of wakefulness is through a sudden and dramatic transformation triggered by intense psychological turmoil.

Over the last twenty years or so, psychologists have become increasingly aware of the phenomenon of posttraumatic growth. A great deal of research has shown that people who go through traumatic events such as accidents, serious illness, or divorce often experience positive aftereffects. In the long term, after the initial intense shock and stress have passed, many people report feeling more resilient and confident, and more appreciative about their lives. They feel that their relationships have become more authentic and fulfilling, and that they have a stronger sense of meaning and purpose. They often become interested in spirituality and have a more accepting attitude toward death.

In my own research I found that trauma can lead to *transformation* as well as growth — a phenomenon that I call posttraumatic transformation. Intense psychological turmoil and trauma can generate a sudden and dramatic shift into a new, higher-functioning identity, with a new perspective on life, a new awareness of reality, different cognitive and perceptual functioning, new values and goals. This shift isn't always *completely* sudden — some people report undergoing some gradual development (including some temporary awakening experiences) before a sudden shift occurs. Other people report a few different "shift" experiences rather than a single one.

In my book *Out of the Darkness*, I call people who undergo this transformation *shifters*. Shifters feel that they have become different people, that their previous selves have dissolved away and new selves have replaced them. As two of them told me, "It's like there are two people — there's a before and after"; "There's no going back. I'm a different person now, for the rest of my life."[1]

In my research for *Out of the Darkness* and in many other cases of posttraumatic transformation I've investigated since then, I found that shifters share a number of major characteristics. They feel an intense sense of well-being, appreciation for the ordinary things of life, and gratitude for life itself. They feel less afflicted with worry and anxiety than before their transformation, and they have a wider sense of perspective, which means they don't ruminate over small problems as much. They also experience intensified perception so that the world around them appears more vivid and beautiful; they feel a strong connection to nature, other people, and other living beings. They report that their minds have become quieter, with less involuntary mental chatter. If the chatter is still there, they feel less identified with it. They can observe it without becoming immersed in it or letting it affect them.

In terms of their lifestyles, shifters tend to be less focused on personal gain; they're less interested in material things or in their success or achievement. Instead, they're more focused on their personal and spiritual development and more concerned for the well-being of others, which expresses itself as kindness and altruism. This new focus often leads to changes in career — in many cases, they leave behind traditional career paths and begin to work in helping professions. For example, a man who once ran his own architectural business retrained as a counselor and college tutor. A woman gave up her job as a high-powered marketing executive for a medical company and retrained as a therapist for cancer patients.

All of these are, of course, characteristics of the wakeful state.

I've found that this sudden awakening can be triggered by a wide range of different types of turmoil and trauma: intense stress and upheaval, depression, bereavement, serious illness, disability, alcoholism, and encounters with death (through medical conditions or accidents). The type of turmoil doesn't seem to be so important as long as it's intense and prolonged.

Investigating these cases was an incredibly inspiring experience. I met people who had been through some of the most tragic and distressing experiences possible for human beings to undergo. They didn't just manage to cope with their predicaments but actually emerged from them in transcendent states. Instead of repeating experiences I discussed in *Out of the Darkness*, I'll describe some of the most striking cases of posttraumatic transformation I've come across in my PhD research and from other sources since that book was published.

Spiritual Emergencies

Spiritual awakening is often a fairly smooth and trouble-free process when it occurs gradually, as we saw over the last two chapters. As with all processes, a slow and gradual progression gives you the opportunity to adjust to the new experiences you're undergoing and the new environments you're encountering. It gives you the opportunity to reflect on the process, and to accept and understand it. The new characteristics you develop can be integrated without disturbing your stability. The cases of Daniel and Ed in the last chapter are fairly good examples of this. Although their awakenings were initiated and impelled by some degree of turmoil, their development seems to have been fairly harmonious and well integrated.

However, sudden and dramatic awakening can sometimes involve difficulties. When a transformation happens suddenly, there's usually no opportunity for understanding, adjustment, or integration. You could compare it to becoming rapidly famous and successful. Many people who become famous or successful very quickly find it difficult to deal with the drastic changes it brings to their lives, such as constant attention and pressure, and the sudden lack of privacy. Some people find the change so difficult to cope with that they turn to drugs or alcohol, or they become alienated and depressed. Success or fame is much less likely to be destabilizing or disorienting when it builds gradually over a long period.

The transpersonal psychologist Stanislav Grof makes a useful distinction between spiritual emer*gence* and spiritual emergen*cy*. Spiritual emergence is gradual spiritual awakening, a slow unfolding that causes little disruption. However, a spiritual emergen*cy* is a sudden spiritual awakening that causes major disruption to a person's psychological functioning and impairs their ability to function in everyday life. In some cases, the disruption may be so severe that it resembles psychosis.[2] (Interestingly, Grof notes that spiritual emergencies are most frequently triggered by intense emotional and psychological turmoil such as bereavement, failure, and loss. As he describes it, "This can be loss of an important relationship, such as death of a child or another close relative, divorce, or the end of a love affair. Similarly, a series of failures or loss of a job or property can immediately precede the onset of spiritual emergency."[3])

Over the next two chapters we'll see some examples of spiritual emergencies.

Marita

Marita's awakening occurred during a period of intense turmoil when her children were babies. After her second baby was born (while her first baby was two years old), she began to suffer from postnatal depression. Her two-year-old child became disruptive and demanding, and she found it impossible to cope. As she described it:

> I entered in retrospect what was probably a psychotic state....My mind was fixated on scenarios of misunderstandings and suffering and torture of millions of children and I stopped sleeping at night, my mind just kept spinning these stories. I spent my days just holding my children and crying with them.... Needless to say, after four nights of not sleeping I was not in great shape. Physically I was wrecked. My sinuses were completely clogged, and my lungs were very congested. I was talking in whispers, because my throat was so tight. My husband was very alarmed and was threatening to get me some help. I had ceased to function. No groceries had gotten bought, and no laundry got done that week.

Marita's shift was so sudden and dramatic that she can pinpoint the exact moment when it occurred: "March 2, 1993, about 8:30 AM, Eastern Standard Time US." It happened when her husband was getting ready to go to work and exploded in frustration because he couldn't find any clean clothes. As Marita described it:

> With a cry of absolute despair he left the bedroom, slamming the door and then he proceeded to destroy the house. He ripped curtains off the walls, he threw things down the stairs. I'd never seen

anyone go berserk like that before. His explosion, and the release of his anger freed something tremendous in me! It was at that moment that I had an experience of enlightenment.

This experience came with feelings of such perfect joy and peace. I remember thinking afterward "so that's what I'm supposed to feel like!" This experience was multidimensional. It was physical. I felt a tremendous amount of energy coursing through my body and with the energy came healing. My sinuses cleared instantly, and my lungs cleared out and started working perfectly again. I watched this instant healing with amazement. It was intellectual. The final puzzle piece dropped into place. It was "eureka" of course!

Spiritual knowledge was revealed to me. I "knew" it in an instant and am still to this day learning in a linear conscious fashion what was revealed to me in that instant. I also felt like a ton of stuff went blowing by me and I didn't pick up on most of it — though I have spent seventeen years actively studying and seeking to put this information together into a state that can be perceived with the human mind and heart....

I understood about why mystics have talked about "for all eternity." In a mystical consciousness, within that one instant, you sense forever and ever, and are forever changed. I guess that was also what was meant by being born again, to see with the eyes of a child. It was amazing that these forgotten teachings from a Christian upbringing were springing to life for me. I had never "got it" before, looking at it in a logical way.

[The next few weeks] were an incredible time that I will never forget and can still access. I felt like I had broken through a barrier, and I was talking back to people left on the other side, and I so wanted to grab them and pull them through with me! I remember feeling a tremendous sense of urgency that I had to write a book and get this information out.... The "spiritual" experiences that I had had previously to this experience I had never connected with, since they didn't fit into my worldview. They now immediately took on tremendous significance, as I realized how every moment in my life had led up to that moment.

As is often the case with posttraumatic transformation, Marita's initially intense wakefulness faded slightly, but this less intense wakefulness became her normal state, which, at the time I spoke to her, she had remained in for seventeen years. One of the most significant changes brought on by her new state is a strong sense of connection, an awareness of what she described as an "energetic space" that links living beings together. Another significant change is her love of doing nothing, which she sees as an opportunity to "listen and be open and connect to something peaceful." Although she still experiences thought-chatter, she feels less identified with it and less affected by it. If negative thoughts arise in her mind, she is able to let them pass by before they create anxiety or worry. Her attitude toward death has also changed. Not only is she no longer afraid of it, but she also thinks of death as a return to that timeless, expansive state she experienced initially: "Being in that 'outside of time / outside of space' place, I guess you'd have to say that [death] is like stepping outside of prison walls, of which it will be very nice to go back home again."

However, Marita's transition from normal consciousness to an ongoing, stable state of wakefulness wasn't easy. Despite the intense well-being she experienced and her newfound insights, she felt confused by her new state. It took a long time for her to integrate the new aspects of her identity. As she told me, "I was really blown apart and needed to do a lot of work and seeking to integrate and figure out how to live with this new person I was." She found relationships particularly difficult; she lost the social and communication skills she'd previously had and hurt and offended people by being too honest. Even after seventeen years, she felt that this process of integration was still ongoing, although largely complete. (We'll examine the difficulties that often arise with sudden transformation in more detail in chapter 8.)

JC's Transformation

JC Mac, as he calls himself, is a Canadian in his late fifties who underwent a dramatic and difficult awakening at the age of forty-five. Before this time, he had some psychic experiences but not any spiritual experiences that he can recall. He had been a musician — not a very successful one, despite his best efforts — and his rock-and-roll lifestyle had led to problems with drugs. However, he had managed to overcome drug addiction and had worked as a drug and alcohol counselor in detox and treatment centers, designing rehabilitation programs for addicts. At the same time, he still pursued his musical ambitions and eventually recorded an album. He recognizes that throughout his early life he had a strong need for affirmation and attention, which he channeled into music.

Partly due to his overpowering desire for success, J C became estranged from his wife. His marriage broke down, and he left the family home, including his three children. Following his counseling role, he developed a career as a personal development coach, but his business began to fail, leaving him with financial problems. He felt under intense stress and struggled with the disruption to his previously stable life.

In the midst of this upheaval and turmoil he underwent a sudden shift in consciousness. One day he found himself crying, without knowing exactly why, and experienced a strange slowing down of time, along with a sense of inner peace. There were physical manifestations, too: a sensation of pins and needles in his arms and legs, which made him think he was having a heart attack or stroke. Naturally, he was afraid, but then he remembered a phrase from a Zen monk: "All fear is illusion, walk straight ahead." This encouraged him to stop resisting and allow himself to flow with the process that was unfolding. He described the process as being "like a set of dominoes falling over. I began to let go everything in life...and went into this state of bliss. All mentation disappeared and everything began to radiate this stunning sense of beauty, stillness, and silence."

This state of bliss became ongoing for JC, but there were problems, too. He began to find the practical, organizational side of life difficult to deal with. He couldn't work and found it difficult to relate to other people. He often forgot to eat and lost a lot of weight as a result. There was a "dark night of the soul" period in which he felt that he was "being abandoned by God" and returning to a state of painful duality. However, he began to realize he was actually undergoing a process of integration, of relearning mental functions and practical abilities at the same time as retaining his sense of peace and new identity.

This process of integration was a long one. At the time I spoke to JC, it had been six years since his shift, and he felt that he was "still working on it." As he described it: "I've been in and out of mind for the last six years. The sense of peace and stillness is always pervading [but] it's difficult to function sometimes, with the things that require mind, organizing. It's inconvenient, in a linear Western world when things are run on schedules, to be in a nonlinear state."

JC described the main ways in which his awareness and his perspective have changed as a result of his shift:

> I have no sense of identity. If you have a sense of identity, you cut off the alternatives. I don't consider myself American or Canadian. There is no particular place which is home. There's an all-pervading still silence, and it's always there wherever I go.
>
> My mind is very quiet most of the time. . . . There is nothing there apart from a still silence, a very peaceful still unifying silence that permeates everything. Then you ask a question and the faculty of speech is triggered. It's beautiful but inconvenient. Thinking is highly overrated. I don't have a problem with thinking, but if you can't distinguish your thinking for what it really is you're going to suffer. The ego is just something that has developed over millennia to help us survive.
>
> There's no attachment to material things, which is a relief. Before I was attached to my body, to success, or what I wanted to become. Being of service to all things is all, in the name of the highest good. To serve humanity, that's my intention.

Encounters with Death as Triggers for Sudden Awakening

Although a wide range of traumatic experiences can give rise to sudden awakening, one particular type is more strongly associated with the shift than any other: an intense encounter with death. This may mean encountering death personally through an illness or accident, or encountering it through the death of a person close to us — that is, through bereavement.

Research shows that encounters with mortality are a powerful source of posttraumatic growth. In particular, studies show that cancer patients who become aware that they may only have a short time left to live often experience it. In the months following diagnosis, many cancer patients report feeling more self-confident and appreciative of life, and that their relationships are stronger and more authentic.[4] (They also report a higher level of spirituality.) Studies of people who have experienced other chronic illnesses, natural disasters, and life-threatening combat situations show similar findings.[5] Bereavement has been shown to generate posttraumatic growth, too.[6]

People who survive near-death experiences also feel permanently changed for the better. As described in chapter 2, in near-death experiences, people "die" for a short time (most frequently due to a cardiac arrest) but find that they continue to be conscious. In most cases, they leave their bodies, feel that they are moving or gliding through darkness toward a light, and encounter deceased relatives or "beings" of some form who speak to them. As you would expect, these experiences have powerful aftereffects. The Dutch cardiologist Pim van Lommel followed sixty-two people who had near-death experiences and found that almost all of them experienced a major shift in perspective and values. After their near-death experiences they became less interested in material wealth and personal success; they felt an increased sense of connection to nature, together with an increased capacity for love and compassion, both for themselves and others. As van Lommel puts it, "The long-lasting transformational effects of an experience that lasts only a few minutes was a surprising and unexpected finding."[7] Another researcher, Michael Sabom, found that people who had had near-death experiences several years ago reported an increased sense of meaning, a greater capacity for love, and a greater involvement with their family.[8] There's no doubt that this shift is largely due to the *content* of the near-death experience and the new picture of reality that it reveals; that is, there may be life after death, and the nature of the universe is love and harmony. But it's also likely that the shift is partly due to encountering death.

Cancer and Sudden Awakening

In addition to generating posttraumatic growth, a diagnosis of cancer can (although not as frequently) lead to posttraumatic transformation. I reported some cases of this in *Out of the Darkness*. For example, Irene was diagnosed with breast cancer and told she probably had only one year left to live. Her transformation was almost instantaneous. The morning after being told that she had cancer, she woke up to a different world in which "the air was so clean and fresh and everything I looked at seemed so vibrant and vivid. The trees were so green and everything was so alive. I became aware of this energy radiating from the trees, and had this tremendous feeling of connectedness. It was fantastic. I just felt so fortunate to be alive on this planet."[9] Although it was especially intense for the next few weeks, this expanded and intensified awareness became Irene's normal state for the next thirteen years. At that point, sadly, her cancer came back and she died soon afterward.

Hugh Martin, who was seventy years old at the time I interviewed him, is another example. He underwent posttraumatic transformation in his midtwenties after being diagnosed with Hodgkin's disease — cancer of the lymph system — and told that he had no more than two years left to live. He defied his doctors and recovered, and although it has been over forty years since his diagnosis, the shift he experienced then has never faded. As he told me, "It's a great blessing to experience first-hand the brevity of life. It teaches you to savour every moment, and inspires you to live life at a level you never dreamed possible."[10]

There was also a powerful example of posttraumatic transformation through cancer in the British media recently. Rock guitarist Wilko Johnson, best known as a member of the band Dr. Feelgood, was diagnosed with stomach cancer and told he only had eight or nine months to live. Speaking a few weeks after his diagnosis, Johnson said that he had been feeling "vividly alive" and experiencing a sense of euphoria, with "this marvellous feeling of freedom." In a similar way to Irene, his sense of euphoria began as soon as he was told the news. As he told the BBC:

We walked out of [the consulting room] and I felt an elation of spirit. You're walking along and suddenly you're vividly alive. You're looking at the trees and the sky and everything and it's just "whoah!" I am actually a miserable person. I've spent most of my life moping in depressions and things, but this has all lifted.... The things that used to bring me down, or worry me, or annoy me, they don't matter anymore — and that's when you sit thinking, "Wow, why didn't I work this out before? Why didn't I work out before that it's just the moment you're in that matters?"

Worrying about the future or regretting the past is just a foolish waste of time. Of course we can't all be threatened with imminent death, but it probably takes that to knock a bit of sense into our heads. Right now it's just fantastic; it makes you feel alive. Just walking down the street you really feel alive. Every little thing you see, every cold breeze against your face, every brick in the road, you think "I'm alive, I'm alive."[11]

There's a twist to Wilko's story. He calmly accepted the fact that he was going to die and refused chemotherapy. However, after nine months his health still hadn't begun to deteriorate, and he became puzzled. He went to see a cancer specialist, who told him that he had a rare type of tumor that was actually operable, although there was just a 15 percent chance of surviving an operation. During a nine-hour-long procedure, a giant tumor was removed from his stomach, and, after a period of convalescence, he was recently pronounced cancer-free. So now — at the time of writing — he is adjusting to the fact that he isn't facing imminent death after all.

Awakening through Bereavement

The death of a person close to us is the only experience that has a similar capacity to induce sudden awakening as encountering death ourselves. Bereavement can create a seismic shock, completely upturning the stability of our lives and minds. The world suddenly seems like a completely different place, in which nothing is certain or permanent and all of our previous ambitions and activities seem meaningless and absurd. The searing pain of loss may make it difficult to carry on living ourselves. The pain may take years to heal, or perhaps it will never heal. But at the same time, the intense and destabilizing experience of bereavement can have a powerful transformational effect.

I also included some examples of awakening through bereavement in *Out of the Darkness*, most notably, the case of Glyn Hood, who underwent a sudden shift into wakefulness eighteen months after the sudden death of her daughter. Since then, I've come across other striking cases, two of which I'll describe here.

The first case is one of the most tragic — and, at the same time, most inspirational — stories I've ever come across. Graham Stew contacted me when I was looking for participants for my PhD research project on spiritual awakening. He was a university lecturer, like me, although since his shift he had become less identified with this role and now only taught part-time. He was different from most of the people I spoke to in that he had a deep interest in spirituality before his shift occurred. He learned meditation as a teenager and followed the path of Buddhism for many years. As a result, he had some understanding of spiritual awakening and some degree of spiritual development. This was good preparation for the shift he experienced that, in his words, "gave me the final push which helped me realize the truth of everything I'd been reading."

Graham's shift was triggered by two bereavements in close succession. His wife was diagnosed with advanced and untreatable lung cancer. Her condition deteriorated quickly — within a few months, she was dependent on oxygen and had difficulty walking more than a few steps. Nevertheless, she was determined to survive at least until the end of the year so that she could spend a final Christmas with their seventeen-year-old son.

However, that October their son was killed in a car crash on his way to a party. The shock brought about a rapid decline in his mother's condition — in fact, she passed away the evening of his funeral.

Apart from the pain and shock of these events — and having to deal with the practical business of organizing the funerals, registering the deaths, and writing to friends and relatives to let them know about the deaths — Graham felt a loss of identity. As he put it, "Almost overnight I had lost two important roles in my life: I had been a husband for twenty-two years and a father for seventeen years. The sense of who I was had been stripped away, and I was left staring at emptiness."

Graham was helped by Buddhist teachings on impermanence and change and also by the Buddhist practice of observing and exploring mental and emotional states. He was aware of the importance of acknowledging his feelings of emptiness and knew that he had to let go of resistance to them. Through doing this, he became aware that, in his words, "within the emptiness there was a stillness that somehow reassured me that all was well."

In *Out of the Darkness* I highlighted the importance of acceptance in these experiences. Acceptance has an alchemical power that releases the transformational potential of turmoil and trauma. A person has to let go of their resistance to their predicament, to surrender to it and accept it. In many cases, a shift occurs at exactly the same moment that a person lets go and surrenders to their predicament.

Through exploring and accepting his pain and emptiness, Graham underwent a shift. The emptiness he experienced was a positive state of ego-transcendence rather than a bleak or hostile vacuum. As he described it: "It shattered the thin shell of my ego....I could see through the illusion of separateness. All those years I'd been looking for a pair of glasses which I was already seeing out of. The idea that all was one had been an intellectual concept, but now it's become real. It's what it is. I can't imagine not seeing it now."

I interviewed Graham eleven years after these tragic but transformational events. He described how, since his shift, he feels much more present-centered, with a heightened awareness and a greater appreciation of simple pleasures. He is filled with a sense of ease and acceptance and less identified with his own thoughts and emotions:

> Life has become a lot easier. I'm able to live more in the present moment and value that. Attachments that I had before have been loosed a great deal. Worries about money, about future work, about relationships, have lost their strength.... Now everything that comes along is okay. I can say yes to life whatever it brings whereas before I used to have conditions.

It gives me a sense of ease. Life just seems easy. There are still problems; it's not a state of bliss. Moods come and go. But I can see it, I'm aware of it. I can let it go. There's a sense of appreciation of the simple things — a simple cup of tea, looking out of the window, the sunshine on the leaves, the wonderful green of the trees. I never bothered to pay much attention in the past. I'm struck by how fresh everything seems, how wonderful it is to be here at all. There's a sense of wonder, like a young child — I've got it back. I can appreciate just walking out the front door, feeling the wind on my face....

My mind still chatters away — that's part of being human. Sometimes I need to listen to it because I have things which need planning — going shopping, paying the bills. It's a useful machine. I can pay less attention to it now. It's like walking into another room, with the TV playing in the background. I don't have to pay attention to it. Before thoughts that were emotionally charged used to come up and I'd get hijacked by them, taken away on trains of thoughts into the future and the past. I don't do that now; I tend to get less caught up in it now....

I'm happy to sit in my garden and just watch the flowers and listen to the birds. I can happily listen to music and read for hours. I am less sociable than I was, not that I was ever party-loving, and am quite content with a simple life. I can relish a simple cup of tea, and marvel at the sheer miracle of being here at all.

I don't have any ambition anymore — that all slipped away. I wasn't worried anymore about how I appear to colleagues, about publishing articles. One day I might write a book, but there doesn't seem to be any urgency....[12]

Time has changed in that it's always now. Everything that I'm aware of arises out of this awareness. The world arises in us. It's also a mystery because we can't describe it.

Graham described how his relationships have changed, too. He is more friendly and relaxed, less prone to becoming annoyed or irritable with people. As he told me, "It feels more comfortable because I don't have an ego which I need to protect and defend. Without that worry everything seems a lot easier."

Phoebe

Phoebe, who contacted me after reading *Waking from Sleep*, is another striking example of awakening through bereavement. Phoebe wrote to me to say that she'd had a "very high-intensity awakening experience" following the death of her friend.

Amanda, Phoebe's friend, was only twenty when she was killed by a drunk driver while riding her bike. At Amanda's funeral, Phoebe's initial shock and sorrow gave way to a sense of "total bliss and peace with the impermanence of all bodies and forms." While she was writing a farewell note to Amanda, she sensed her presence. In Phoebe's own words:

> I saw her face, except it wasn't physical. In fact, I completely lost the sense that there was a physical world around me. We were together, and we were one and the same. Her presence was one of pure love and peace. There were clearly no differences between us even though I was still in a body and she wasn't. She said, "Phoebe, live your life to the absolute fullest while you're still on Earth." Her voice felt like it was being spoken through me rather than to me.
>
> For the next two or so days, I was in a state of total peace and bliss. Everything physical was unstable and subject to decay, and that was completely okay with me. I was at peace with the fact that I was going to die, and it truly didn't matter to me when that would happen. I felt profound love and gratitude toward everyone in my life, everyone who was alive, and for everything I saw and experienced. It was clear to me that negativity of any kind had no power and was infinitely small compared with the vastness of life itself.

After this initial awakening experience, Phoebe felt that she was looking at her life with new eyes, with a completely different perspective. As she said, "When I went back to the small Quaker liberal arts college I was attending, I felt as if I had been dropped there from another planet." Her previous life seemed alien to her, and she had a strong sense that she was "awake" in some way, even though she didn't fully understand what that meant. She became, in her words, "highly sensitive to the energies of spaces and people," able to perceive subtle vibrations outside solid forms.

She experienced an opening of consciousness, which brought revelations about the nature of human life. She had visions of the cycles of human life, human history, the whole evolution of life on this planet, and how they are all interlinked. As she described it:

> I could see cycles within larger cycles within even larger cycles: a day between waking and bedtime, a year between early spring and the next winter, a stage of development between its beginning and end, a lifetime between birth and death, an era between its beginning and end, and the life spans of planets and stars. Even the life of the universe between the Big Bang and its final contraction mirrors these. I could see that in the evolution of life, life-forms and living systems increase in complexity, cooperation, efficiency, intelligence, and awareness.

Soon after this she had what she described as a "great opening" in which she became aware of "the Source of all existence." In her words:

> This came right after several days of sensing deeply that everything I encountered — furniture, hair, paper, clothes, music, food, soap, bodies, minds, thoughts, reactions, plans, cities, cars, trees, clouds, and more — had an unspeakably complex history that was inseparable from the history of the whole universe and everything else in it. Everything simple looked magnificent in still observation. I saw that bed sheets, jeans, and wood floors were incredibly complex, and I felt that I was seeing many secrets of life that had been hidden in front of my eyes all along.... I saw that there was a vast life that was the Source of everything that was and ever will be. I was not seeing with my eyes, but with the core of my being. I saw our universe, all physical space, all other universes, and everything that changes as one tiny dark finite speck surrounded by an infinite sea of life and light. I saw even more clearly life's nature of pure love, bliss, creativity, and wisdom. This sea of pure life is formless and spacious, and yet it is fully conscious and intelligent.

It is the only true experiencer, the only true "I." The Source is present everywhere and in every moment whether we are aware of it or not.

As this great being showed Him/Herself to me, I could see that the pure divine life that is Him/Her is the same life that is the essence of every being through all space and time. The formless gives birth to all forms. Every taste, opinion, personality, and experience grows out of pure divine....

I absolutely knew without a doubt that this is God. God showed me that S/he is creating, shaping, and evolving forms and worlds in much the way an artist creates masterpieces. God/spirit exists outside of time and does not need anything in order to be, and yet life expresses itself through form because of its creative nature.

But there were difficulties, too. Phoebe's experience was a spiritual emergency that caused an earthquake-like disturbance to her psyche. Such a sudden and powerful opening inevitably disrupted her normal psychological functions. She became highly emotional and often felt disoriented and exhausted. She had problems with memory and found it difficult to communicate and do simple everyday tasks.

However, Phoebe was fortunate in that she had some knowledge of Buddhism and spiritual Christianity and had read modern spiritual authors such as Eckhart Tolle. She had a framework to make sense of her experiences and was aware that she was undergoing a profound positive transformation rather than a breakdown. Like JC Mac, she had to go through a process of relearning and rebuilding as the shift began to settle.

At the time Phoebe wrote to me, it had been four years since her awakening. She had recovered her psychological functions and was able to operate pretty well in the everyday world again, even though she still felt that the process of integration wasn't yet complete. The intensity of her initial transformation had faded and settled into a steady and stable ongoing form of wakefulness. As she described it, her awareness of a "spacious presence behind and within all experience has never left me, though sometimes it is more in the foreground or background.... The space of now — life itself — transcends all phenomena, experiences, and circumstances. The light is infinitely greater and more powerful than all burdens, darkness, and suffering. God is all there is."

Understanding Posttraumatic Transformation

Why is there such a strong relationship between turmoil and transformation? In psychological terms, what actually happens when a person undergoes awakening in the midst of intense stress or trauma?

We touched on this issue in chapters 5 and 6, in relation to renunciation and letting go of psychological attachments. We saw that gradual spiritual awakening is often related to a process of loss in which a person's psychological attachments are slowly dissolved away. This might happen as a result of illness, professional failure, alcoholism, and other negative events. Attachments such as hopes, beliefs, status, and possessions are the building blocks of our identity, so as they are broken down, our identity — in fact, our whole self-system — breaks down, too. This can lead to intense turmoil and despair, but it can also allow a new self to emerge. As the old self breaks down, a new, higher-functioning self emerges to replace it — that is, the wakeful self-system. We also saw that people who follow traditional spiritual paths often practice renunciation; that is, they make conscious efforts to dissolve their psychological attachments through voluntary poverty and celibacy, turning away from worldly ambitions, and so on.

The same process occurs in posttraumatic transformation, but the new wakeful self-system emerges suddenly and dramatically rather than gradually. The most important aspect of the process is the breakdown of the old self-system. While this can occur gradually, it's much more common for it to occur suddenly. This can happen through intense stress, when the old self-system can no longer withstand the pressure and suddenly breaks down, like a building in an earthquake. Or it can happen when the old self-system is so weakened by the loss of its attachments that it simply gives way, like a building that has lost so many bricks that it can no longer keep its form and falls down. As a result, there's suddenly a great open space of being that was filled by the previous self-system. A new, higher-functioning self-system — an awakened self with softer boundaries, heightened awareness, and reduced cognitive activity — emerges to fill the vacuum, like a butterfly emerging from a chrysalis.

Why Some and Not Others?

Why does this higher-functioning, awakened self emerge in some people but not in others? After all, almost everyone goes through intense turmoil at some point in their lives, but most people experience a breakdown without a shift-*up* into a new state of being. In doing my research in this area, I was constantly surprised at how easy it was to find examples of people who had undergone this shift. This led me to conclude that posttraumatic transformation — and therefore the state of wakefulness itself — is much more common than is generally believed. I found that most people who underwent the shift had no previous knowledge of spiritual traditions or practices (which sometimes meant that they were confused by their new state). I now have a strong feeling that there are many unknown awakened individuals all around us who don't fully understand what has happened to them. Nevertheless, posttraumatic transformation is still quite rare; the great majority of people who go through intense turmoil and trauma don't experience transformation.

Whether we experience posttraumatic transformation or not depends largely on how we *respond* to turmoil and trauma. There are two important prerequisites of transformation: acknowledgment and acceptance. In order for transformation to occur, a person first has to face up to their predicament rather than divert or distract themselves from it. All too often, people who are suffering from trauma don't do this, as a self-protective mechanism. They deceive themselves that their predicament isn't as serious as it actually is or simply avoid contemplating it. Acknowledgment (or facing up) is an act of courage. It means confronting intense loss and pain. But without it, the positive transformational effects of turmoil and trauma can't manifest themselves.

Once a person has found the courage to face up to the reality of their predicament, they are able to take the second step of *accepting* their predicament. This attitude of acceptance — of ceasing to resist their predicament, of letting go or surrendering to it — is absolutely essential in posttraumatic transformation. The moment of acceptance is often also the specific moment when transformation occurs. An attitude of acceptance has a seemingly alchemical power of transmuting suffering and turmoil into positive transformation. Acceptance is often the trigger that allows a person's latent higher self to emerge and replace the broken fragments of the old self that has been damaged so badly by loss or turmoil.

I've come across a lot of cases of posttraumatic transformation triggered by therapy. Of the twenty-five cases of spiritual awakening I studied in my PhD thesis, for example, five occurred while people were undergoing some form of psychotherapy or counseling.[13] Therapy seems to unlock a person's turmoil and create an opening through which a new self-system can emerge. If the therapeutic environment is safe and supportive — and if the therapist is skilled — counseling may create the right conditions for a person to acknowledge their turmoil and trauma and then let go of their resistance to it. They may feel able to step back and surrender to their predicament, which allows transformation to take place.

Perhaps most fundamentally though, transformation through psychological turmoil is related to a person's *readiness* for spiritual awakening.

I interpret awakening and wakefulness in evolutionary terms. I see the wakeful state as an evolutionary progression, the next phase of human development. Wakefulness is a more expansive and intensified state of awareness in the same way that our present normal state is more expansive and intensified than, say, a sheep's or a dog's state of awareness. As I will explain in the final chapter of this book, I believe this state will one day become human beings' normal one.

The wakeful state is therefore latent inside the human race as a whole and is beginning to manifest and express itself. We see its expression in the increasing frequency of temporary awakening experiences in people, the buildup of the *impulse* to awaken in people (which expresses itself through the impulse to follow spiritual practices and paths), and the increasing *latency* of wakefulness in individuals. The higher self-system of wakefulness is latent in some people; it has already formed but has not yet manifested itself. It may be unable to express itself because it's being blocked by their present self-system. However, when their psychological attachments dissolve away and their normal self-system breaks down, this latent higher self is able to emerge and establish itself. It becomes their new identity. Many people who undergo posttraumatic transformation describe feeling as if they have been reborn, as if they are a different person inhabiting the same body. And in the same way that actual physical birth can be a difficult process, this birth of a new identity is often problematic.

In most people, the wakeful self-system is probably not *ready* to emerge. It has not yet become fully formed or integrated as a structure. So when these people experience turmoil and trauma and the dissolution of their psychological attachments, they experience a breakdown without a shift-up. Their normal self-system breaks down with nothing to replace it. There's just a psychic vacuum inside them, which is not filled by a latent higher self. Their higher self isn't yet ready to be born.[14]

When Transformation Is Both Gradual and Sudden

As I noted at the beginning of this chapter, there's no hard and fast division between gradual and sudden transformation. In my PhD research, I found six cases where transformation was both gradual and permanent; that is, the sudden transformation was preceded by a long period of gradual awakening. In fact, a long period of gradual awakening may make a person more likely to undergo sudden transformation.

In most cases, posttraumatic transformation occurs when the person is *in the midst of* intense turmoil and stress. However, there may be a delay in some cases. A person may initially experience only the traumatic aspects of their experiences, but a long period of spiritual practice, which induces gradual spiritual awakening, may allow a sudden posttraumatic transformation to occur later.

My friend and mentor Russel Williams is a good example of this delay. His awakening was undoubtedly connected to the intense turmoil and trauma he underwent in his early life. As he describes in his book *Not I, Not Other Than I* (which I edited), Russel was born in 1921 and left school at the age of eleven, following the death of his father. Even more tragically, his mother died shortly afterward, and he spent the next few years struggling to survive, doing incredibly hard manual and menial work for very low pay. He also experienced intense trauma during the Second World War — he was at Dunkirk, in London during the Blitz, and came close to death on several other occasions.

His sudden transformation occurred five years after the war, after he had spent three years in a kind of involuntary spiritual practice of looking after horses in a circus (as described in the previous chapter). This is how Russel describes his moment of transformation:

> I woke up one morning and looked across at the horses, watching the steam rise out of their nostrils the way it does on a cold morning. The next thing I knew I wasn't just observing the horse, from the outside. I was the horse. I was looking inside it. I was it. I could look through its eyes and mind. I was aware of its true nature. I was aware that all things are one. There was a sense of profound peace within me.
>
> It was a revelation. I looked at another horse, and another, and I was inside them as well. I looked at one of the dogs, and saw it in its true nature, too. I saw everything in its true nature. I went outside to look at the lions and it was the same with them — looking from the inside out, not the outside in. We were all the same nature, all arising from the same source. My own nature was just as theirs was, in a different form, with one consciousness linking us all together. They were only separate in terms of form and structure. It was the same essence, the same emptiness, in all of them — in all of us. I went outside to look at the trees, and they were the same nature. Then I looked at my own body, and inside myself, and there was nobody there. My normal sense of self had disappeared. At that moment there was no more anger, no frustration, just a sense of peace. There was no desire, no aversion; everything was as it should be.[15]

It seems, then, that Russel's three years of involuntary spiritual practice created the conditions — including the attitude of openness and acceptance

— that allowed the transformation potential of his traumatic experiences to manifest itself.

Another way in which transformation can be both gradual and sudden is when the process is spread over several different transformational experiences rather than concentrated into one sudden shift. The normal self-system doesn't dissolve in one fell swoop but over a few separate incidences of loss or turmoil, like a castle that's broken down over a few separate attacks. One person I interviewed described three individual transformational experiences — each triggered by intense psychological turmoil — over a period of nine years. Each experience led to a more intense state of wakefulness; the last one led to a permanent and stable state. Another participant described "five or six moments of clarity" that were followed by what he describes as "the usual spiritual seeking," until a period of intense turmoil generated a shift into a permanently wakeful state.

However, it's fitting that different varieties of wakefulness merge into one another and are sometimes difficult to distinguish. After all, we're dealing with a state in which duality falls away and boundaries no longer exist. The experiential landscape of wakefulness is *terra incognita* for most of us, so it's important to try to map it to some degree, to provide some orientation and direction so that we don't become lost or confused. But at the same time, we should avoid unnecessary dividing lines and distinctions.

8. Sudden Awakening:
Kundalini and Energetic Awakening

The cases of sudden awakening that we've looked at so far can be described as experiences of ego-dissolution in which loss, trauma, and turmoil dissolve away a person's psychological attachments and, in the process, their ego and their entire self-system. But some sudden awakenings occur in a slightly different form. I call these energetic awakenings, which are more explosive and dramatic. Energetic awakenings also lead to a breakdown of the normal self-system, but this occurs in a more violent way.

You could use an analogy of the destruction of a house. In ego-dissolution, it's as if the house is slowly dismantled — the building blocks of psychological attachments are gradually taken away. But in energetic awakening, it's as if the house is suddenly demolished, like a beach house swept away by a tidal wave. These are spiritual emergencies of the most intense and dramatic kind.

Kundalini Awakening

In the Indian spiritual traditions of Yoga and Tantra, sudden energetic awakenings are depicted as *kundalini* awakening. As described in chapter 5, *kundalini* — derived from the Sanskrit word *kunda*, meaning "to coil" or "to spiral" — is an intense and explosive form of energy that lies dormant in the first and lowest of the seven chakras (or energy centers), the *muladhara*. When this energy travels up to the highest chakra, near the crown of the head, it results in spiritual awakening.

Many contemporary spiritual researchers and transpersonal psychologists have studied the phenomenon of *kundalini* awakening, mainly focusing on the negative effects that occur when *kundalini* rises suddenly and dramatically. According to the researcher Bruce Greyson, for example, this can cause major disruptions to psychological functioning that resembles psychiatric disorders and often result in a misdiagnosis of mental illness.[1] Other researchers note that it can also cause physical problems, including involuntary spasms and vibrations, burning or itching sensations, and lethargy. People may hear voices, see visions of light, and have psychic experiences.[2]

Interestingly, traditional Indian texts devote very little attention to these problems. At most, they hint at the potential volatility of the energy, describing it as "a ring of lightning, folds of flaming fire"[3] or as "fiery energy" that releases "dazzling sparks."[4] The *Vijnanabhairavatantra*, a Tantric text, describes how depression and fatigue can occur if *kundalini* energy happens to move back down through the chakras instead of rising up. This text also mentions that if the yogi hasn't entirely transcended their sense of identification with the body, they may experience uncontrollable trembling.

Presumably the reason why these texts don't explore the difficulties of *kundalini* awakening is because the awakening process occurred in the controlled context of monastic and spiritual traditions, under the supervision of gurus, with a great deal of understanding and preparation. Under these circumstances, such difficulties are probably less likely to occur. This highlights the point I've already made (and a subject we'll investigate fully in chapter 10): awakening is much more likely to be disruptive when a person isn't prepared for it and doesn't have a framework to make sense of it, and also when it occurs in a nonsupportive environment.

Cases of Energetic Awakening from My Research

Energetic awakenings — or *kundalini* awakenings — are common, although not as common as awakenings through ego-dissolution. In my PhD research, for example, I found five clear cases of energetic *kundalini*-like awakenings out of twenty-five, as well as two other possible ones. Like most other cases of sudden awakening, the cases I investigated were mainly triggered by intense psychological turmoil, with the slight difference that they were more likely to be triggered by intense *stress* (often manifesting as sleeplessness) rather than through factors such as failure or loss.

Kimberley, a case from my PhD research, experienced awakening through explosive energy release shortly after the death of her mother. One morning, while lying in bed, she sensed her mother's presence and suddenly she felt she couldn't move her body or open her eyes. She felt heat and bright light around her body and felt frightened but somehow reassured at the same time. Over the next few days, she had a feeling of "energy rising through my body with a loud screeching sound." At night, when she closed her eyes, she saw visions of colors and symbols, and "random information at a very, very high speed, like a slideshow, showing frames throughout human history." During her waking hours, she was acutely sensitive to other people; she was able to sense their feelings and thoughts and see colors around them.

Kimberley had no knowledge of spirituality or esoteric ideas and so struggled to make sense of her experiences. She suspected that she had "gone mad," even though she was sure that her experiences were real and that she had entered a heightened reality rather than a hallucinatory one. For several weeks, she was unable to work or function in everyday life. She was diagnosed with depression and found it difficult to sleep. She had problems focusing her attention and holding on to information with her mind. Sensing that conventional medicine couldn't help her, she turned to alternative therapies, which she felt helped to integrate her new state of being. Overall, it "took two to three years to feel stable and finally understand what was happening." Now that this integration has taken place, she describes her normal state as featuring a constant psychic and spiritual awareness:

> Once it stabilized I realized I was left with abilities that could help other people. I started to get a sense of what the purpose of it was and what good it could do for others. With enhanced sensory awareness I can read what's going on with people at the unconscious level, and help make those things conscious and help transform them. There's an awareness of energy or vibration or consciousness, an ability to read that fundamental level of reality, what's going on beneath the surface....

There's also a more expanded awareness and a realization of our context in the universe, an expanded understanding of the journey of the soul and the continuity of consciousness, an understanding that physical life is just one dimension of reality.

I walk between two worlds a lot of the time. I'm learning to enjoy physical reality and family life, and just the simple things in life. That's become heightened — an appreciation of everyday life. I always had a sense of beauty but it's become more heightened now. There's certainly a connection with nature and because of the openings and awareness of energy and vibration, I can certainly delight in nature and feel its forces and its cycles. When that first happened I thought I was losing the plot, when I thought I could almost feel a tree speaking to me, but now I realize I was just picking up on the energy....

What was interesting was that I moved back down to Devon (my home town) and was fully expecting to walk into the room and for family and friends not to recognize me. I felt so different, like a completely different person to be honest. All my internal frames of reference have changed. I no longer experience life as a random sequence of disconnected, separate events of which I am merely a passenger or victim. I experience life as an interconnected co-creative partnership with some kind of intelligent force or ever-present sentiency. I live as a timeless soul enjoying my physical experience. That is my daily reality.

As another example, Simon experienced energetic awakening during a very stressful period in which he was forced to do a job that he intensely disliked, and while his wife was undergoing tests for cancer. He "literally did not sleep at all for a week due to worry and stress....[Then] out of nowhere at 5 AM one morning I had what I now realize was a sudden uncontrolled *kundalini* awakening." There were shooting pains and convulsions of energy going up and down his spine, and he had the experience of regressing to previous lives, and "had the clearest understanding of God and the universe."

Even though Simon knew almost nothing about spirituality, he, like Kimberley, was sure he was undergoing some form of transformation. But there was no one to give him any guidance. He went to see a doctor, who transferred him to a psychiatric hospital where he was locked up and medicated. Initially he went along with the doctors' diagnosis, believed that he had gone mad, and took all the medication he was given. But after a few months, once his condition began to stabilize, his certainty that he had undergone some form of positive transformation returned. He read the work of Eckhart Tolle and other authors (including *Waking from Sleep*, which was how he came to make contact with me), which helped him make sense of his new state of being. He began to attend a Sahaja Yoga center and to realize that he had undergone a spiritual awakening.

Simon described the changes his awakening brought to him as follows:

> I found I wasn't able to work full-time anymore. I had to work part-time. I was a service manager at BMW car dealers and I just couldn't do it anymore, physically and mentally. I had a different perspective, a different outlook on life.... Now I have lost all material desires. I used to think my life would only be complete if I had a newer, faster motorbike and drove my wife mad for years with impulsive purchases of dozens of different bikes. At the time of my original breakdown I was consumed with having the latest biggest car and gadgets. This has all dissolved into thin air.

It took several years for Simon to feel that his wakeful state had fully settled and integrated and that the disruptive effects of his sudden transformation had faded away completely. But finally he began to feel a powerful ongoing sense of contentment and fulfillment, one of the effects of which was a new enjoyment of inactivity and solitude. He recognizes that this is one of the biggest changes he has undergone: "Now I look forward to nothing better than sitting and meditating in thoughtless awareness.... I don't get bored anymore. I only work two days per week and all I do otherwise is read books, go for walks, and meditate. In the past, I couldn't sit still for five minutes. I had to be doing something or going somewhere. The transition from that to being able to sit and do nothing is massive."

As a final example, Eric experienced an energetic awakening after a yoga retreat. He had suffered from serious psychiatric problems earlier in his life, and shortly after the retreat he experienced his "first manic episode for ten years," probably triggered by the intensive yoga practice. He had "several experiences where my consciousness seemed to rise suddenly, the energy meridians in my body were energized, and my mind became sharper and clearer." He was sure he was undergoing a spiritual transformation but was admitted to a psychiatric ward where the staff was skeptical and hostile. However, he managed to persuade them to discharge him after a few days, and on the same day he had a "breakthrough" experience: "My mind was becoming quieter, and at the same time the world was becoming sharper, more real, and the experience was lasting. I went for a swim while my friend taught a class at the gym, and for the first time in my life I experienced myself as consciousness. I went home that night still feeling very clear, and my mind was still quiet."

This was followed a few weeks later by another shift in consciousness, which led to a stable, ongoing state of wakefulness. This occurred while he was having a shower one morning:

> I was in a vibrant dimension of clarity, laughing my head off, absolutely elated. I realized a profound truth, what it meant just to be alive and to be able to have a shower, and have a bed to sleep in, and food to eat.... I was amazed at the quality of the colour of the sky, it had never looked like that before, and the warmth on my skin, it was like the world had been made anew.
>
> I felt like a new person. The things that used to bother me didn't anymore. I spend a lot of time in the present now, more than I ever did, and I can quiet my mind easily when I want to. My family has often remarked on my positive changes, and my psychiatrist told me recently that I'm one of the most psychologically healthy people she's ever met.
>
> Life is simple. And life is precious. All forms of life are sacred. Life is a miracle, and it's to be enjoyed. Every moment is different; every moment is alive with possibilities. If I was to lose everything tomorrow, I'd be okay. The greatest way I can use my life is to contribute toward the well-being of all forms of life.... I spend most of my time in the moment, and in many ways encourage others to do the same. There's nothing lacking from my present situation. I don't feel uneasy when I'm lacking direction or stuck. All

of the difficult things in my life happened to get me to where I am today — and I'm very happy with who I am and where I am — so I no longer label experiences as good or bad.

Integration

Although all sudden awakenings are often disruptive and can take a long time to fully integrate, this seems to be particularly true of energetic awakenings. (Kimberley said it took her two to three years, while Simon said it took several years.) Because energetic awakenings are so powerful and explosive, they are especially likely to cause psychological disturbances — and physical problems — that may take years to settle. As we can see in the examples above, people who undergo energetic awakenings are likely to be diagnosed with psychiatric problems. Spiritual awakening is certainly *not* a form of psychosis, but sometimes it may resemble it. It's easy for psychiatrists who aren't aware of awakening as a phenomenon to misdiagnose it as psychosis and to prescribe medication or hospitalization.

However, in *all* the cases of energetic awakening I investigated, the psychological disturbances and physical difficulties eventually became less intense or faded away all together, even if it took several years. This was partly due to people's increased understanding of their experience but also because energetic awakenings seem to be a process that naturally plays itself out, slowly settling over time like a very long, drawn-out earthquake.

Again, it's difficult to make a clear distinction between these energetic awakenings and the experiences of ego-dissolution we looked at in the previous chapter because the latter usually have an energetic aspect to them, too. When the normal ego dissolves, the energy that it monopolized is freed up and flows through our being. We feel intensely alive and our perceptions are energized so that our surroundings appear intensely vivid and beautiful. But the experiences we've looked at in this chapter seem to be different in the sense that they are so overtly and intensely energetic.

However, the real difference between these two modes of sudden awakening may be that the energy that they feature is of a different nature and has a different source.

Sexual Awakening Experiences
and Energetic Awakening

I've been referring to the experiences in this chapter as "*kundalini*-like" rather than *kundalini* experiences. This is because I don't believe the concept of *kundalini* awakening is *literally* true. I don't believe that there really is a mysterious energy source located at a chakra close to the bottom of the spine. My feeling is that what Yogic and Tantric traditions called *kundalini energy* is actually sexual energy, or *libido* (to use the Freudian term). In Daoist terms, this energy is *xing*. And I believe that this is the energy that flows explosively through people in these experiences, so forcefully that it demolishes the normal self-system like a tidal wave.[5]

Many researchers have identified a connection between energetic *kundalini*-like awakening and sexuality. In studying reports of *kundalini* awakening, transpersonal psychotherapist Bonnie Greenwell found that the experience could sometimes be triggered by powerful sexual encounters and that its aftereffects can include spontaneous orgasms and heightened sexual desire in general.[6] Some people also describe energetic awakenings as having a sexual quality. Here, for example, is a report of a temporary awakening experience of a highly energetic nature, which I collected for my book *Waking from Sleep*. This occurred after a long period of meditation, during which the person felt a "forceful, pushing sensation near the base of my spine." And as she continued breathing:

> This sensation continued to rise in my spine, getting higher with each in-breath. It was *a magnificent but intensely intimate and sexual experience*. It was at that point where the sensation was arriving at my neck that I panicked. I knew that if I did not resume control, this force would pass through my head and out through the crown and as a result I would scream and be forced to run around the room like some crazy person....[*For weeks afterward*] my face shone with a new happiness and many people commented on the "new image" — lively, awake, and laughing. I had boundless energy and required little or no sleep. I was surrounded by people wanting to talk to me.[7] [italics mine]

The connection between energetic awakening and sexuality is perhaps clearest in reports of sexual awakening experiences. These often involve an explosive release of energy shooting through one's body and filling one's being with heat and light. This is illustrated by the following intensely energetic experience, which was sent to me after I wrote a blog article on transcendent sexual experiences:

> I was making love and suddenly the pleasure was all throughout my body, then I was nothing but the pleasure. I was no longer in my body in a physical sense, I was energy. My partner's energy and mine merged together, and I saw that energy while simultaneously being that energy. Then I began seeing a pattern, maybe an energy pattern, maybe a light pattern, but nonetheless it was something I had never seen or heard of before in reality so I have nothing to compare it to. Then, I passed through "something," into another universe, dimension, realm or whatever, and became the pattern that I was seeing. I was no longer in the room, I wasn't anywhere, I was in an all encompassing void, only existing as the energy or light pattern. Instinctively I knew, not believed, that this was where I was before my first memories and first became conscious in human form.[8]

The transpersonal psychologist Jenny Wade collected ninety-one reports of sexual awakening experiences, many of which showed similarities to energetic awakening. As Wade describes it, "Some people report strange energies coursing through the body. Sometimes it starts with a sense that the sexual charge normally rooted in the genitals is spreading throughout the entire body, lighting it up with crackling power and fireworks."[9] One person spoke of an "electric charge," while another person described an "electrical feeling that moves up my body and just goes out my eyes. When it's intense, it's almost blinding."[10]

Energetic awakening and sexual awakening experiences are connected, in my view, because they involve the same type of energy — sexual energy, libido, or *xing*. Energetic awakening experiences involve an explosive release of energy that normally expresses itself through sexual desires and impulses.

Energy and Development

In order to understand this connection between awakening and sexual energy, we need to consider how the distribution of the energy of our whole being changes as we develop from childhood to adulthood.

Young children possess an abundance of free-flowing energy. In Yogic terminology, this can be described as *pranotthana*, a state of uplifted or intensified life-energy. Or as the transpersonal psychologist Michael Washburn describes it, young children are "bathed in the water of life. Ripples and waves of delicious energy move through the infant's body, filling it with delight. When its needs are satisfied and it's otherwise content, [it] experiences a sea of dynamic plenitude, blissful fullness."[11] Because of this abundance of rich energy flowing through their being, young children naturally possess some of the characteristics of the wakeful state, such as intense perception, a sense of meaning or of an atmosphere of harmony, and a sense of inner well-being, bliss, or joy. (We'll discuss this more later.)

But when the child reaches adulthood, this free-flowing energy begins to be concentrated into two main areas: the ego and libido. The ego, as a part of the adult self-system, begins to use a large proportion of our life-energy. At the same time, roughly in parallel with the ego, we begin to mature as sexual beings. Our previously free-flowing energy becomes centered around sexual desires.

So it may be that the phenomenon of energetic awakening occurs when this libidinal energy is suddenly released from its sexual center and flows wildly through our whole being, so explosively that it dislodges and demolishes our normal self-system. For some people this may simply lead to a breakdown or a state of psychosis, but for others it may allow a latent wakeful self-system to emerge.

Sexual energy is extremely intense and concentrated, which is why its repression can have such harmful consequences (as Freud, Wilhelm Reich, and many other psychologists have pointed out). And whereas egoic energy is used continuously, sexual energy is often dormant, awaiting a stimulus to be aroused. This can make its release even more explosive. Certainly sexual energy seems to have a more volatile nature than egoic energy, which may be why energetic awakening is more disruptive than awakening through ego-dissolution. Even when it flows freely through our whole being, this energy may still retain some of its original sexual quality, which explains why *kundalini*-like awakenings may sometimes have a sexual element to them.

———

It does, therefore, seem to make sense to think in terms of two different modes of sudden spiritual awakening: one related to the ego, the other to the libido (or, if you prefer, one coming from above and the other from below). However, as I mentioned at the end of the previous chapter, I'm aware of the danger — and the artificiality — of making distinctions in the misty, unmapped landscape of wakefulness. I certainly don't think that there are two cut-and-dried categories of sudden awakening, one ego based and one libido based. It may be that in some cases both modes occur together, indistinguishably. In other words, a person may experience ego-dissolution due to dissolution of psychological attachments, and, at the same time, the sheer stress and pressure of their predicament may trigger an explosive release of libidinal energy. (One possible example of this is JC Mac, whose awakening was both an experience of ego-dissolution and an intensely energetic experience that took many years to settle and integrate.) It's difficult to differentiate them because loss and stress usually occur simultaneously.

Also in the same way that ego-dissolution usually has an energetic aspect to it, energetic awakenings involve ego-dissolution. The only difference is that energetic awakenings dissolve the ego with the sheer force of their explosive, disruptive power rather than through a process of dissolving psychological attachments.

But the end result is the same: the birth of a new self.

9. Other Types of Sudden Awakening: Is It Possible to Awaken through Psychedelics or Technology?

Is psychological turmoil the only way that sudden awakening can occur? According to my research, this varies in relation to the two different modes of awakening we looked at in the previous chapter. Awakenings through ego-dissolution almost always occur in response to turmoil and loss. On the other hand, energetic awakenings can be triggered by a wide range of circumstances. Although they appear to be most frequently by intense turmoil, they may occasionally be triggered by intensive meditation and yoga or even by psychedelic drugs.[1]

But can't awakening just happen spontaneously, too, for no apparent reason? Isn't it possible for us to experience a moment of sudden insight, seeing things as they really are, which permanently transforms us?

Sudden Awakening in Traditional Spirituality

Some spiritual traditions suggest that spontaneous awakening is possible. As we saw in chapter 5, most spiritual traditions see awakening as a gradual process generated by spiritual practice or by following certain lifestyle guidelines (such as the Buddhist Eightfold Path or the eight-limbed path of Yoga). However, some Buddhist schools disagree with this. The Ch'an (Chinese Buddhist) and Zen traditions moved away from the Buddha's original gradualist model. More than anything else, they disputed the view that human beings move slowly toward wakefulness through lifetime after lifetime, until they finally have the capability to awaken within one particular lifetime. They argue that awakening can occur suddenly in *any* lifetime. They don't discount gradual awakening but believe that sudden awakening is also possible, and that it's superior to the former. In Ch'an, in particular, a great deal of conflict existed between the northern sudden schools and the southern gradualist schools.

According to proponents of the sudden view, awakening occurs in a flash of insight, in which one sees the true nature of self and the world (the Zen term *kensho* literally means "seeing into one's true nature"). Hui-Neng, the Sixth Patriarch of Chinese Buddhism who lived during the seventh century CE, describes sudden awakening as perceiving "the right view concerning defilement, delusion and sentient beings, resulting in instant enlightenment."[2] Once a person has experienced this moment of realization, they can never again fall into delusion.

In some respects, however, this debate is based on a false premise. Even if followers of Zen and Ch'an view the actual moment of awakening as sudden, they still recognize the importance of *preparing the way* for awakening, of undergoing training and discipline so that it's more likely to occur. This preparation and discipline includes rigorous study, koans, and meditation. Hui-Neng states that the "right view" that brings about enlightenment is the result of "training the mind." Or as the Buddhist scholar D. T. Suzuki puts it, although awakening may occur in a sudden flash of insight, it's the result of "much piling up of matters intellectual and demonstrative. The piling has reached a limit of stability and the whole edifice has come tumbling to the ground, when, behold, a new heaven is open to full survey."[3]

In other words, even though awakening may seem to occur suddenly, the process itself is a gradual one. A great deal of inner change takes place to enable transformation to occur, just as — to adapt another metaphor that Suzuki uses — a long process of cooling takes place to reach the point where water "suddenly" freezes. These changes may be so gradual that they are imperceptible or they may take place unconsciously, below the surface. It's only the final stage of the process — what appears to be the sudden moment of awakening — that is obvious or experienced consciously.

Sudden Awakening in Contemporary Spirituality

Some contemporary nonduality teachers take a similar approach to Zen and Ch'an but go much further. They suggest that there's nothing we can do to prepare for awakening, and we shouldn't use spiritual practices and paths as a means to attain it. Awakening just happens for no particular reason; we can't force it. According to this interpretation, spiritual practice is actually counterproductive because it implies that we're working toward awakening as a goal. Making an effort to attain this goal strengthens the ego and so takes us further away from enlightenment. Awakening will come when we stop making an effort — when we give up striving and let go of the idea that we're a self that needs to be awakened. Then we realize that we were *always* awakened, that wakefulness is our natural state, and it was only our clinging to the idea of self that stopped us from realizing this.

This argument seems logical, and there is a grain of truth in it, but I haven't come across any cases in which awakening has occurred in this way. In my view, this approach places too much emphasis on the Zen or Ch'an idea that awakening is about realization, about "getting it" or seeing the truth of things. This interpretation is a little problematic even in its original Buddhist context. It suggests that awakening arises solely from "right view" — when it's probably more accurate to see "right view" as a quality that arises *with* awakening. When a person wakes up, they see the world in a different way, with a revelatory sense of understanding and knowledge. But awakening is the condition of this realization rather than the other way around. Awakening is primarily an *experience* — a new sense of connection or oneness, a new perception of the phenomenal world and a new sense of identity. The understanding or insight follows *from* this experience.

Nevertheless, it's perfectly possible to imagine this "right view" emerging as an aspect of wakefulness, following a long period of spiritual training, as recommended by Zen and Ch'an teachers (and then perhaps being misinterpreted as the cause of the awakening rather than just an aspect of it). It's more difficult to imagine how this revelation could occur for no reason, without a long preparation of spiritual practice. Since the revelation occurs as an aspect of awakening, the process of awakening already has to be under way for it to arise.

Through long-term spiritual development, changes quietly take place within the psyche at an unconscious level. And my feeling is that when sudden realization seems to occur for no reason — apart from simply "letting go of the spiritual search" — this is what has been happening. For example,

Tony Parsons, one of the most radical nonduality teachers, spent many years investigating different therapies, practices, and religions to no evident benefit. Then, one day while he was walking across a park, he experienced a flash of insight that apparently came unbidden. As he describes it:

> I noticed as I walked that my mind was totally occupied with expectations about future events that might or might not happen. I seemed to choose to let go of these projections and simply be with my walking. I noticed that each footstep was totally unique in feel and pressure, and that it was there one moment and gone the next, never to be repeated in the same way again.
>
> As all of this was happening there was a transition from me watching my walking to simply the presence of walking. What happened then is simply beyond description. I can only inadequately say in words that total stillness and presence seemed to descend over everything. All and everything became timeless and I no longer existed. I vanished and there was no longer an experiencer....
>
> I felt I had been suddenly overtaken and everything took on a new sense. I looked at grass, trees, dogs and people, moving as before, but now I not only recognized their essence but I was their essence, as they were mine. It was in another way as if everything, including me, was enveloped in a deep and all-encompassing love, and in a strange way it seemed that what I saw was also somehow nothing special...it is the norm that is not usually perceived.[4]

This is a beautiful description of a powerful awakening experience, but although Tony writes that "this illumination had occurred without any effort on my part,"[5] it's highly likely that his previous years of exploration, spiritual practice, and therapy helped prepare the way — or create the necessary conditions — for this shift, in the same way that Zen and Ch'an practices were designed to cultivate the conditions that allow flashes of awakening to occur. It's probably *impossible* to spend years investigating spiritual practices and therapies without gaining some degree of positive development, even if this only means heightened powers of introspection and self-observation.

Tony's shift is similar to Russel Williams's experience of waking up one morning and realizing that he was one with the horses he was looking after and with everything else. But Russel was clearly aware — at least in retrospect — that the three years he spent looking after the horses was a form of spiritual practice that created the conditions for his awakening to occur.

Actively seeking spiritual development — or awakening itself — *can* be problematic. It depends on the nature of one's seeking. In some cases, it may be a rigid egoic process in which a person sets their sights on the goal of awakening much as they would on a goal of becoming rich or successful. Or seeking may be a diversionary tactic in which a person explores spiritual practices and sets their sights on awakening as a way of escaping from difficulties in their life or psychological issues. In these cases, seeking certainly can be counterproductive and can take us further away from harmony and well-being.

However, spiritual seeking can be — and most frequently *is*, in my experience of seekers — more organic, generating not from the ego but from the core of our being. Ideally, seeking stems from an impulse to expand ourselves, to transcend our psychological discord and our narrow egoic desires and engender a more integrated and connected identity — that is, an impulse to wake up. Fundamentally this impulse is an *evolutionary* one. Ever since the beginnings of life on earth there has been movement toward the expansion and intensification of consciousness, and the impulse for spiritual growth is part of this. It's an expression — in us as individuals — of the same impulse that has given rise to ever more complex and conscious life-forms over countless millions of years.

Ideally, spiritual seekers act on behalf of evolution, allowing this impulse to express itself through them. They may not even have a clear idea of where this impulse is leading them; they may not even be conscious of spiritual awakening as a goal. They may not necessarily *strive* to become awakened but simply allow their impulse for growth to express itself and follow where it takes them. They use spiritual practices — unconsciously or consciously — as technologies of transcendence, methods of facilitating an impulse for growth and transformation that is much larger and older than they are.

Awakening through Psychedelics?

In the 1960s, psychedelic pioneers such as Timothy Leary popularized the belief that drugs such as LSD could provide chemical enlightenment, a way of circumventing the years of arduous spiritual practice that monks and other spiritual seekers put themselves through to attain wakefulness. Why spend years meditating and practicing self-denial when you can simply alter your brain chemistry directly by taking psychedelics?

It soon became apparent that this was naive and that regular LSD use was much more likely to generate psychological breakdown than spiritual awakening. Many of those who originally used LSD as a way of expanding consciousness — including Timothy Leary himself — eventually began to use drugs hedonistically, as a way of escaping boredom and discord after their chemical enlightenment project had failed.

Nowadays, psychoactive substances such as ayahuasca and DMT (N,N-Dimethyltryptamine) are widely used with a spiritual intention, as a means of self-exploration and self-expansion. Ayahuasca in particular has the status of an elixir of enlightenment, as LSD had in the 1960s.

As I suggest in *Waking from Sleep*, psychedelics can certainly generate temporary awakening *experiences*. Some writers on mysticism — usually with religious backgrounds — have argued that psychedelic awakening experiences are facsimiles of genuine ones, similar to them but devoid of any real spiritual quality.[6] But this is difficult to justify because psychedelic awakening experiences clearly feature many of the same characteristics of other awakening experiences, such as intensified perception and a sense of harmony, meaning, and connection or oneness with the world.

Nevertheless, there are differences between psychedelic awakening experiences and other types. In awakening experiences generated by an intensification and stilling of life-energy (such as through meditation or contact with nature), we often have a sense of energetic serenity, as if we've made contact with a deep energy of being that has a natural blissful quality. Related to this, we often sense the onset of a deeper identity, a new self that is somehow more authentic than our normal self. Psychedelic experiences tend not to feature these inner aspects. They are mainly perceptual and visionary experiences rather than inward experiences of peace and wholeness. In fact, this applies to *all* awakening experiences caused by homeostasis disruption, that is, the intense disruption of our normal physiological and neurological functioning through practices such as fasting, sleep deprivation, self-inflicted pain, unusual breathing patterns, exposure to extreme temperatures, and so on. Drug-induced awakening experiences are simply a variety of these.

Psychedelics can bring temporary awakening experiences but it's very unlikely that they can lead to permanent awakening, either gradually or suddenly. (Equally, one could say that it's doubtful that other methods of homeostasis disruption such as fasting or sleep deprivation can lead to permanent wakefulness.) Psychedelics (like all other homeostasis disruptors) are basically *dissolutive*; that is, they dissolve the normal self-system and put its psychological mechanisms out of action. When the normal self-system dissolves, the desensitizing mechanism no longer functions so that our perceptions become intensely vivid. The boundaries of the normal self-system fade away so that we no longer experience separateness. Our normal concepts of ourselves and reality also fade away so that we feel we're looking at the world and ourselves in a completely new way. In addition, with the boundaries of the self dissolved, a great deal of unconscious mental phenomena may emerge. This dissolution is sufficient for temporary awakening experiences, but permanent wakefulness can only occur if there's a new self-system to replace the normal one. It's not enough to dissolve the sense of self — a new self has to replace it.

As we saw in chapter 7, for people who have been through long periods of intense turmoil and trauma, this new self-system may be ready to emerge. As their psychological attachments progressively dissolve away, the new self-system slowly prepares itself to supplant it, slowly taking form in the same way that a butterfly prepares itself to emerge from its chrysalis. But it's unlikely that a new self is ready to emerge inside people who take psychedelics in normal situations. Their self-systems will simply dissolve away temporarily and then their normal self-systems will simply reform and reestablish themselves.

This explains why psychedelics (including ayahuasca) can't generate gradual awakening either. If you regularly ingest psychedelics, you may experience regular awakening experiences, but it's highly unlikely that a higher self will slowly emerge or form. Prolonged spiritual practice *will* gradually form a new self that slowly supplants your old self; spiritual practice slowly facilitates the creation of a mold of a new self that already exists as a potential. But ingesting psychedelics doesn't entail any training or discipline in itself.

You could say that spiritual practice is basically *constructive* — it gradually changes the structures of consciousness, remolding your self-system into a higher functioning form. But because psychedelics are basically dissolutive (or *de*structive), they don't facilitate the emergence of a new self-system. The danger with regular use of psychedelics is that the structures of the normal self-system will completely dissolve away and, without another self-system to supplant it, there will simply be a psychic vacuum that equates to a state of psychosis. Unfortunately, cases of this are not uncommon. In fact, psychosis, not awakening, is really the only permanent psychological change caused by regular use of psychedelics.

In every area of human experience, *readiness* is important. If you haven't attained a sufficient level of development (including sufficient understanding) to process and integrate an experience, it may be overwhelming and damaging. This is a particular problem with psychedelic experiences because they can be so powerful. Just one powerful psychedelic experience can permanently damage a person whose self-system is fragile and delicate. As the ancient Neoplatonist philosopher Iamblichus warns, not all experiences of ecstasy are elevating and transformational. They may have the opposite effect. Unless a person's inner being is properly prepared, ecstasy can make "the soul degenerate, confused, and even more alienated from reality."[7] And this can certainly happen with the ecstasy of psychedelics.

However, psychedelics can sometimes be a *contributory* factor in awakening, both gradual and sudden. They may contribute to gradual awakening if a person takes them at the same time as following a program of spiritual practice. In that case, the stability and integration provided by spiritual practice may minimize the disruptive potential of psychedelics and make positive effects more likely. (At the same time, though, I feel that if a person's practice is effective, it's unlikely that they will feel the need or impulse to take psychedelics.)

In terms of sudden awakening, psychedelics can be a contributory factor by creating a psychic opening that unlocks the transformational potential of turmoil or trauma in a way similar to therapy. As Stanislav Grof suggests, psychedelic substances may be the *final trigger of* spiritual emergencies (or psychospiritual crises, as he also terms them), following a long period of loss, failure, or traumatic emotional experiences.[8]

In my research, I came across one case of sudden energetic awakening that was triggered by psychedelics. Helen took a small amount of ecstasy during a long period of depression and intense stress. Immediately before her transformational experience, a relationship with a close friend had broken down. After taking the ecstasy she suddenly "felt a rush of love, like I was burning up. My whole body was flooded with light." This was a transformational experience, which remained even after the effects of the ecstasy had faded away. There was a sudden and dramatic opening of her psyche, which took her many years to integrate. As she described it:

> After that my whole senses opened up, and I found everything overwhelming. I was completely blown open too fast. I had no filter. I was so open and so delicate. Whenever I went out it was very chaotic. I was having psychic episodes but I didn't understand them. I could sense other people's thoughts.
>
> I thought I was going bonkers, but I was aware that I was going bonkers, and I had a sense that I needed to work through it, that it would play itself out. It lasted for about two years, before it started to stabilize. I was working in a bookshop at the time but had to stop because I was ill. I was diagnosed with ME [myalgic encephalopathy, or chronic fatigue syndrome]. I was too ill to go out.
>
> The past seven years have been about integrating the old and the new. Over the last three or four years I've reached a more stable state. I've worked through the chaos and I don't feel vulnerable anymore. I feel a lot more peaceful and stable now.
>
> I feel like a completely different person. I used to be very cynical and intolerant and judgmental. I was also anxious and neurotic and insecure. I'm a lot more intuitive and in touch with myself, a

lot more aware of my own energies. People are so surprised at how sorted I seem. People who knew me in the past can't believe that I'm the same person, they're amazed at how calm and centred I am. Now I'm really happy being me. I used to feel a general anxiety all the time.

Ecstasy appears to have been the catalyst for this experience, but it certainly wasn't the sole cause of it. And in my view, this is true of psychedelics in general — they can possibly have a *catalytic* but not a *direct causal* effect in terms of awakening.

The Primary and Secondary Shifts

Nevertheless, there is a way in which psychedelics can be transformative, even by themselves. There's an important distinction between what I call the *primary shift* and the *secondary shift*. The primary shift is the transformation we've been speaking about throughout this book — the shift into a state of wakefulness in which the normal self-system is supplanted by the higher-functioning wakeful self-system so that a person has a new sense of identity. The secondary shift is a less fundamental kind of transformation. A person doesn't experience a shift in identity — or a state of oneness with the world or heightened awareness — but their values, beliefs, and attitudes are transformed. They have a new perspective; they look at life in a different way. For example, they might start to believe in life after death, become less materialistic and more altruistic, and become more optimistic and more trusting toward other people. They may begin to investigate spiritual teachings with a sense that there's much more to life than they previously realized, that the world isn't the same place it was before and their previous lifestyle no longer seems meaningful.

You could compare the distinction between the primary and secondary shifts to inhabiting a house. The primary shift — actual awakening — is like moving into a different house or, perhaps more strictly, creating a new house on the same plot of land where your previous one stood. A secondary shift is like remaining in the same house but giving it a complete overhaul, renovating and redecorating it. In a secondary shift, your previous self-system and sense of identity remain intact. Since your ego-boundaries remain essentially intact, you don't experience the intense connection, oneness, or intensified perception of the wakeful state. You feel that you are the same continuous ego-self as before, although you may possess a different cognitive map of reality.[9]

John is a good example of this secondary shift. He had a successful career as a computer programmer and described himself as very materialistically oriented: "I was motivated by the money, the possessions, and the status that came along with 'success.' I was very anti-religious and I had donated money to the National Secular Society to support their work. My car was a very expensive 'look at me' sports car." Although he had experiences of lucid dreaming he was "not very interested in anything remotely spiritual."

However, John decided to attend a lucid dreaming workshop, where there was an option to take ayahuasca. As a result of his ayahuasca experience, his vision of reality and his values were transformed. After believing that he "knew it all," he became aware of how limited his normal perspective was. As he described it:

> I saw that the seemingly endless desire for more money, things, and success was not the key to happiness. My motivation changed to "give something back" to the world that had been so good to me. I retrained as a counsellor and worked as a volunteer with cancer patients at my local hospital. I became interested in "spirituality" and the underlying message of religion, and I donated money to the Lucidity Institute to support their work. My car is now an ordinary and very practical seven-seater. These changes have proved to be long term and the date of the experience, the 28th of January 2005, is as important to me as my birthday.

Indeed, a great deal of research shows that psychedelics can bring about a long-lasting shift in perspective and values. As Aldous Huxley famously writes of psychedelic awakening experiences in *The Doors of Perception*, "The man who comes back through the Door in the Wall will never be quite the same as the man who went out."[10] This was illustrated by the theologian Walter Pahnke's famous "Good Friday Experiment" in 1962, in which a group of theology students were given doses of psilocybin (the active ingredient in "magic" mushrooms) in a religious setting. They all had powerful mystical experiences, including feelings of ecstasy, awe, and oneness. In a follow-up study six months later, eight of ten students said that the experience had had a powerful long-term effect, deepening their sense of spirituality and enriching their lives. And remarkably, this was still the case twenty-five years later. In a follow-up study by the psychedelic researcher Rick Doblin in 1987, most of the original participants reflected that the experience had changed them permanently, giving them a deeper appreciation of life and nature, an increased sense of joy, a reduced fear of death, and greater empathy for minorities and oppressed people.[11]

There have been similar findings in relation to ayahuasca. The author and proponent of psychedelics Dennis McKenna found that use of the plant "may result in profound, lasting, and positive behavioral and lifestyle changes."[12] He gives the example of an ayahuasca group whose members had a history of addiction and domestic violence. These negative traits fell away with the use of ayahuasca. This recalls the findings of psychedelic therapy programs in the early 1960s, when alcoholics were given LSD. Around a half of them responded positively to the treatment and either became long-term sober or began to drink much less.[13]

This research makes it clear that psychedelics can have a powerful transformative effect, although not in the sense of generating full-fledged wakefulness. Nevertheless, the secondary shift generated by psychedelics may indirectly lead to a primary shift in the sense that it may encourage a person to follow spiritual practices or paths — or to generally live a lifestyle that is more conducive to wakefulness — in an attempt to recapture their experience. Like awakening experiences in general, psychedelic experiences can provide a glimpse into a new, unsuspected dimension of harmony and meaning, and ideally generate an impulse to return to that dimension on a permanent, stable basis. One of the best examples of this is Ram Dass, formerly a psychology professor at Harvard University (under his birth name, Richard Alpert) and one of the pioneers of research into psychedelics. His experiences with LSD encouraged him to investigate meditation and yoga and to travel to India to study with spiritual teachers.

He began a long journey of spiritual awakening that has led him to become one of the most revered spiritual authors and teachers of our time.

The important thing to realize is that *psychedelics are not a permanent means of providing us with what they offer us temporarily*. In a sense, they are deceptive. They show us the place where we should be heading, but they don't provide us with the means of getting there. They show us the destination but not the route. If you try to use them as a route to awakening, you're more likely to end up in a state of psychosis rather than wakefulness.

Ideally, psychedelics can be wise guides, especially at the beginning of the spiritual journey. But once they have shared their wisdom with us, we should move on and try to apply the knowledge we've gained. Or in the words of Alan Watts: "Once you get the message, hang up."

Technological Wakefulness:
The Fallacy of the Materialist Model of Mind

The only perspective from which chemical enlightenment really makes sense is if wakefulness is seen as a *neurological* state; that is, if it's explained as being generated by a particular type of brain functioning, such as the activity of certain neurotransmitters or other chemicals, or enhanced or decreased activity in certain areas of the brain. If wakefulness is just a brain-state, then it should be possible to produce this brain-state through chemical interventions.

From this point of view, it might also be possible to generate wakefulness by technological means. Perhaps we could use machines to alter brain functioning or stimulate different parts of the brain and so create the neurological conditions that produce the wakeful state. Perhaps we could even use neurosurgery in this way, too. If we know that wakefulness is associated with increased activity in a certain part of the brain, perhaps surgery can alter our neurological functioning so that these parts become more active. Or if we know that wakefulness is associated with higher levels of certain chemicals (such as DMT), then perhaps we can tweak the brain's functioning so that it produces higher levels of these chemicals.

This sounds absurd, of course — but then, for me, it's absurd to think of wakefulness as a neurological state. Of course, many people do assume that mental activity is produced by neurological activity or, from a slightly different perspective, that consciousness is produced by the brain. This is the standard materialist model of the mind, closely related to the biological approach to psychology, which sees psychiatric problems (such as depression or ADHD) as produced by imbalances or dysfunctions in brain activity. This model assumes that matter — physical "stuff" such as atoms, molecules, and cells — is the only reality, and that what appears to us as "mind" or "consciousness" is an epiphenomenon produced by the activity of the molecules and cells in our brains. And so all of the different psychological states we experience such as depression, joy, love, and wakefulness are the result of different variations of activity among these molecules and cells.

This isn't the place for a full discussion of the shortcomings of this model — philosophers such as David Chalmers and Thomas Nagel have written powerful texts exposing its flaws and inconsistencies.[14] But it's strange to think that, twenty years or so ago, when scientists began to investigate consciousness intensively, most were confident that it wouldn't be long before we solved the mystery of how the brain gives rise to conscious experience. They believed that brain-scanning technologies would enable us to see how the brain's billions of neurons work together to generate our subjective experience. But despite more than two decades of intensive research and theorizing, very little (if any) progress has been made. The so-called hard problem (in the phrase coined by David Chalmers) of how the brain might give rise to the richness of our subjective experience seems to become ever more intractable. No neuroscientist has ever made any reasonable suggestion about how the brain might produce consciousness or even about which parts of the brain might be involved in producing it. Phenomena such as near-death experiences (when the subjective experience seems to continue when the brain is clinically dead) and terminal lucidity (when people with severe brain damage experience a return to normal consciousness shortly before death) also argue against a straightforward link between the brain and consciousness. In addition, there doesn't seem to be an exact or reliable correspondence between mental states and neurological activity, which we would expect if the latter produced the former. For example, more and more research suggests no clear relationship between brain-states and psychological conditions such as depression or ADHD, and no real benefit of drugs designed to increase the brain's serotonin uptake (or to change the activity of the neurotransmitters supposedly associated with ADHD).[15]

There's a growing sense that the materialist model of the mind is far too simplistic. Philosophers are taking seriously the alternative panpsychist model, which holds that consciousness is a primary quality of the universe. In this model, consciousness is a fundamental force embedded into the fabric of reality so that it pervades everything — and even seemingly inanimate things are conscious (or at least possess a kind of protoconsciousness). This view obviously fits well with high-intensity awakening experiences in which one perceives a radiant spirit-force pervading all things and bringing all things into oneness as manifestations of the force. (It also fits well with the worldview of many of the world's indigenous peoples that the whole world is pervaded by a spirit-force.)

This doesn't mean that the brain isn't necessary for consciousness. The function of the brain may be to pick up and "canalize" an all-pervading consciousness so that we can become *individually* conscious. Consciousness then becomes *localized* within us, in a particular point in time and space. This applies to other living beings as well, even if they only possess consciousness in the sense of being aware of their surroundings to some degree. Even if they don't have brains or nervous systems, the function of their cells may be to pick up and canalize consciousness so that they become individual entities with some awareness of their surroundings. As living beings become more complex, with larger numbers of cells interacting with each other in more complex ways, they are able to receive and canalize consciousness more fully so that their own consciousness becomes more intense and at the same time more subtle and intricate.

This also doesn't mean that the state of wakefulness — or any other psychological state such as depression or ADHD — isn't related to neurological functioning. Perhaps the wakeful state is associated with higher or lower levels of activity in certain parts of the brain. But there is no need to assume that the brain activity *generates* the state of wakefulness. We could just as easily reverse the causal direction and suggest that the wakeful state generates the neurological state. This actually makes sense in terms of the panpsychist model, which suggests that mind is more fundamental than matter.

In my view, therefore, the idea that you can chemically engineer a state of wakefulness through technology or drugs — and the idea that wakefulness is fundamentally a neurological state — is as false as the idea that depression is caused by a chemical imbalance that can be cured by drugs.

10. The Aftermath of Awakening:
Spiritual Crisis

When we undergo awakening, doesn't it mean that all our problems are at an end? Doesn't wakefulness mean that finally we're at peace, in a state where there's no more striving, discord, or anxiety? Surely, if wakefulness means anything, it means a state of permanent ease and bliss. After all, aren't all our problems created by the ego so that when the ego dissolves away, all our problems dissolve away, too? The Upanishads state, "When [the soul] discovers the Atman, full of dignity and power, it is freed from suffering" and "when a man knows the infinite, he is free; his sorrows have an end."[1]

I'd never wish to disagree with the sages of the Upanishads (it's my favorite spiritual text, after all). But the sages were speaking generally and poetically, without dealing with the intricacies of the awakening process. They were also part of a culture much more accepting and understanding of wakefulness. Certainly for modern Westerners (such as Europeans or Americans), awakening can involve challenges and difficulties. When it occurs gradually — usually through following spiritual practices or paths — it often *is* smooth and easy. Sudden awakening can also be smooth and easy, especially if the person has some knowledge of spiritual practices and traditions to help them make sense of what's happening and a supportive environment around them. (Perhaps it also depends on how well established their new self-system is as a structure and how prepared it is for emergence.) But in most cases, when awakening occurs suddenly, it's problematic to some degree. As the twentieth-century Christian mystic Bernadette Roberts describes it, the wakeful state is "a new dimension of knowing and being that entails a difficult and prolonged readjustment."[2]

In this chapter, we're going to summarize these potential difficulties, focusing on three main areas: confusion, psychological disturbances, and physical problems. It's important to remember that the difficulties related to the *process* of awakening tend to fade away, as we saw in relation to *kundalini*-like energetic awakenings. The birth of a new self can be painful and dangerous, but eventually the difficulties pass and the new self settles into its new state.

But even then, wakefulness as a settled, ongoing state may not be *completely* blissful and easy. Old behavior patterns may take some time to die away (or may not die away at all), and life may still throw up challenges that destabilize us. Certainly we'll have a much deeper and steadier sense of well-being than before. We'll be much less affected by negative or stressful events, just as we'll be much less selfish and more altruistic than before. But this doesn't mean that our lives will be *completely* trouble-free and that we'll be completely perfect as individuals.

Confusion

Gradual awakening provides ample opportunity for people to build a framework to make sense of their experience. There's time for people to gain knowledge and support — perhaps to gravitate to spiritual groups, explore spiritual practices and traditions, read books, and meet other people who have had similar experiences. But sudden awakening provides little or no opportunity to do this. Unless a person already has some knowledge of spiritual traditions, they will likely be confused by their new state, possibly even to the extent of thinking that they've gone mad.

It might seem strange to stress the importance of a conceptual understanding of wakefulness because it's fundamentally an *experiential* state, and in some senses conceptual understanding can be an obstacle to it. Aren't concepts what we're trying to transcend? Don't they stop us from seeing the world in its is-ness? Don't they mean that we've become caught up in the intellect, with ideas and beliefs?

This is true, but a *basic* conceptual understanding of wakefulness is essential. A map is important so long as we *just* use it as a way of orienting ourselves, of checking that we know where we are and that we're heading in the right direction. The map only becomes a problem when we spend all our time looking at it, thinking about where we've been and where we're heading instead of experiencing the reality we're in at this moment. If awakened individuals don't understand the process they're going through (or have been through), their wakefulness will be overlaid with doubt, and they may even try to suppress it.

Again, you might think, how is it possible to suppress a process as powerful as awakening? And how is it possible for such a powerfully positive experience to be negated by confusion? But this is probably another example of idealizing wakefulness. I've come across countless cases where lack of a conceptual framework has caused difficulties. We've already seen that this confusion can be a problem with natural wakefulness, too. It was certainly a problem for me and for Peace Pilgrim because we didn't have the background knowledge to make sense of our state, and the wakeful perspective is so opposed to the values of the cultures we grew up in.

Confusion caused difficulties even for Russel Williams, who is one of the most intensely awakened individuals I've come across. I described in chapters 6 and 7 how Russel experienced awakening after an early life of great turmoil and trauma and following three years of "accidental" spiritual practice while he was looking after horses as a member of a traveling circus. But there's an interesting postscript to Russel's story. His sudden awakening occurred in 1950, when he was twenty-nine years old, at a time when there was little knowledge of spiritual traditions in Europe. After an initial honeymoon period, he began to doubt his newly awakened state because of the confusion he encountered whenever he tried to explain it to people. As he traveled around with the circus, he sought out local vicars and clergymen, hoping that they would understand. As he describes it in *Not I, Not Other Than I*:

> I told them I only saw wholeness, with no separation, this natural state of being which was nurturing and kindness. I thought it would interest them, but they didn't understand. They thought it was far-fetched, or that I was being blasphemous....
>
> The lack of understanding from others had the effect of making me very confused. I had a lot of knowledge but I couldn't communicate it to anybody. I began to doubt myself. I thought,

"If nobody can appreciate this, I must be mad. I'm so different to everybody else." I knew deep down that I wasn't mad, that I had something that was profoundly important to other people, but it was overlaid with this confusion.[3]

The frustration became so intense that one night, in desperation, Russel cried out, "For God's sake, somebody help me!" Right at that moment, he felt a "massive flood of peace, a vast emptiness full of love. There was no substance. It was the same serene feeling I'd had before with the horses, but in greater depth. It was as if someone had dropped a soft warm blanket over me."[4] Just a few days later, he felt impelled to go to a talk about spiritual healing in London, and there he met John Garrie, one of the founders of one of the first Buddhist groups in England. As Russel describes it:

He was the first person I ever met who could understand me. I could explain the way I experienced the world and he could relate it to the teachings of Buddhism. I felt a deep rapport with him.... It was a massive relief, to find out that I wasn't mad after all. I found out later that he'd been drawn to that meeting in a similar convoluted way to me. He had felt impelled to go too, even though he wasn't keen.[5]

This gave Russel the confirmation he needed — or, more strictly speaking, the understanding and the support he needed — and from that point on he had a strong sense of orientation and purpose. Soon afterward he began to take on a role as a spiritual teacher, which has continued for over fifty years.

William Murtha, whose awakening I described in *Out of the Darkness*, is an example of a person who attempted to suppress his wakefulness because he couldn't make sense of it. William almost drowned after being swept into the sea by a freak wave. He had a near-death experience in which he floated outside his body and encountered beings who answered every question he had ever had about life. But the experience — and the insights he learned — didn't fit into the materialistic model of reality he had always accepted. He couldn't make sense of what had happened and didn't know how to explain it to other people, and so acted as if nothing had changed. For eighteen months he suppressed his wakefulness. He tried to carry on

living the way he had before — in fact, he clung even harder to his previous habits and values, working even harder and drinking even more than
before. But finally, and inevitability, the new self that he had been trying so
hard to suppress burst through his resistance:

> All of a sudden I heard this little voice at the back of my head, say-
> ing, "Bill, this is not who you are, you are not meant to be here."
> And I can just remember stopping in my tracks and I sobered
> up, just like that. All of a sudden I just got it. Everything became
> crystal clear. I just thought: What am I doing? I am running away
> from the truth of what happened to me....I was running away
> from it because of my narrow worldview, my conditioning, what
> I'd learned at school....It was like a switch going on. I could feel
> a shift inside me.[6]

Most shifters I interviewed described similar difficulties to Russel and
William. Many shifters described how the positive aspects of their new
state of being were offset by incomprehension and confusion. As one person put it, "I didn't understand at all what was going on. I had no concepts
to help me understand it. Something was happening which felt very strong
spiritually but I didn't know what was going to happen at the end of it."
Another person described how she "needed to do a lot of work and seeking
to integrate and figure out how to live with this new person I was. I was
very confused." More graphically, another person described how his transformation "opened up a can of worms because I had to find out what I had
experienced and nobody I knew had the slightest clue what I was talking
about."

As with Russel, shifters' initial confusion is often intensified by the incomprehension they receive from others. In some cases, their own confusion may *wholly* be the result of the incomprehension of others. They may
try to explain the way they see the world now, only for people to shake their
heads and say something like, "Wow — have you been taking drugs?"
So many people might tell shifters that they "sound mad" that they may
start to believe it themselves. One woman told me how she had a sudden
spiritual awakening one morning in which it was "as if I was seeing it for
the first time. Everything shone with beauty and clarity no matter what

it was. It was as if I had a new pair of eyes and there was a light that was exquisite." At the same time she had no idea what had happened to her and tried to explain it to other people in the hope of some guidance. "I asked everyone that I thought would understand if they could explain this. No one knew what to say."

In the worst-case scenario, wakefulness may be so catastrophically misunderstood that it becomes pathologized, seen as a mental illness rather than as a higher-functioning state. A shifter who doesn't understand their new state may go to see a psychiatrist who knows nothing about spiritual awakening and only sees signs of mental abnormality. The psychiatrist may prescribe drugs, which will suppress the awakening process, or even send the awakening person to a psychiatric hospital.

In retrospect, many shifters were aware that the main source of their confusion was their lack of knowledge of spirituality, which meant that they had no framework to make sense of their experiences. As one person told me, "I had never read a spiritual book or meditated, never done any spiritual practice, so I had no framework or reference point at all. It was all new. I documented as much as I could but there was so much happening so quickly." And indeed, as I've already mentioned, I found that sudden awakening was less likely to be problematic for individuals who already had some knowledge of spiritual traditions and concepts. (Perhaps this was also because they already had contact with spiritually minded people or groups who could provide them with some understanding, guidance, and support.) This also suggests that sudden awakening is less likely to be problematic in cultures that are more accepting of spirituality or where spiritual ideas and practices are a part of everyday life. (As I suggest in chapter 8, this is perhaps why the ancient Yogic and Tantric texts devote little attention to the potentially problematic aspects of *kundalini* awakening.)

This period of confusion is only temporary. Almost everyone who undergoes sudden awakening eventually begins to understand their new state. Sooner or later they find clues and signposts that give them a sense of orientation. They open books of spiritual teachings and realize, "Yes! This is what I've been through!" They find themselves chatting to someone who meditates or follows a Buddhist or Daoist path and feel a sense of connection. Or they may remember a conversation they had years ago — or a poem or passage from a book they read, or a documentary they saw — that now seems to make sense. They begin to build up a conceptual framework to make sense of their wakefulness. Their own certainty begins to override the doubts of the people around them.

For example, one person described how after her awakening she felt "a little in the wilderness, trying to understand what had happened to me" and began a process of "seeking, searching for answers." She eventually discovered meditation and yoga, which she felt were instinctively right for her, and enabled her to understand and integrate her new state. Another person felt drawn to study counseling and discovered spirituality through psychotherapy and transpersonal psychology.

More than sixty years ago, when Russel Williams underwent his awakening, this process of orientation could take a long time (several years in Russel's case) simply because knowledge of spirituality was so hard to come by. But now that spiritual knowledge is much more accessible, the process is easier.

Difficult Relationships

In general, when people wake up, their relationships improve. People usually become more empathic, compassionate, and considerate; they are better able to express love and affection. But their transformation may be so drastic and incomprehensible to the people around them that relationships can sometimes be problematic, too. The awakened person changes so fundamentally that it can be almost as if they're a different person inhabiting the same body. For example, in chapter 8 we saw that Kimberley underwent such a dramatic shift that when she went back home she didn't expect her friends and family to recognize her.

Relationships that were once close and harmonious may become discordant. Often old friendships and family ties break down, and sometimes marital partners separate. A gulf opens up — shifters have changed so fundamentally while their old connections have remained the same. Typically, relatives and friends are bemused by the awakened person's new behavior and new personality. One shifter told me that after her transformation, "I had very little in common with a lot of people who I knew....Over time I have renewed some old relationships in a different way and let some go completely."

In some cases, friends and relatives resent the shifter's new personality and feel that they're behaving selfishly, now that they're living more authentically and honestly and exploring new avenues to make sense of their transformation. For example, one shifter created resentment because she felt the need to spend a lot of time alone, to create as much space for herself as possible, rather than giving her time to her family. Another woman was accused of being selfish because "I sometimes say no — I might have to say no because now I'm trying to take care of myself. I need to take time out."

The sense of authenticity shifters experience — and the responsibility they feel to be truthful — is another potentially tricky issue. They are sometimes *too* honest and hurt other people's feelings. They may be less willing to placate people, to tell people what they want to hear or sympathize with problems that seem trivial to them. One shifter told me that she had less patience for friends who complained about problems but didn't do anything about them. Another woman told me that "my eighteen-year-old niece lives with me and sometimes I say things which she may perceive as hurtful — but I'm just being truthful....She'll be making excuses but I'm asking her to take responsibility."

Relationship difficulties can add to the confusion and discord that often follow sudden awakening, but it's usually not long before shifters begin to form new connections to replace the old ones. As they search for understanding of their new state, they meet people who share their spiritual interests, who are also exploring and expanding themselves and may have already experienced some degree of wakefulness. Shifters usually form deep, open, and authentic relationships with these fellow self-explorers and so establish new friendship groups that are often more fulfilling than the previous relationships.

Psychological Disturbances

Confusion can be difficult enough to deal with, but sudden awakening can be even more problematic when it causes psychological disturbances. As

mentioned in chapter 8, psychological disturbances are especially prev-
alent in energetic *kundalini*-like awakenings, but can sometimes occur in
ego-dissolution, too. The awakened person may find it difficult to think
clearly or concentrate because their mind is overwhelmed with new impressions, thoughts, and visions, or with subconscious mental material that
was previously repressed. They may have problems with memory and difficulty organizing their lives and making plans and decisions. They may
find social interaction difficult. In extreme cases, they may even have problems speaking. It's quite common for them to have to take extended time
off work or to give up their jobs all together. If the incomprehension of the
people around them has made them think that they might have gone mad,
these disturbances may confirm it.

These problems are the result of the sudden dissolution of the person's
previous self-system, together with their new sensory openness, which
overwhelms them with new impressions and perceptions. Psychological
functions such as memory, concentration, and cognition are performed by
the self-system, so when it dissolves these functions are disrupted, in the
same way a computer crashes when its programs are disrupted. The new
self-system usually takes over these functions fairly quickly, but the transition may not be smooth. You could compare it to a new political party
winning an election and taking over a country's governance — there's an
initial period of uncertainty as the new politicians take over their new roles
and find their footing.

Some shifters find that they have to effectively *retrain* themselves to
think conceptually and relearn basic mental functions. This parallels the
way that stroke victims sometimes have to retrain themselves to perform
basic functions. Stroke victims, however, are mainly retraining the *brain* —
reforming neural connections, training different parts of the brain to take
over functions that used to be performed by the now-damaged parts of the
brain — whereas shifters are training their new self-system to take over
mental functions that used to be performed by the previous one.

One of the most dramatic examples of psychological disturbance is JC
Mac's, which I described in chapter 7. His basic psychological functions
were so disrupted that he couldn't work. He found it difficult to hold con-
versations and often forgot to eat. Even several years after his sudden shift

he found it "difficult to function sometimes with the things that require mind, organizing." Kimberley said she had "a short-term memory cycle of about thirty seconds and everything was just sort of slipping through my mind." In the same way, Phoebe, whose sudden awakening in response to the death of her high school friend was described in chapter 7, said she "had a lot of trouble with long- and short-term memory, with work and simple tasks, and with communicating." On her twenty-first birthday she kept forgetting that it was her birthday; she only remembered when people wished her happy birthday. While in chapter 8, we looked at the examples of Simon and Eric, whose psychological disturbances led them to be diagnosed with mental illness.

As with confusion, these psychological disturbances are usually only temporary. In extreme cases such as JC's, they make take several years to fade away, but in almost all cases shifters become psychologically integrated again and able to function in the everyday world. It's partly simply a question of allowing the earthquake of sudden awakening to settle down and relearning conceptual and mental abilities. As shifters relearn the ability to concentrate, they learn to deal with their sensory openness and heightened perception by narrowing their awareness when they need to. They learn the ability to control their attention so that they can screen out their heightened reality when they need to focus on the practical business of everyday life. For Kimberley, it was "two to three years" before she began "to feel stable and finally understand what was happening." Similarly, Helen, whose sudden awakening we looked at briefly in the previous chapter, told me how initially, "I thought I was going bonkers, but I was aware that I was going bonkers, and I had a sense that I needed to work through it, that it would play itself out. It lasted for about two years, before it started to stabilize."

Physical Problems

The third — and most severe, but also the rarest — type of difficulty that can arise after sudden awakening is physical problems. Even more than psychological disturbances, physical problems are associated with energetic awakening because of the disruptive effects of the powerful explosion of energy that occurs. And like psychological disturbances, these physical difficulties can greatly exacerbate the confusion that often comes after sudden awakening and increase the likelihood of people being diagnosed with mental illness.

The most common physical difficulties reported to me are sleeplessness, fatigue, and unexplained pains. (Not coincidentally, transpersonal psychologists have identified similar difficulties with *kundalini* awakening.) For example, Kimberley described how "I started to develop physical symptoms which stopped me in my tracks and that forced me to reassess. . . . My body was in pain. I was fatigued but couldn't sleep. I didn't sleep properly for about eight months." She was diagnosed with fibromyalgia, but began to recover with the help of alternative therapies like Reiki. Similarly, Helen began to suffer from unexplained pain and extreme tiredness and was eventually diagnosed with ME, or chronic fatigue syndrome. As she told me, "I was working in a bookshop at the time but had to stop. . . . I was too ill to go out." Another person experienced sleeplessness together with a complete loss of appetite and an inability to feel heat or cold.

When an energetic awakening occurs, it creates a massive upheaval that may affect a person's whole organism, throwing it completely out of balance. The carefully regulated mechanisms that maintain homeostasis and health may be disrupted. At the same time, the explosive energy that has been released inside the person may make them feel too restless to relax or sleep, as if they've taken a powerful stimulant. In *Waking from Sleep*, I suggest that homeostasis disruption can cause awakening experiences (such as when a person fasts or intentionally goes without sleep) but here the causality is reversed: the intense energetic awakening itself causes a major disruption to homeostasis.

The Importance of Understanding and Support

These difficulties illustrate how vital it is that people who experience sudden awakening are given support and understanding to help alleviate their confusion and help them deal with their psychological disturbances and any physical issues. If they don't realize that they're undergoing a transformation into a higher state then it'll be all too easy to mistake their shift-*up* for a break*down*. Unless they are familiar with the signs of spiritual awakening, it's possible that they will misread them. It will be easy for them to agree with relatives and friends who suspect that they've gone mad. They may resist or suppress the awakening process, and it's more likely that they will fall into the hands of uncomprehending psychiatrists.

I'm a great admirer of such organizations as the Spiritual Crisis Network (based in the UK) and the Spiritual Emergence Network (in the US) because of the support they provide. The express purpose of these groups is, as the website of the Spiritual Crisis Network states, to promote "understanding and support for those going through profound personal transformation."[7]

A *spiritual crisis* is essentially what I've been calling sudden spiritual awakening. The symptoms of spiritual crisis, as identified by the Spiritual Crisis Network, are similar to the difficulties I've described in this chapter: feeling full of energy, hypersensitivity, the inability to sleep, and feeling alienated and adrift."[8] Perhaps most importantly, these organizations provide advice on how to minimize the disruptive aspects of the shift, and how to ensure that it stabilizes and becomes integrated. For example, the Spiritual Crisis Network advises people to cut down on their activities and responsibilities, to slow down and give themselves time and space to deal with their shift. It cautions against seeking therapy straight away — partly because there's no need to open up and explore ourselves even further — but rather emphasizes the importance of getting support from sympathetic and understanding people.

It's also important for us to remain as grounded as possible so that we don't lose ourselves in the transpersonal phenomena we're experiencing and lose contact with everyday reality. In order to keep ourselves grounded, the network recommends a diet of "heavy" foods such as grains, root vegetables, pulses, dairy products, and meats. Sleep is often disturbed during spiritual crisis so sedative herbs, or even — if all else fails — the occasional conventional sleeping tablet, can be useful to help establish normal sleeping patterns. Exercise can also help to keep us grounded, as well as doing everyday tasks such as cleaning, cooking, gardening, or walking the dog. Creativity is important as an outlet for our heightened sensitivity and our insights and impulses.

If we remain grounded and receive support and understanding — and so are able to build a conceptual framework to make sense of our new state — then we should hopefully reach what the Spiritual Crisis Network calls the stage of reentry and reintegration. At this point, we're stable enough to function in the everyday world, even if we may need to undergo further adaption and integration.

Of all of these different aspects of support, the single most important is probably *understanding*. The simple realization that you *are* undergoing a positive transformation can be enormously affirming. It can immediately transform confusion into clarity and discouragement into determination. I've had this response many times to my own books and articles. I regularly receive appreciative emails from people telling me that my writings have helped them to make sense of their own experiences and made them realize that they're not going mad or having a breakdown. For example, I recently received an email from a woman who was helped by reading an article about spiritual awakening on my website. She told me that she is from a small town in Pennsylvania and had "what I now understand to be a spiritual awakening." As she wrote to me:

It was such a strange experience. I have only told five people. Three of them are members of my immediate family whom I know are spiritual....I have not even told my husband.

My experience was almost the same as you described in your article on your website. It made me feel good to know others have gone through this. In my case, it started while I was in church and continued as I was driving home from church. (I was by myself.) The powerful feeling lasted a couple of days though the most intense moment lasted about 30 minutes.

I have basically become a different person since. It's like God zapped my insides with a laser and all my past emotional pains are gone...like I had an emotional detox. During the experience I had a feeling of oneness with the universe, not feeling fear, not feeling afraid of dying. Before I used to always think about my dream condo and dream car. After the experience, I wasn't so interested in these things....I don't have the need to impress others.

Before reading the article on your website, I was afraid people would think I was crazy.... I still don't plan to broadcast this experience all over, but I know that if I choose to tell someone, I can show them this article.

Now that more and more people are experiencing wakefulness — having temporary awakening experiences, feeling the impulse to wake up, or undergoing sudden awakening — increased understanding and acceptance of the state is imperative. As a culture, we must begin to accept wakefulness as a natural and healthy state — one that is actually much healthier and higher-functioning than our normal state and therefore more desirable for us all to move toward.

Awareness is definitely spreading. Spiritual ideas are increasingly entering the mainstream of our culture, as witnessed by the popularity of mindfulness meditation and of figures such as Eckhart Tolle and the Dalai Lama. Some psychiatrists are even beginning to recognize the importance of spiritual experiences and to view spiritual awakening as a valid psychological process rather than treating it as a form of psychosis. (In the UK, for example, a Spirituality and Psychiatry Special Interest Group exists within the Royal College of Psychiatry.) So hopefully the kind of misunderstanding that we've encountered so often in this chapter — and the confusion it creates in newly awakened people — will soon fade away.

Sudden Awakening and Psychosis

This is a good point to look at the relationship between spirituality and psychosis in more detail. In chapter 8, we saw a number of examples of people who, after sudden energetic awakening, were seen by psychiatrists, given medication, and/or confined to psychiatric hospitals.

This misinterpretation of awakening as psychosis is a great shame, for two reasons. First, it means that the awakening process is pathologized. The awakening person is officially confirmed as having something wrong with them, that they are "going mad." Any doubt and incomprehension they may have received from their friends is substantiated by the medical profession. As a result, they are more likely to try to deny or suppress their awakening and less likely to receive support and understanding. Second, medication may interfere with the organic process of restabilization and integration that should follow awakening. Ironically, although medication may suppress some of the psychological disturbances that sometimes arise with sudden awakening, it may actually perpetuate them in the long term — that is, stop them from fading away naturally.

Such misinterpretation is unfortunate but perhaps not surprising because sudden energetic awakening can certainly resemble psychosis. Unless a psychiatrist is aware of spiritual awakening as a process, which is still rare, then it's all too easy for them to misread its symptoms.

Differentiating Psychosis and Awakening

Some researchers believe that there's no fundamental difference between psychosis and spiritual awakening. Instead, they see a fundamental experience of going beyond the boundaries of the normal self, which can become either a psychotic or a spiritual experience depending on different factors. Isabel Clarke, one of the UK's leading researchers on spiritual crisis, believes that the most important factor in determining whether a transpersonal experience becomes "a life-enhancing spiritual event" or a "damaging psychotic breakdown from which there is no easy escape" is how strong and stable a person's sense of self is — or, in her terms, the "well-foundedness" of the self, or "ego-strength."[9] In other words, if a person doesn't have a strong sense of self, they're more likely to have a psychotic experience. Clarke believes that, rather than make a distinction between spirituality and psychosis, we should think of a whole spectrum of "transliminal states of consciousness." Other researchers argue that the only difference between spiritual awakening and psychosis stems from how the experience is contextualized and labeled; that is, whether it's supported or pathologized by the person's peers or wider culture.

However, other researchers — including me — take the view that there *is* a basic difference between psychosis and awakening. They aren't just two variations of the same fundamental experience but two fundamentally different experiences that have some similarities. The transpersonal psychologist Stanislav Grof, for example, acknowledges that what he calls a spiritual emergency can resemble psychosis in that the sudden eruption of new spiritual energies and potentials may feel threatening — even overwhelming — and cause disruption to normal psychological functioning. However, Grof believes that a spiritual emergency is fundamentally different in that it usually features an "observing self" who stands apart from the psychological disturbance so that the person can rationalize and understand their experience to some degree. In psychosis, however, there's no observer; the self is completely immersed in the experience and so can't control or integrate it. A person who is having a spiritual emergency has a sense of grounded detachment that is absent from psychotic episodes.[10]

Other researchers have identified a number of essential differences between psychotic disorders and spiritual experiences. People who have visionary spiritual experiences have good pre-episode functioning; that is, unlike people with psychotic disorders, they tend to be well-adjusted and integrated individuals without a history of psychological problems. The onset of their symptoms also occurs more quickly — usually during a period of three months or less — and they usually have a positive and curious attitude toward the experience. In addition, people who have spiritual experiences are more likely to have a sense of ecstasy and revelation, and they have a much reduced risk of homicidal or suicidal behavior.[11]

All of these descriptions certainly fit with the experiences we looked at in chapter 8. Kimberley, Simon, and Eric were all convinced that they were undergoing some form of spiritual or transformational experience even though everyone around them believed they were having psychotic experiences. Kimberley and Simon had little or no previous knowledge of spiritual ideas or practices but still intuited that they were undergoing an important positive process. They were not completely caught up in their psychological disturbances; they knew what was happening to them and were able to observe the process with some degree of objectivity. Both Kimberley and Simon had had good pre-episode functioning until bereavement (in Kimberley's case) and stress (in Simon's case). Eric had had psychiatric problems in the past but had been free of them for ten years, until he went to India to learn yoga.

But perhaps the difference between psychosis and spirituality is more simple and fundamental than these researchers suggest. The similarity between them lies in the fact that they both involve a disruption of the normal self-system and its normal functioning. When the normal self-system is disturbed by spiritual awakening, its functions also become disrupted, in the same way that an earthquake disrupts the basic infrastructure and amenities of a city. But this isn't strictly a breakdown because a new self-system emerges, however problematically, to replace the old one. The disruption to psychological functioning is usually temporary since the new self-system soon takes over (again, even if this takeover is a difficult process) and the awakened person soon relearns to conceptualize, concentrate, communicate, and so on. What might have appeared to be a breakdown is now revealed to be a shift-up, the birth of a latent higher-functioning self-system — that is, the wakeful self-system.

In psychosis, no latent self-system emerges. There's simply a breakdown, without a shift-up. The normal self-system dissolves into a vacuum. No new self-system emerges to bring order to the disrupted psychological functions and structures. To continue with the political analogy I used earlier in this chapter, it's as if a government dissolves itself without arranging for anyone else to take over. As a result, the country descends into chaos. Its infrastructure begins to fall apart, and its basic amenities and systems no longer function. In awakening, of course, a new government takes over.

This isn't to say there aren't similarities between psychosis and spirituality, besides the initial psychological disturbances that sudden awakening can cause. In both states we step outside the normal self-system, so it's natural that they should share some characteristics. The main one is the intensified perception or heightened awareness that is often associated with schizophrenia. But even here the difference is that, for a person with schizophrenia, heightened awareness may not necessarily be a positive phenomenon. It's likely that a person with schizophrenia will lack the ability to control it so that it constantly intrudes on their attention. It's also likely that they will interpret this heightened reality as threatening because of their general sense of anxiety. Heightened energy and creativity are sometimes associated with both schizophrenia and wakefulness too. But again, a person in psychosis usually isn't able to control their energy and may feel overwhelmed by it.

The wakeful state and psychosis also share an altered sense of time. In wakefulness, this may appear as a sense of transcending the past and the future and becoming intensely present, or perhaps as an expansive sense of time in which time moves slowly or may not even seem to exist. But people in psychosis often experience a sense of being lost in time, of being unable to estimate it or control it.

It seems, therefore, that some of the same basic characteristics appear in both psychosis and awakening but in a different guise — in a positive manifestation in wakefulness and in a negative manifestation in psychosis. (I don't want to stretch these similarities too far, though. Most of the major characteristics of the wakeful state such as heightened well-being, empathy, mental quietness, and a reduced need for group identity don't occur in psychosis at all.)

Psychosis and spiritual awakening may also sometimes overlap and merge. In some situations, the relationship between them may be more complex than I suggest here. For example, there may be a period of psychosis before a new self-system begins to establish itself. Or perhaps there may be occasions when an emerging self-system is overwhelmed by psychotic disturbances and so temporarily dissolves away before returning and establishing itself properly later.

11. After the Storm: Lingering Traits and Questionable Teachers

The previous chapter makes clear that the process of awakening can be difficult, particularly when it occurs suddenly. But even once the initial awakening process has run its course — even once a person has built a conceptual framework to make sense of their state, and even once the wakeful self-system has become stable and well integrated — difficulties can still arise. Although we like to idealize enlightenment as a state of perfect bliss and ease, this is rarely the case. Life certainly becomes *more* blissful and easy, but challenges and discord can still occur.

One issue is that an awakened person may have preestablished behavioral traits that carry over into their new state and may take a long time to fade away (or may never fade away completely). In some cases, awakening may be a completely new beginning, free of previous habits and traits. But in others, behavioral traits associated with our old self-system may become attached to the new one. As a result, despite the general background of serenity and ease that comes with wakefulness, we may be surprised to find that we still experience some fears, anxieties, and other forms of psychological discord. For example, we may still lack self-confidence in certain situations, or experience fear of flying or public speaking, guilt about some past events, self-aggrandizement, or ambition. (Such unwholesome mental states are called *kleshas* in Buddhism.)

These traits don't automatically fade away, even if we aren't *as* affected by them as we were before. They usually become less intense, and we're usually less *identified* with them. We're aware that these traits are *just* habits, mental phenomena that aren't part of our real identity. Our true self stands apart from them in the same way that it stands apart from thoughts that may pass through our mind. We're much less likely to latch onto the fears or feelings of guilt or ambition, and so they're less likely to become inflated. As a result, this karmic laundry does normally fade away over time.

American philosopher Robert Forman underwent a shift into a wakeful state at the age of twenty-five. He had suffered from intense anxiety for as long as he could remember (at least since the age of eleven) and had had a breakdown while at university. He seriously contemplated committing suicide and spent several hours standing at the edge of a high bridge over the Chicago River with the intention to jump off. He had his first glimpse into wakefulness during this period of turmoil — a powerful awakening experience that occurred while driving a racing car. As he describes it, "I was careering at some ungodly speed and all of a sudden, everyone else in my life seemed to drop away. All my anxieties, all my thoughts and feelings, even the loneliness just disappeared."[1]

Soon after leaving university Forman began to practice Transcendental Meditation and, after two years of regular practice, he woke up while on a Transcendental Meditation teacher training course in Spain. (His story is similar to Russel Williams' in that many years of psychological turmoil were followed by a long period of intensive spiritual practice, leading to a moment of awakening.) As he describes his sudden shift in his book *Enlightenment Ain't What It's Cracked Up to Be*:

> My experience, indeed my life, became noticeably different than
> it had been before that date: behind everything I am and do now
> came to be a sense of silence, a bottomless emptiness, so open as
> to be without end. The silence bears a sense of spaciousness, or
> vastness, which extends in every direction.... Though it rapidly
> became too normal or everyday to seem amazing or ecstatic, it is
> quite pleasant and peaceful. Since that day, it has been what I am....
> Vast silence has been the me that watches and lives and holds it all.
> I am, strange to say, infinite.[2]

Since then, Forman has experienced a permanent inner quietness, with no thought-chatter running through his mind. Whereas before he had a "localized" sense of self, since then his sense of identity has been "strangely non-personal yet infinite openness," with a strong sense of connectedness to his surroundings.[3] In other words, he no longer experiences himself as a separate self, enclosed in his own mental space. At the same time, he has had a strong sense of disidentification with his experience, of witnessing it without being involved in it.

However, Forman also admits that his transformation at the age of twenty-five didn't bring an end to negative emotions, nor did it make life easy or perfect. He still suffered from anxiety, still had relationship problems, still felt incompetent in his job, still daydreamed about having extramarital affairs, and even went shoplifting on occasion. As the title of his book suggests, Forman concludes that this is a problem of expectation, and that the idea that spiritual awakening leads to a state of constant bliss — as well as a life of ethical perfection — is misleading. At the same time, he says that these traits have faded over the decades, and now his enlightenment is much more integrated and less problematic.

Even people who are naturally awake may experience these difficulties. They too may have karmic laundry — negative traits and tendencies that are innate to them, and have perhaps been carried over from previous lives. (In Hindu philosophy, these are known as *samskaras*.) It's extremely rare for a naturally wakeful person to be completely free of negative behavioral traits. D. H. Lawrence, for example, was certainly not a perfect human being — he had an explosive temper, sometimes betrayed the trust of his friends (for example, by casting them as unsympathetic characters in his novels), and could be vitriolic and bitter toward his critics. Even Walt Whitman resorted to unethical ways of drawing attention to his work, such as publishing articles under pseudonyms in praise of his poetry and printing a eulogizing letter from Ralph Waldo Emerson without the latter's permission. Whitman was sometimes accused of being vain and self-absorbed, too. When his contemporary Henry David Thoreau met him, for example, Thoreau complained that Whitman talked about himself and his work almost continuously for three hours.

Even aside from the carryover of negative traits, the belief that awakened people sail through life in a state of bliss and ease is romantic. They may sometimes feel sad, bitter, or irritated. They may sometimes suffer what might be called *reactive negativity*; that is, they may be affected by challenging circumstances such as stress, rejection, relationship issues, or professional failure. They may feel hurt when relationships end or when projects fail. They may feel irritated when flights are delayed or when acquaintances exploit their good will.

But even if they're not wholly immune to this reactive negativity, wakeful people are certainly *less* affected by it. They have a more accepting attitude toward negative situations. When they experience emotional pain due to failure, upheaval, or bereavement, for example, they accept the pain as inevitable and natural and simply allow it to express itself, just as physical pain does. And closely related to this, just as with their negative personality traits, they're less *identified* with negative emotions. They have the ability to observe them without being immersed in them. Without resistance or identification, they can allow them to pass through them naturally and easily, without leaving any psychological damage.

All of this depends to a large extent on *how* awakened a person is. The further along the spectrum of wakefulness a person is, the less affected they are by negative emotions and situations. People who experience a high degree of wakefulness *may* be almost entirely free of reactive negativity, though I feel that this is extremely rare. Even Eckhart Tolle, who I'd say experiences a high degree of wakefulness, admits that he very occasionally experiences irritation. He once told an interviewer in response to the question, "Do you ever get irritated?" that the last time he could remember becoming irritated was a few months ago. As he told the interviewer: "I was walking, and there was a big dog, and the owner wasn't controlling it and it was pestering a smaller dog. I felt a wave of irritation. But what happens is it doesn't stick around, because it's not perpetuated by thought activity. It only lasted moments."[4] This is also a good example of how quickly irritation fades away when we don't identify with it.

The same applies to thought-chatter. People at a high degree of wakefulness may experience no thought-chatter at all (like Robert Forman) and have the ability to just think when they need to. Others at a lower degree of wakefulness may experience some mental chatter (although significantly less than normal) without being identified with it. As with emotions, they view their associational chatter as an automatic process that they're not obliged to pay attention to. When negative thoughts arise, they don't latch onto them but allow them to pass by so that they don't generate negative states of mind.

The Dangers of Becoming a Spiritual Teacher

Another problematic aspect of wakefulness relates back to the carryover of negative traits from our previous self-system. Until wakefulness is properly integrated, these traits may actually be *amplified* and — paradoxically — become more of a problem than they were before awakening. This is a particular danger if an awakened person becomes a spiritual teacher.

We tend to idealize spiritual teachers in the same way that we idealize the state of wakefulness. We think of wakefulness as a state of perfect bliss and we like to think of awakened individuals as perfect people incapable of behaving badly. We assume that anyone who attains the state — whether they decide to become a spiritual teacher or not — is incapable of selfishness, unkindness, or mistreatment of others.

And these assumptions aren't groundless. Wakefulness predisposes people to ethical behavior. Wakeful people are more likely to treat other people with compassion and fairness. Other people's well-being often becomes as important as — or even more important than — their own. They're often less likely to exploit people for financial gain or to use them as a means of satisfying their desires for power or sex.

There are two reasons for this. First, in wakefulness we feel a heightened sense of empathy now that our self-boundaries are more fluid. We have a heightened sense of connection with other people, a heightened ability to sense what they're experiencing, which means we're much less likely to inflict suffering or harm on them. Second, because we no longer have a separate sense of self, we no longer need to strive to accumulate wealth and power (or fame or status) to mitigate our sense of insignificance and incompleteness. As a result, we no longer need to exploit other people to satisfy these needs.

Indeed, in chapter 2 we saw that most of the world's spiritual traditions see compassion and altruism as characteristics of the wakeful state.

In Buddhism, once a person becomes enlightened it becomes impossible for them to act impurely. They live in a state of effortless *sila*, or "right conduct."

And yet…many spiritual teachers don't behave in this way. They mistreat and exploit their followers, become prone to narcissism and megalomania, and sully their personal lives through excess and impropriety. Admirers of such gurus sometimes try to defend them as exponents of "crazy wisdom" who test the loyalty and resilience of their disciples or practice some form of divine play or obscure Tantric exercises. But these attempts at justification often seem desperate and deluded. As Andrew Cohen, a spiritual teacher himself, writes:

> How could a spiritual genius and profoundly Awakened man like Da Free John, who makes such a mockery of his own genius through his painfully obvious megalomaniacal rantings, leave so many lost and confused? And how is it that his teacher, the Guru of gurus, the extraordinarily powerful Swami Muktananda, who literally jolted so many thousands far beyond what they imagined possible, could leave behind him so much skepticism and doubt as to the actual depth and degree of his attainment? How is all this possible?[5]

The sad irony here is that in recent years Cohen himself has suffered many accusations of impropriety and misconduct from his followers, including allegations of bullying and financial extortion. In 2013, as a result of these accusations, Cohen decided to step down from his role as a guru, after realizing that "in spite of the depth of my awakening, my ego is still alive and well."[6]

As Andrew Cohen asks, how is all this possible? Perhaps we shouldn't be surprised if some spiritual teachers are narcissistic attention seekers. After all, what better role could there be for a narcissist than one that enables you to collect admirers and followers so easily, who are willing to sit in silence while you speak and obey you unquestioningly?

But, as I've suggested, I don't think this is the whole story. At least to some extent, the failings of spiritual teachers are the consequence of the role itself. Teachers who are genuinely awakened to begin with can easily become corrupted by their power and authority, to the point that their wakefulness dissipates and they become lost in self-indulgence and delusion. Their egos become inflated by the projections of their followers, who treat them as perfect beings even when they behave unethically. Cruel or exploitative behavior is explained away and the teachers lose their moral compass. The egos that they were supposed to have dropped a long time ago become inflated to monstrous proportions.

The problem is that, as I mentioned earlier, awakening doesn't necessarily wipe the slate clean. Lingering tendencies to narcissism or authoritarianism can become amplified by the role of spiritual teacher. What might originally have been a tiny germ of a negative trait, which wasn't even evident before, becomes a grossly obvious personality defect. A very slight predilection toward self-indulgence inflates into excess and degeneracy on the scale of a rock star.

A person who decides to become a spiritual teacher soon after their initial awakening, before there has been time for negative traits to fade away, is in particular danger of this. It's also more likely to happen when Eastern spiritual teachers move to the West, particularly if they are from a monastic tradition. They may well be unused to permissive Western attitudes toward sex and find themselves unable to control their sexual impulses. They may have no experience with wealth or be unable to deal ethically with the money that flows freely from their disciples. They may also be unable to cope with the overt hedonism and materialism of Western culture. This certainly helps to explain the questionable behavior of teachers such as Chogyam Trungpa Rinpoche and Osho.

It's important to remember, though, that only a small proportion of awakened individuals become spiritual teachers. Most awakened individuals are content to live quietly and simply, without drawing special attention to themselves. The Indian philosopher and teacher Vivekananda once said that the enlightened teachers we know of — like Ramakrishna or Ramana Maharshi — make up only a tiny fraction of the enlightened beings who have lived. Most awakened individuals have passed by unrecorded because they didn't make an effort to proselytize or draw attention to themselves. Some awakened people may feel an impulse to spread their teachings, to establish themselves as gurus, and (in modern times) promote themselves through social media, but others may be content to remain unknown. Some people may feel that they can help people best by sharing their insights with them as spiritual teachers. Others may feel that they can help best in other ways — for example, by expressing themselves through creativity or altruism; by working as counselors, community volunteers, or therapists. That awakened individuals become spiritual teachers is by no means automatic.

One of the problems here is that the role of spiritual teacher is unregulated. Regulations to ensure that teachers behave responsibility or guidelines to protect vulnerable people don't exist. There's no reliable means of distinguishing fraudulent or deluded teachers from genuine ones. In fact, one of my aims in researching the wakeful state was to identify all its main characteristics so that it's easier to distinguish genuinely awakened people from frauds or narcissists. This was also my motivation for creating — with my co-researcher Dr. Kelly Kilrea — the "Inventory of Spiritual/ Secular Wakefulness" that appears as an appendix to this book.

And this — the characteristics of the wakeful state — is going to be the topic of the next chapter.

One point I'd like to re-emphasize here, though, is that wakefulness isn't a state but a *process*. It's not an end point but a different journey. It doesn't mean reaching the end of the road but rather switching to a different road. To extend the analogy, you could say that this road is higher up the side of the mountain; the view is more panoramic and the scenery is more beautiful and vivid. There's more space and time, and the journey is both calmer and more exhilarating. But it's still a journey, and there's still movement and change. There's still the possibility of progression or — in the case of some spiritual teachers — *re*gression. There are still challenges to face. Our wakefulness can become corrupted and fade away. Or it can become more integrated, more refined and intense, depending on the course we take.

12. What It Means to Be Awake: A New World and a New Self

Following our investigation into the different ways in which wakefulness can manifest itself, I think it would be useful to highlight exactly what it *means* to be awake. We've already looked at the characteristics of the wakeful state in relation to spiritual traditions, but here I'll summarize the characteristics as they've emerged from my own research. Then we'll look at *where* these characteristics come from — that is, try to identify how the self-system of wakefulness gives rise to them.

For ease of understanding, I've divided the characteristics into four categories: perceptual, affective, conceptual (or cognitive), and behavioral. I'll discuss the first two of these in this chapter, and the second two in chapter 13. As a reminder, these are the same categories I used to describe the characteristics of our normal sleep state in chapter 1. The only difference is that in chapter 1 I discussed affective characteristics first and perceptual second. I've switched them around in this chapter because I think the affective aspects are most prominent in sleep, whereas in wakefulness it's the other way around: the perceptual aspects are more prominent.

Let me point out again that these categories shouldn't be seen as hard and fast. There's a lot of overlap between them, and some of them are interdependent in the sense that they help to generate one another. But as I've already said, because the landscape of the wakeful state is uncharted, I think categories can be useful to provide some orientation.

These characteristics are uniform. Typically, permanently awakened people experience *all* of these characteristics and usually at roughly the same degree of intensity. This uniformity is one of the most striking things to emerge from my research and emphasizes the validity of seeing wakefulness as a distinct psychological state. The only significant variation is in terms of the *overall* intensity of wakefulness. As I've hopefully already made clear, the continuum of states of wakefulness ranges from less intense to very intense. The intensity of the characteristics of wakefulness obviously varies according to the intensity of a person's overall wakefulness. That is, if a person experiences a high intensity of wakefulness, they will obviously also experience a high level of well-being, a high degree of mental quietness, a very pronounced tendency toward altruism, a very pronounced lack of group identity, and so on. The reverse obviously applies to someone with a lower intensity of wakefulness.

It's also worth noting that many of the characteristics I'm going to highlight are common to temporary awakening experiences, too. This particularly applies to the perceptual and affective characteristics, such as intensified perception, increased presentness, and transcendence of separation. The conceptual and behavioral characteristics that we're going to look at in the following chapter aren't as strongly associated with temporary awakening experiences. These are less immediate and more long-term traits, which take some time to manifest or establish themselves.

A New World: Perceptual Characteristics

The clearest way in which wakefulness manifests itself is in terms of the wakeful person's different perception and experience of the world around them. Awakened individuals don't perceive the same world as other people do. The world is as different a place to them as the world of a child is to the world of an adult — or, you might say, as the world of a pre-civilized indigenous person is to the world of a modern Westerner.

Intensified Perception

In wakefulness, perception is vivid and direct. Awakened people see the world in a very childlike way — struck by the wonder, beauty, and intricacy of phenomena that other people take for granted and don't pay much attention to. The world is a brighter, more fascinating and beautiful place to them. In particular, they are captivated by nature — the amazing is-ness and beauty of the natural landscape, the sky, and the sea; the strangeness, complexity, and intricacy of animals, plants, and other phenomena.

This childlike worldview is part of the reason for the connection between wakefulness and art, and why so many poets and artists are awakened individuals. When you're awestruck by the is-ness and beauty of your surroundings, you often have an impulse to express or frame the experience, perhaps in a poem or painting. Certainly this sense of awe was the mainspring of the work of poets such as William Wordsworth, Walt Whitman, and D. H. Lawrence, and painters such as William Turner and Caspar David Friedrich.

This intensity of perception is sometimes experienced as an *openness* to experience or, in slightly different terms, an increased *sensitivity*. It's as if filters have been removed or shutters have been opened and, as a result, more impressions *come into* our minds and affect us more powerfully. What is normally a "measly trickle" of information, as Aldous Huxley calls it in *The Doors of Perception*, becomes a powerful flood.[1] As we've seen, intensified perception can sometimes feel overwhelming in sudden awakening (as it can also be in psychedelic experiences), but it usually isn't a problem once wakefulness becomes established. We learn the ability to turn off our attention to such impressions when we need to concentrate or think abstractly. In other words, we learn to consciously close down the shutters when we need to.

All of the awakened individuals I interviewed commented on this intensified perception. One person told me how the world had become "sharper, more real," while another was "struck by how fresh everything seems." Another person remarked that "colours seemed brighter, more alive." Others described a sense of awe and a new appreciation for simple pleasures and activities like walking, cooking, eating, and simply attending to their surroundings. One person described vividly how she had come to relish "simple things — a simple cup of tea, looking out of the window, the sunshine on the leaves, the wonderful green of the trees."

Why does the wakeful state feature this intensified perception? The best way to describe this type of perception from a psychological point of view is *nonautomatic*. We've seen how, in the sleep state, our powerful ego consumes massive amounts of energy and perception becomes automatic as an energy-saving measure. But in the wakeful state, our sense of "I" is much softer and weaker, and isn't surrounded and maintained by a constant whirl of thought-chatter. As a result, it doesn't consume as much energy so there's no need for automatic perception. Our perception remains fresh and intense.

Increased Presentness / Timelessness

Wakefulness also brings a different perception of time or, you might say, a shift in time orientation. In wakefulness, the past and the future become much less important, and the present becomes correspondingly more important. Awakened individuals spend much less time recalling past experiences or ruminating over past events, just as they spend less time looking forward to the future, daydreaming about future events or focusing on future goals. Instead, they focus on their present experience, on the surroundings they're in, the people they're with, and the sensations and impressions they're having.

For some people, this increased presentness leads to a sense of the *expansiveness* of time. Time seems to somehow open up, slow down, or even disappear all together. Kelly, the co-author of "An Inventory of Spiritual/ Secular Wakefulness," described how, because of her presentness, "every day seems full. A day seems to last for such a long time." Another person described an awareness that "there is no time....No past, no future, just things appearing and happening. Everything just is." Even more intensely, Lynn, who had a sudden awakening after the deaths of her husband and her mother (in quick succession), described "an intense mind-boggling feeling of the past, the present, and the future all existing at once." This is the sense of the eternal now that is sometimes described by mystics, when the past, future, and present all merge into one.

Why does wakefulness bring this different time orientation? It's partly related to the awakened person's intensified perception. Because their surroundings and their experience are more real and vivid, they naturally pay more attention to them in the present. It's also related to the inner quietness of the wakeful person, particularly their lack of (or reduced) associational thought-chatter. One of the main reasons we normally spend so little time in the present is simply because we spend so much time immersed in thought-chatter. Ultimately, the past and the future are concepts created by the human mind. We never actually *experience* either because our minds and bodies are always in the present. The past and the future only exist in thought, whereas the present does *not* exist in thought. A large proportion of thought-chatter is related to the past or the future in some way. So the quieter our minds are and the less immersed we are in thought-chatter, the more present we are.

In addition, as I suggest in my book *Making Time*, our normal linear perception of time is a mental construct generated by our strong sense of ego. The weaker our sense of ego becomes, the more linear time seems to fade away. Our perception of time slows and expands — and eventually disappears into now-ness.

Awareness of "Presence" or an All-Pervading Spiritual Energy

At *higher* intensities of wakefulness, we become aware of a spiritual force that pervades all things and the spaces between things. In my research, one person described this as "a deep sense of a living presence within that is both magnificent and also very ordinary." Another person described "a vast presence which is just infinite and pretty mind-blowing. Especially in nature." Another person spoke of an "awesome presence" that he referred to as "God." This force is sometimes described in terms of a "source," something underlying and fundamental that doesn't just pervade all things but gives rise to them, too. In a sense, all things are the manifestation of this force.

This force is clearly the same as what the Upanishads refer to as *brahman* — the spiritual force that pervades all things and the space between all things, and that also manifests itself in human beings as *atman*, our own spiritual essence. Elsewhere, it's conceptualized as the Dao (the Way) in Daoism, as the *dharmakaya* of Mahayana Buddhism, or in the energetic all-pervading form of "God" described by Christian, Jewish, or Sufi mystics. It's also fundamentally the same as the all-pervading spirit-force perceived by most of the world's traditional indigenous peoples. (As I describe in chapter 1, the Hopi Indians call it *maasauu*, the Lakota *wakan-tanka*, and the Pawnee *tirawa*; the Ainu of Japan refer to it as *ramut*, while in Africa the Nuer call it *kwoth* and the Mbuti call it *pepo*.)

Our normal automatized perception prevents us from perceiving this all-pervading spiritual energy. In our sleep state, when we look at the sky, we don't see a spiritual energy shimmering through space; we just see *empty* space. When we look at rocks or rivers or trees, we aren't able to sense spiritual energy radiating through them; we just see them as inanimate objects that we're entitled to use for our own devices. Due to the massive energy demands of the ego, our attention is switched off to this spiritual force. As a consequence, the world that seems to be so sacred and spiritual to indigenous peoples becomes a mundane, inanimate place to us.

Aliveness, Harmony, and Connectedness

At a lower intensity of wakefulness, a person may not be aware of this all-pervading spiritual force *directly* but they may still be able to indirectly sense its effects.

One of these effects is a sense of *aliveness*. To the awakened person, there are no such things as inanimate objects. Even natural phenomena that aren't biologically alive (such as clouds, sea, or stones) and manmade objects (such as pieces of furniture or buildings) shine with the radiant aliveness of spirit. Objects that are biologically alive become *more* powerfully animate. One woman described how "everything looked and felt ultra real and alive. I kept staring out of the window and just marveling....I could almost *see* the atoms in everything I looked at. I had the strongest feeling that everything was perfectly okay and perfect in the universe."

This woman's recollection touches on another indirect effect of this all-pervading spiritual force — a sense that "all is well." As spiritual texts and mystics tell us, the nature of this energy is blissful. It has a quality of bliss or joy in the same way that water has a quality of wetness. So when we perceive its presence in the world, there's a sense of harmony — again, an awareness that is commonly described by indigenous peoples. We sense that the universe is a benevolent place and that harmony and meaning are its fundamental qualities.

Finally, this spiritual energy underlies and pervades all things and so creates a sense of connectedness or oneness. All things are folded into oneness in its embrace. So even if an awakened person isn't able to directly sense *brahman* in the world, they may still have the sense that the boundaries between superficially separate and distinct objects have melted away. They may still sense what some of my participants described as "the oneness of everything" or "the oneness of the universe."

A New Self: Affective Characteristics

When we wake up, our *inner* life changes. There's a shift in how we *feel* inside, in our psychological experience.

This shift changes us so profoundly that, in a general sense, we feel as if we have a new identity, as if we have been reborn. Russel Williams describes this vividly: "I felt like I wasn't myself anymore, and began to wonder if I really existed, because it was such a different existence. I had the same body, was still doing the same work, but with a completely different nature of mind. It was a new life, without a future."[2]

We *do* take on a new identity as the wakeful self-system emerges and replaces the old self-system of sleep. In cases of gradual awakening, this identity shift happens very slowly, as the old self-system is gradually remolded into a different form. It may not even be noticeable, except in retrospect. In sudden awakening the shift is so abrupt and dramatic that many people can pinpoint the exact moment it occurs. In chapter 7, for example, Marita reported that her shift began at "March 2, 1993, about 8:30 AM, Eastern Standard Time US." Another person described her shift as "very sudden — instantaneous really. It happened in February '98."

So in this section we'll examine the inner changes that contribute to this overall sense of becoming a completely different person.

Inner Quietness

With wakefulness comes a dramatic reduction of the inner noise of our thought-chatter. In our normal state, this streams through our mind almost constantly — a whirl of associations and images, worries and daydreams that only usually stops when our attention is absorbed in external things. This thought-chatter is such a normal part of our experience that many of us take it for granted. We're so immersed in it — and so identified with it — that we don't even realize it's there, and we certainly don't realize how powerfully it affects us. In my view, it's one of the main sources of psychological suffering. It disturbs our inner world, giving rise to negative thoughts and emotions. It disconnects us from the essence of our being, constantly reinforces our ego-identity, and strengthens our sense of separateness.

For both Eckhart Tolle and Russel Williams, the dramatic reduction of this inner noise was one of the most palpable immediate effects of their transformation. Russel describes how "I noticed that I wasn't thinking anymore. My mind had gone quiet. I realized that knowing and thinking are two different things, and that you could know without thinking. I wasn't forming opinions or jumping to conclusions anymore. I began to do things spontaneously, to live in the moment."[3] Similarly, Eckhart told me, "My mind had slowed down. It was far less active. There were long periods in my daily life where there was no thinking or very little thinking or only important thinking. I was no longer identified with thought processes."[4]

Almost all of the awakened individuals I spoke to described similar experiences, although with variations. Some people — a small proportion — reported that their minds had become *completely* quiet, with a complete cessation of thought-chatter. For example, one person described how her mind was "so calm and still it's absolutely wonderful. Sometimes I just sit and I wish everyone could have a quiet mind. When I see people getting impatient in a queue I think 'I wish you could have that quietness.'" Another person described how inside him "there is nothing there apart from a still silence, a very peaceful still unifying silence that permeates everything."

More typically, though, people reported that there was still some thought activity in their minds but much less than before. One person told me that he had "nowhere near as much" thought-chatter as before, and that "a lot of the time my mind is very still." Another person also described an awareness of a background of "silence" inside him and remarked that "because I notice the thoughts, because they are set against silence, they are not always there and I no longer have the chatter endlessly."

Others reported that while thought-chatter was still there (although not as much as before), they felt less identified with it. They were able to stand back, observe their thoughts, and let them flow by without becoming immersed in or overly affected by them. For example, Graham described his discursive thinking as "like walking into another room, with the TV playing in the background. I don't have to pay attention to it." Another described his thoughts as "clouds drifting by. The point would be to let them drift; not invest life-force in them."

When we speak about the *thought-mind* and aim to quiet it, it's important to remember that thinking can be useful. In fact, being *completely* unable to think would make our lives impossible. We often need to consciously deliberate in order to make plans and decisions and to organize our lives. At a deeper level, streams of thought can also be useful in a creative sense, as a way of generating ideas and insights.

As an author and poet, I know how important both of these types of thinking are. A lot of my ideas come from a kind of deep daydreaming state, when impressions and associations are flowing through my mind. And at later stages in the creative process, it's important to be able to edit and organize this raw creative material, in order to mold it into a coherent, well-structured form (hopefully like this book!).

Thought should be a tool that we use whenever we need it and then set down once we no longer need it. We should be able to think voluntarily and consciously rather than have a constant stream of involuntary associations and images running through our minds. Several people I spoke to described being able to "use" thought in this way. Graham remarked, "Sometimes I need to listen to [my mind] because I have things which need planning — going shopping, paying the bills. It's a useful machine." Similarly, another person said, "To use my mind, I have to zoom into a task. My mind is still, but it's still used as a tool."

Some of these variations in the quality of inner quietness may be due to different degrees of wakefulness. Perhaps those who experience little or no thought activity are generally at a higher intensity of wakefulness than people who still experience a significant degree of thought-chatter but no longer feel identified with it.

The question of identity is quite important because thought-chatter is *fueled* by our identification with it. In reality, our involuntary thought-chatter is just a process, not dissimilar to biological processes like breathing or the circulation of blood through our body. The process is just taking place within our consciousness rather than within our bodies. In the sleep state, we immerse ourselves in the process; our thoughts become part of our identity and help to determine our moods and feelings. This immersion keeps the thought-chatter active, like gas fueling a car. But in the wakeful state, our identity is detached from this process. We step back from it and, as a result, it loses some of its momentum. It becomes more subdued and less disturbing.

Transcendence of Separation / Sense of Connection

In wakefulness, the sense of otherness between us and the world fades away. We no longer feel that we're "in here" looking out at a world that seems to be "out there." We no longer observe from a distance — we're part of the flow of the world's unfolding is-ness. Separation dissolves into connection. In the same way that we sense that all things are connected to each other, we feel that we're connected to all things. We're part of the oneness of all things.

This sense of connection manifests itself in different ways and at different degrees of intensity. At the most basic level, a person may feel strongly connected to other human beings, other living beings in general, or to the whole natural world. For example, Eric, whose energetic awakening I described in chapter 8 — told me that, "I feel a part of nature. . . . I feel a connection with people, but I also feel connected with trees and birds and grass and hills." A sense of connection to the spiritual force that pervades the whole universe and that forms the essence of our being may occur at higher intensities of wakefulness. In other words, we may not just be *aware of* this spiritual force but also feel connected to it. For example, one person told me that she experiences life as "an interconnected co-creative partnership with some kind of intelligent force or ever-present sentiency."

At a still higher intensity of wakefulness, a sense of connection may intensify into a sense of *oneness*. A person may feel that they exist in a state of unity with all things — even that they *are* all things. They may not just feel that they are *one* with the world but also that they actually *are* the world. Their sense of separation may dissolve away to the extent that there's no distinction at all between them and what they perceive. For example, Kelly described how "the deep aliveness of space is so amazing it takes your words away. I don't feel connected to it. I feel like I am it."

All of this stems from the softer boundaries of the wakeful self-system. The awakened person's sense of identity isn't confined to their own body or mind but stretches out and incorporates other phenomena. In our normal state, we're like a wave that has somehow deluded itself into thinking that it's a separate entity, distinct from the ocean that has given rise to it. But in the wakeful state, we realize our true condition, as a part of the ocean.

In this way, the sense of connection or oneness of the wakeful state is a direct apprehension of the essential sameness of our being with the being of everything else that exists. It's a direct apprehension of the oneness of our own *atman* with the all-pervading *brahman*. The essence of our own being is also the essence of every other being and the whole universe itself.

Empathy and Compassion

This sense of connection is closely linked to the high levels of empathy and compassion associated with wakefulness. When we're connected to other beings — animals and the natural world as well as human beings — we're able to sense what they're experiencing, to feel what they're feeling. If they're suffering, we sense it and feel the impulse to comfort them or try to alleviate their pain. We're touched by other people's pain because there's no separation between our being and theirs.

In this sense, empathy is more than just a cognitive ability to imagine what other people are thinking or feeling, or to look at the world from their perspective. Empathy, in its deepest sense, is the ability to "feel with" other people by experiencing a shared sense of being with them. This ability to "feel with" other beings gives rise to compassion and love. Love stems from a sense of connection and oneness, a sense that you *are* another person — or other people — and so you belong to them and share their experience. Irene, who experienced a sudden awakening after an abusive childhood and years of addiction, told me, "I feel a strong sense of compassion. I love people. I love helping people, love encouraging people, love being around people."

Empathy gives rise to forgiveness, too. It enables us to understand the reasons why a person hurt or exploited us. It generates an impulse to establish a bond with the person and eradicate the negativity between us and them. In addition, if a person behaves unkindly to us now, our empathy means that we're less likely to respond with hatred, desire revenge, or create conflict. Another woman who suffered abuse described how "one of the major effects of awakening was coming to a place of love and forgiveness for those who abused me and the understanding that came about what was going on — I began to see all that happened in the light of the bigger picture. A great love grew inside me for them."

Well-Being

Well-being is perhaps the most obvious affective change generated by wakefulness, but I've saved it until now because it's partly the result of two of the previous affective characteristics, "inner quietness" and "sense of connection."

Awakened individuals may not live in a state of complete uninterrupted bliss, but they are generally *much* more content than other people. One major source of this well-being is freedom from the psychological discord that plagues human beings in our sleep state — habitual worry about the future, feelings of negativity about the past, and a general sense of unease. Awakened people are much less prone to negative states such as boredom, loneliness, and dissatisfaction. The atmosphere of their inner world is less charged with negativity and much more harmonious.

Many people I spoke to commented on this freedom from worry and anxiety. As one person described, "Something inside me has changed in the way that I don't worry about anything — I know everything's okay....I feel a huge sense of peace." Similarly, Irene described how "I'm at peace. I'm free, I don't worry about a thing. I don't have anything to worry about. I don't live with stress." More generally, others described an "inner contentment" and "peace and a sense of freedom." Even more powerfully, a person described how "most of the time there is absolute bliss. A deep lingering peace which is unshakeable, which is just anchored."

This freedom from psychological discord is mainly the result of the awakened person's inner quietness and their transcendence of separation. After all, the discord is generated by the disturbance and negativity of our normal thought-chatter. Our normal sense of separation creates a sense of lack and fragmentation, as if we've broken off from the whole. So to experience an inner quietness and a sense of connection means freedom from psychological discord.

This inner quietness and lack of separation have another effect that is related to well-being: they allow us to experience the spiritual essence of our being. In the sleep state, we're usually cut off from this essence because we're enclosed within the strong boundaries of our ego. In the metaphor I use in chapter 1, the ego is like a big city that is separated from the whole landscape and can't sense the fresh radiance of the countryside.

But since the wakeful self-system is so subtle and unobtrusive, like a small eco-town rather than a big city, and is largely free of the fog of thought-chatter, we can sense the radiance of the whole natural landscape. We can feel the spiritual energy of our being flowing through us freely. This energy is essentially the same spiritual force that pervades the universe. As the Upanishads put it, *brahman* is also *atman*, our own spirit. The nature of this energy — whether in us or in the world — is bliss. When we experience this energy inside us, we experience its bliss. It fills us with a natural and very palpable sense of joy.

Finally, the well-being of wakefulness is related to a sense of appreciation. In wakefulness, people are more likely to feel a sense of gratitude for their health, freedom, loved ones, and other good things in their lives. In our sleep state, we likely take these things for granted and fail to appreciate their true value. (I'll explore this in more detail in the discussion of conceptual characteristics in chapter 13.) Appreciation is important in terms of well-being because it helps free us from *wanting*. In the sleep state, our dissatisfaction with our lives as they are — together with the impulse to escape from our psychological discord — puts us into a state of constant *wanting*. We feel a constant desire to escape our dissatisfaction by getting more of what we already have or different things to replace what we have. We desire pleasures, possessions, success, status, and many more things as a way of trying to alleviate our dissatisfaction and discord. And we often get trapped in a vicious circle. Wanting is generated by dissatisfaction, and the very act of wanting creates *further* dissatisfaction. Envisaging our desires and striving to satisfy them makes us even more dissatisfied with our present lives, in the same way that looking at photographs of a rich person's lavish house makes us feel more dissatisfied with our own house. But in wakefulness we're free of this cycle of wanting. In Buddhist terms, we become free of craving and so free of the psychological suffering this creates.

Absence of (or Decreased) Fear of Death

Absence of (or decreased) fear of death is another contributing factor to the well-being of awakened individuals and, at the same time, a significant characteristic of the wakeful state.

Fear *in general* decreases in the wakeful state. A great deal of fear comes from anticipating the future, so the presentness of awakened individuals mitigates this. A great deal of fear also stems from the fragility of the separate ego — a fear of being psychologically or emotionally wounded by disrespect and a fear of psychological attachments being taken away. The increased inner security of the wakeful state (a characteristic that I'll discuss very shortly) diminishes this. As the Upanishads tell us, when we become one with the world, fear disappears. In other words, fear is created by our sense of separateness, which makes us feel vulnerable and threatened by the world.

Fear of death is our most fundamental fear. The ego feels especially fragile in the face of death. The fact that death could strike us down at any moment — and will eventually reduce everything we have achieved and accumulated to nothing — creates a basic sense of meaninglessness, especially if we don't believe in the possibility of life after death. It's therefore not surprising that, in modern secular Western cultures, death has become a taboo subject. We try to avoid contemplating or talking about it.

To lose one's fear of death is therefore a powerful and liberating experience. For example, Eric described how he had "no fear of death anymore. I'm not in a rush to die, but I'm not attached to the body and the life and the possessions. Life is a miracle and a mystery, and I'm happy with that." Similarly, Chris, who experienced gradual awakening following a long period of turmoil in his life, told me that he felt "very calm about [death]....I would quite be willing to accept it if I was told my death was to come, even though I don't want to die just yet."

This decreased fear of death is related to the transcendence of the separate ego. Because our own ego isn't the epicenter of our universe anymore, its demise no longer seems such a tragic prospect. We know that our own death isn't the end of all things; the world that is part of our identity will continue.

The awakened person's freedom from psychological attachments is important, too. In the sleep state, we try to accumulate attachments like possessions, achievements, and success to support our fragile sense of self. We fear death, in part, because we know that it will take all of these attachments away from us. In wakefulness, we don't cling to these things so much and so it's easier for us to let go of our lives and accept death.

However, perhaps the main reason why the awakened person loses fear of death is because of a different attitude toward — and understanding of — death. Awakening brings an understanding that death isn't the end, that the essence of our being will continue to exist after the dissolution of our bodies. Maylene, who underwent awakening a few years after the death of her young daughter, told me, "We're just like little fireflies — bursting forth from this main energy. We're just sparks and we go back to that source and we spark some more."

From the materialistic worldview derived from our sleep state, it seems completely clear that there's no life after death. Our consciousness is just the product of brain activity; when our brain stops functioning, our consciousness ceases, too. But from the awakened perspective, reality is more complex than this. The essence of our being transcends our brain and our individual identity. Death isn't the end of consciousness but a transformation of consciousness. As one person told me, "I believe that death is a part of life. It's just a transition to a different state." Another person, Andreas, described death as "just a passing to another state where the soul separates from the body and unites with the universal soul." In this sense, the duality between life and death seems to fade away in the wakeful state, in the same way that the duality between us and the world or between us and other human beings fades away.

Along with not seeing death as an end, the wakeful state brings a new sense that *dying* isn't a painful process to be dreaded but is potentially a positive process of liberation. Helen, whose energetic awakening I described in chapter 9 — explained how she "used to think there was absolutely nothing. I thought people who believed in life after death were idiots.... I'm not afraid of death at all — in fact, in some ways I think it's something to look forward to, a kind of liberation." Marita, who underwent sudden awakening amid the turmoil of having a new baby (as recounted in chapter 7), described dying in terms of going "back home again," of being "outside of time, outside of space... like stepping outside of prison walls."

———

There are two further affective characteristics that I should mention, even though they didn't show up as major themes in my research. The vast majority of the characteristics I describe in this chapter were reported by all (or almost all) of the people I interviewed, but these two were only mentioned by around a half of my participants. This doesn't mean that the others didn't experience them; perhaps these themes didn't strike them as being so significant and so they were less likely to mention them.

Heightened / Increased Energy

It's not surprising that some people mentioned having more energy following awakening. We've seen that the dissolution of the normal self-system makes available a large proportion of energy previously monopolized by the ego. We've also seen that there is an explosive release of highly concentrated libidinal energy in sudden energetic awakenings.

In *Waking from Sleep*, I suggest that most awakening experiences are linked to an "intensification and stilling of life-energy (ISLE)." And in ongoing wakefulness, we experience this ISLE state continuously. One person told me that his high level of energy was the result of the "freeing up" of energy that previously had been used in *seeking*, that is, in trying to find happiness and fulfillment. Now that his seeking had fallen away, he found that "it frees up my energy to find out what I'm really interested in, just for the sheer enthusiasm of it." Maylene told me how, since her awakening, she had "incredible amounts of physical energy." She described how this energy had helped to heal her physical problems and enabled her to lose "close to a hundred pounds in the last three years."

Inner Security

Awakened individuals feel as if they have uncovered a core self that is somehow deeper and *truer* than the self they knew before. In retrospect, their previous self seems a construct, made up of environmental influences and other people's expectations. As Kimberley put it, "Now I'm more authentic and more aligned and in tune with who I really am." This new core self is firm and strong, less easily swayed by other people's judgments and less affected by slights and perceived disrespect and negative (or even positive) life events. It gives awakened individuals a sense of equanimity, which means that, in the words of the Bhagavad Gita, they are "the same in pleasure and pain... what is pleasing or displeasing leaves [them] in peace."[5]

13. What It Means to Be Awake: A New Mind and a New Life

Most of the perceptual and affective characteristics I discussed in the last chapter are probably familiar to you if you already have some knowledge of spirituality. You've probably heard spiritual teachers talk about the presentness and inner quietness that awakening brings. You've probably read spiritual texts that describe the serenity that awakened individuals experience or the radiant all-pervading spiritual force that they perceive. However, the conceptual and behavioral characteristics we're going to look at in this chapter probably aren't so familiar to you. They're rarely mentioned by spiritual teachers and authors, most of whom view wakefulness purely in perceptual and affective terms — that is, involving a different vision of the world and a different experience of being. The classic studies of mysticism by Evelyn Underhill, Walter Stace, or Richard M. Bucke barely touch on these aspects either.

Part of the reason why these conceptual and behavioral characteristics aren't so familiar is because, as I mentioned at the beginning of the last chapter, they don't feature in temporary awakening experiences. They're also less obvious than the perceptual and affective characteristics. The conceptual characteristics in particular are more deep-rooted and subtle, and less frequently expressed. Whereas characteristics such as intense perception and a sense of well-being express themselves fairly constantly, the conceptual characteristics are underlying psychological traits, which may only become manifest in certain circumstances.

In addition, these characteristics have been neglected due to the influence of otherworldly spiritual traditions, which imply that wakefulness doesn't belong in everyday life. After all, according to some spiritual traditions, we have to separate ourselves from the everyday world — take refuge in monasteries and hermitages — in order to wake up. And when we wake up, don't we realize that the everyday world is an illusion and that its goings-on are trivial? Some modern teachings promote a similar attitude by suggesting that both the world and the self are illusions, and that the events and concerns of our daily lives are just insubstantial "stories." Such attitudes discourage us from considering how our lifestyles and attitudes might be transformed by waking up.

As a consequence, the conceptual and behavioral characteristics are some of the most interesting findings from my research. It is fascinating to learn how awakening changes people's outlook on the world, their attitudes, and their lifestyles.

A New Mind: Conceptual and Cognitive Characteristics

The conceptual characteristics we're going to look at refer to how awakened people see themselves in relation to the world and other human beings, and how they conceive of the world and other human beings. It's useful to think in terms of *perceptual* awareness, which is the direct awareness of the phenomenal world around us, and *conceptual* awareness, which is our *understanding* of the world, our own lives, and the whole human race. We've seen that wakefulness dramatically changes our perceptual awareness and the same is true of our conceptual awareness.

Lack of Group Identity

As I mentioned in chapter 1, in the sleep state we have a strong tendency to *identify* ourselves, to give ourselves labels in order to enhance our fragile sense of self. We like to define ourselves in terms of our religion, ethnicity, nationality, and political affiliation, and also by the labels of our careers, achievements, and qualifications. Defining ourselves in these ways gives us a sense of belonging, and bolsters our egos. We feel that we're not alone; we're part of something bigger than ourselves.

In wakefulness this need for identity and belonging fades away. People no longer feel affiliated with any particular religion or nationality, just as they no longer feel defined by their careers or their achievements. They no longer feel that they *are* Americans or Jews or scientists or socialists. They don't feel any pride in their nationalities, ethnicities, or qualifications. And they don't have a sense of otherness or feel enmity to members of other groups. They feel that such labels are superficial and meaningless. They don't see any difference between Americans or Iraqis, Christians, or Muslims; they treat all people with equal respect. If they see themselves with any kind of identity, it's as global citizens, inhabitants of the planet Earth, beyond nationality or border.[1]

In my research, Simon and Graham exemplified this lack of identity and the need for belonging. They both used to be big fans of soccer teams. After their transformation, they no longer feel the need to support their teams, although they still feel a strong enjoyment for the game itself. As Simon, whose energetic awakening I described in chapter 8, reported, "Even my love of football has waned. It was a massive part of my life but that desire to belong has pretty much gone. Everyone seems to need to belong to a particular group but I don't need that anymore." Similarly, Graham told me that "I don't support a football club anymore.... Now I just watch football matches and I just think 'I hope they all win.' I enjoy the game for its own sake." Graham also said that he no longer thinks of himself as English or even as male.

Ed, whose account of awakening through regular spiritual practice combined with professional failure was covered in chapter 6, described a similar attitude. Living in the Midwest of the United States, Ed identifies himself as "a citizen of the cosmos. I don't have any sense of regional or political identity — and around where I live a lot of people do."

Awakened individuals often have a similar attitude toward different spiritual traditions, too. Even if they are affiliated with a particular tradition, they don't feel that this tradition is the only true and valid one, as religious fundamentalists do. They have an open and ecumenical attitude, and they recognize that different traditions are simply expressions of the same underlying truths. In the words of the Indian mystic Ramakrishna, who frequently read the Christian Gospels and the Qur'an, "All religions are true — as many faiths, so many paths."[2]

Wide Perspective: A Universal Outlook

Awakened individuals have a wide sense of perspective, a macrocosmic outlook. They aren't preoccupied with their personal problems and concerns to the exclusion of everything else. They know they're not the center of the universe.

This means that they have an awareness of the wider impact of their individual actions. They're aware of how their life choices affect others, or the earth itself, and so are more likely to live ethically and responsibly. For example, they may decide not to buy or use goods that are produced by exploited workers or oppressive regimes. Aware of how their own lifestyle could contribute to damage to the environment, they're more likely to adopt an environmentally friendly lifestyle.

This wide perspective also means that, for awakened individuals, social or global issues are as real and important as their own personal concerns. They're likely to feel a sense of concern for oppressed groups, social problems like poverty and inequality, or global problems like climate change and the extinction of other species.

Heightened Sense of Morality

This wide sense of perspective has moral implications. As we have seen, awakened people tend to be more ethical and responsible, more compassionate and altruistic. But awakening also fosters a more *all-encompassing* and *unconditional* type of morality. Awakened individuals don't practice moral exclusion; that is, they don't just show concern and kindness toward people with whom they share superficial similarities of religion or ethnicity but extend their benevolence to all human beings indiscriminately. (This is obviously related to a lack of group identity.)

Another moral aspect of wakefulness is that the awakened person's sense of right and wrong (or good and bad) isn't culturally determined but stems from an *innate* knowing, a deep moral certainty that transcends their own self-interest and culture. For awakened individuals, justice and fairness are universal principles that transcend laws or conventions. They may even break laws and potentially sacrifice their own well-being — perhaps even their lives — in order to uphold moral principles. It's therefore not surprising that many of the world's great idealists and social reformers such as Mahatma Gandhi, Archbishop Emeritus Desmond Tutu, Martin Luther King Jr., and Nelson Mandela were awakened to some degree (or at least experienced moments of wakefulness).[3]

Appreciation and Curiosity

In the sleep state, the process of familiarization that switches off our attention to the phenomenal world acts on our *conceptual* awareness, too. It switches off our attention to things we should ideally feel grateful for. I call this the "taking for granted syndrome," which means that rather than feeling grateful for what we have, we feel dissatisfied. Rather than appreciating what we have, we want *more*.

But awakened individuals *do* feel grateful. They don't get used to the good things in their lives once they've had them for a while. They appreciate the value of their health and their freedom, the beauty and benevolence of their partners, and the innocence and radiance of their children. They have the ability to count their blessings, no matter how long they have had them. They feel a profound sense of gratitude for small and simple experiences. (As we saw in the last chapter, this is an important factor in the well-being of the wakeful state.) For example, Phoebe, who experienced an awakening following the death of her high school friend, described how she "felt profound love and gratitude toward everyone in my life, everyone who was alive, and for everything I saw and experienced." Cathy, who had an awakening after being diagnosed with breast cancer, described how she "began to feel real gratitude for the birds visiting my garden, the rays of sunshine streaming through trees; the light took on a richness which I found so beautiful." More generally, a person told me how her awakening had led her "to inner contentment and an intensification of gratitude."

This sense of appreciation also leads to curiosity and openness. Because awakened people don't take *life itself* for granted, they are always open to the new and unfamiliar. They don't feel satisfied with what they already know and never feel that their understanding of the world is complete. They're eager to explore new ideas and skills, take on new challenges, travel to new places, and so on. This is another way in which they're similar to children. The world is a fascinating place to them, and they're keen to explore it more deeply.

A New Life: Behavioral Characteristics

The behavioral characteristics we're going to examine now are the outward expression of the perceptual, affective, and conceptual characteristics we've looked at already. They are the fruits of those inner changes, expressing themselves in terms of new traits, habits, and ways of living.

Altruism and Engagement

Spiritually developed individuals are commonly believed to be detached from the world and not particularly concerned about what is happening in it. Their enlightenment supposedly makes them indifferent to the trials and tribulations of ordinary people in everyday life. We imagine them sitting on mountaintops or in monasteries, basking in their own self-realization.

This belief isn't completely without foundation. As we've seen, some spiritual traditions — most obviously the monastic traditions of Buddhism, Hinduism, and Christianity — aspire to otherworldliness and detachment. Some spiritual traditions and teachers (such as the Samkhya school of Hindu philosophy and some modern-day nonduality teachers) also maintain that the world is an illusion and so imply an indifference to pain and suffering. Why should we be concerned with suffering when it's fundamentally unreal?

Or from a slightly different perspective, some teachings hold that although the world may be real in itself, its seeming difficulties are unreal. The world exists in a state of perfection, so how can problems exist? "Everything is just as it was meant to be." Such attitudes certainly promote a detachment from the world and a disregard for social or global problems.

In my research I've consistently found the opposite to this kind of detachment — awakened individuals tend to become more altruistic. Altruism is the natural fruit of the awakened person's strong capacity for compassion, their universal outlook, and their innate sense of justice. We feel a strong impulse to alleviate other people's suffering and to help people fulfill their potential. We have a strong idealistic desire to change the world for the better, an impulse to *serve* other people and contribute to the human race in some way. We may feel a sense of *mission*, to help the human race move through our present phase of chaos and crisis into a new era of harmony. (I certainly feel this; it's the mainspring of all of my writings.) As one person told me, "Now I feel a very strong sense of purpose and sense of spiritual calling. I feel called to serve the evolution of human consciousness, to support others through awakening."

Enjoyment of Inactivity: The Ability to "Be"

Awakened individuals love doing nothing. They relish solitude, quietness, and inactivity. In my book *Back to Sanity* I suggest that this is one of the most obvious differences between living in a state of "humania" — that is, our normal state of human madness — and in a state of inner harmony. In humania, which is equivalent to a state of sleep, people find it difficult to do nothing or be alone with themselves because this means facing the discord of their own being and the turbulence of their thoughts. As a result, they feel impelled to seek distractions and activities   that is, external things in which to immerse their attention — so that their attention doesn't turn inward, into their own being. But in a state of harmony, which is equivalent to wakefulness, this isn't necessary. We can rest contentedly within our own being because there's no turbulence or discord inside us. We don't need to constantly do things just for the sake of it or constantly supply ourselves with distractions. Rather than fear quietness and inactivity, we enjoy them deeply because they allow us to touch into the radiance of our own well-being.

Many of my participants mentioned this. Susan, who experienced gradual awakening due to spiritual practice and self-investigation, described how "I really love my quietude. It gives me the chance to read and delight and meditate in a different way that allows for reflection and for an ever-deepening." Another person gave me a beautiful description of how "the silence is so beautiful. In the silence everything is taken care of. It's so nice just to sit and do nothing. That's one of my favourite times. I can just sit in silence for hours."

Others described how their ability to *be* meant that they were never bored, even if they had nothing in particular to do. Simon, whose energetic awakening I described in chapter 8, noted that "some people cannot sit still and get bored very easily. I don't get bored anymore. I only work two days per week and all I do otherwise is read books, go for walks, and meditate." In a very similar way, some people described that they never felt lonely, even if they were alone for long periods. As one person told me, "I can be on my own for long periods of time and doing nothing and that is okay with me."

This is definitely true of my own experience, too. I'm an active person in some ways — I'm quite productive as a writer; I teach at my university, read a lot, and spend a lot of time with my kids. But I absolutely love quietness and solitude, and I honestly can't remember the last time I was bored. Even before I had a family, I spent long periods without a girlfriend or without a regular job and don't remember ever feeling lonely or bored. I agree with D. H. Lawrence, who wrote:

> I never know what people mean when they complain of lone-
> liness.
> To be alone is one of life's greatest delights, thinking one's own
> thoughts....
> and feeling oneself uninterrupted in the rooted connection with
> the centre of all things.[4]

In the sleep state, the constant need for distraction and activity is like a drug addiction; it's a constant struggle to keep ourselves supplied with what we need, and we often feel uncomfortable and anxious between our fixes. So to be free of this nagging need makes life much easier.

Beyond Accumulation and Attachment / Nonmaterialism

In wakefulness, the impulse to *accumulate* falls away. It's no longer important for us to try to accumulate possessions, wealth, status, success, or power. In sleep, the urge to accumulate is a response to our sense of incompleteness and fragility. We try to *bolster* our sense of self by adding possessions, achievements, and power, in the same way that an insecure king continually builds up a castle and reinforces its walls. Alternatively, we become overly attached to preexisting aspects of our identity, such as our appearance or our intellect. We derive a sense of specialness from them, which also serves to reinforce our fragile sense of self. But these efforts are no longer necessary when we wake up because that sense of incompleteness and vulnerability no longer exists.

Some people I spoke to described the falling away of accumulative impulses as one of the most visible effects of their new state. They recognized that before their transformation they had tried to offset their inner discontent by spending money or accumulating wealth, but those impulses had now disappeared. Marcus described how he had been "absolutely focused on being a millionaire." He had a lucrative career as a health consultant, giving talks around the country and appearing regularly on television. He drove a luxury car and bought the most expensive clothes and consumer goods. At the same time, he was deeply unhappy and reached the point of contemplating suicide. He had had a number of glimpses of wakefulness before, amid his turmoil, but now he underwent a permanent shift of being. After this shift Marcus off-loaded most of his possessions and was happy to share an old secondhand car with the rest of his family.

Similarly, Simon told me that he used to be "consumed with having the latest biggest car and gadgets" but now "this has all dissolved into thin air." Kelly described how "I used to shop and be addicted to home and garden television. . . . I was looking to possessions as a way to feel better but now I don't need to feel better. . . I don't need things."

Awakening brings a shift away from accumulation to *contribution*. The energy that people invested to try to alleviate their own psychological suffering is now redirected to try to alleviate the sufferings of others. As Marcus aptly described it, there's a shift in focus from "what I can get from life to what I can give to life."

Autonomy: Living More Authentically

In the sleep state, most people are products of the environment they are born into. They tend to conform to the values of their cultures and happily go along with the kinds of lifestyles that are expected of them. But awakened individuals tend to be more autonomous and inner-directed. They feel less identified with their culture's values; they are likely to reject them in favor of following their own impulses. They have greater confidence in their choices and preferences, and are more liable (partly because of their inner security) to stand by them, even in the face of ridicule or hostility. They live their lives according to their own sense of what is right, rather than trying to please others or doing what is expected of them.[5]

One person described this sense of autonomy in terms of having "more courage to do what I believe in now. I am going to trust my instincts more and my inner knowing, rather than listening to what others think is the right thing to do." Kimberley told me, "It's very important for me to follow my own rhythms and cycles, whereas before I was disconnected from that, pushing myself based on timescales and diaries and expectations. Now I'm more authentic and more aligned and in tune with who I really am."

Strictly speaking, this sense of autonomy is a conceptual characteristic, but I've included it here because it's difficult to separate from the new way of life it gives rise to. People often realize that, prior to awakening, they weren't *really* living their own lives but largely just following social conventions or trying to please other people. But after awakening it becomes much more important for them to live authentically and follow their own impulses. Other people may see them as rebels or eccentrics because they're liable to disregard social norms and trends. They're likely to reject the consumerist and status-oriented values of their culture in favor of a life of simplicity. They have little interest in watching the latest popular television shows, acquiring the latest gadgets or goods, or trying to impress people with their appearance, their status, or their sophistication. They may shock others with their unconventionality and their willingness to contradict consensus opinions.

There's a connection here with awakened individuals' lack of group identity and their sense of inner security. Many people are reluctant to break cultural expectations because they're afraid of losing status or being rejected by their peers. Their need for belonging is stronger than their need for autonomy. But for awakened individuals, this relationship is reversed — it's important for them to follow their own impulses and intuitions, even if this means being disliked. It's more important for them to be true to themselves than to be accepted. As one person told me, "I feel like I have more courage to do what I believe in now."

Enhanced, More Authentic Relationships

In some cases, friends and relatives resent shifters' new authentic way of living and misinterpret it as selfishness. In chapter 10 we saw that this contributes to relationship problems that can occur after awakening. In general, though, awakened individuals feel that their relationships deepen and become more fulfilling. The authenticity of their lifestyle also expresses itself in more authentic relationships.

Relationships deepen for awakened people partly due to their increased empathy and compassion, which means that they become more tolerant and understanding and less judgmental. For example, Helen told me that her relationships have improved because she has "a lot more compassion and understanding. If people are behaving in a certain way, I'm aware that there are reasons why they are like that." Similarly, a person described how her relationships have improved because "I am more tolerant and less judgmental of other people." As a result, awakened individuals are less likely to react with hostility and animosity to others, and less likely to initiate conflict. As Graham remarked, "Things [about other people] that might have annoyed me or irritated me don't affect me at all. I just let it go."

The ability to be *present* in relationships is a factor, too. If you aren't present to the people you're with — if you're thinking of other things, writing texts, or reading emails while you're talking to them — then your companions will (rightly) feel rejected. This may lead to discord and hostility in relationships. But if you're fully present to people — as awakened individuals are likely to be — you create a bond of empathy that leads to mutual respect and trust.

There's certainly a connection between deeper relationships and inner security, too. If we're insecure, our social interactions are usually self-centered. We're concerned with making good impressions, saying the right things and behaving in the right ways. We often wear social masks to try to make ourselves seem more charming or interesting. But if we feel secure within ourselves, as awakened individuals do, this self-centeredness and role-playing falls away. We shift our focus away from ourselves and give our full attention to the people we're with. Kelly gave me an excellent description of this shift, telling me how she used to be "on guard, ready to defend myself against potential criticism or judgment, always self-conscious, wanting to be seen in the best possible way.... All of that stopped. I could just see people instead of focusing on what they thought of me." And at the same time, the absence of role-playing enables our relationships to become more intimate. We're able to reveal our deepest feelings without pretense, which encourages others to do the same.

Characteristics at Different Intensities of Wakefulness

The intensity of a person's wakefulness can be measured by the intensity of the characteristics we've looked at in this chapter and the previous one. In perceptual terms, you can gauge the intensity of a person's wakefulness by how vivid their awareness of the phenomenal world is or how present they are. From an affective perspective, you can think in terms of the degree of well-being and compassion they feel, how quiet their mind is, or how much they fear death. It's quite common to discuss wakefulness in these perceptual and affective terms, but the conceptual and behavioral aspects offer an equally reliable gauge of wakefulness. You can also think in terms of how wide a person's sense of perspective is, their degree of appreciation and gratitude, and whether they have moved beyond group identity. You can also consider how authentically they live, how much they enjoy quietness, or how altruistic they are.

Wakefulness occurs across all of these areas roughly in parallel. You can't be awake in perceptual or affective terms without being awake in conceptual or behavioral terms (or vice versa). Different intensities of wakefulness express themselves fairly evenly across the different aspects and characteristics.

Consider a person who experiences a low intensity of wakefulness, for instance. They might sense that the world around them is alive and that life is somehow meaningful without being directly aware of the all-pervading spiritual force that is the source of these qualities. They might experience a strong sense of connectedness to other beings, nature, and the world in general without actually feeling *one* with the world or that they actually *are* it. While they might still experience a lot of thought-chatter, they may be aware of it as just a process that they can let pass by without identifying with it. They might feel a general sense of well-being, but one that is sometimes disturbed by degrees of anxiety, stress, or frustration.

In conceptual terms, they may veer between feeling deeply appreciative of different aspects of their lives and sometimes taking them for granted. Although they might generally have a universal outlook, they may sometimes lose perspective and find themselves immersed in a narrow world of personal concerns. In behavioral terms, they may feel a small degree of attachment to material goods or other kinds of accumulation. They may enjoy quietness and solitude, but also sometimes find themselves getting caught up in unnecessary activity.

Now let's consider a person who experiences a high intensity of wakefulness. They can sense spirit-force pervading the whole of their surroundings and can see the whole world as the expression or manifestation of this force. They have a quiet mind with no involuntary thought-chatter. They feel a sense of oneness with the whole world and all things in it. They might even sense that they *are* all things, aware that their own being is also the manifestation of (and is also pervaded by) spirit-force so that they are *of the same essence* as everything else. They have a constant sense of equanimous well-being, including appreciation.

In conceptual terms, the events and issues of their personal lives have little significance to them — certainly less significance than social and global issues and the suffering of others. They are completely free of the impulse to accumulate possessions, wealth, success, or fame. They are content to be, to live harmoniously within themselves, within the present moment, and within the world. At the same time, they live harmoniously *in union* with other human beings, other living beings, the whole of nature, and the whole cosmos.

———

Toward the end of chapter 11 we discussed the problem of distinguishing false spiritual teachers from genuine ones, and hopefully the characteristics I've delineated over the last two chapters will help in this regard. If a person claims to be awakened but doesn't display all (or almost all) of these characteristics, then it's highly likely that they are either self-deluded or fraudulent. A person may claim to live in a state of union with the cosmos or in a constant state of bliss; they may claim that their mind is completely quiet, and that they can set other people free with their insight. But if they live an accumulative lifestyle (that is, if they have an impulse to become wealthy or powerful or influential as individuals), if they behave immorally, if they don't radiate compassion and live altruistically, if they seem to be wounded by slights, if they encourage a sense of group identity among their followers, or if they show signs of prejudice or enmity toward other groups — then you should treat their claims with skepticism.

The Two Metacharacteristics of Wakefulness

All of these characteristics are generated by the wakeful self-system, in the same way that the characteristics of our normal state such as ego-isolation, automatized perception, inner discord, and the need for group identity are generated by the self-system of sleep. This is why the characteristics are so closely linked — they're all related to the same underlying factors. They can all be traced back to the same fundamental aspects of the wakeful self-system.

One way to look at this is in terms of *meta*characteristics; that is, fundamental features of the wakeful self-system that generate a wide variety of other characteristics. These fundamental features appear directly as characteristics themselves at the same time as generate other characteristics.

In my view, there are two metacharacteristics — fundamental features — of the wakeful self-system. The first, and most important, is its lack of boundaries, its fluid openness, which generates connection rather than separation, lack, and vulnerability. In addition to being a characteristic in itself, this transcendence of ego-isolation is closely linked to many other characteristics: increased empathy and compassion, inner security, and stability; loss of fear of death and the need for group identity; universal outlook, altruism; and nonaccumulative lifestyle. All of these characteristics are related to some degree to either an increased sense of connection or a falling away of the separate ego's need to be strengthened or supported.

The second metacharacteristic is the inner quietness of the wakeful system. This is strongly linked to the perpetual aspects of wakefulness. Without thought-chatter, our perception becomes more direct and infused with energy. We also become much more present, which enables us to attend more fully to the world around us. Inner quietness is also strongly linked to the ability to be, to enjoy quietness and inactivity. It's almost impossible for us to do nothing while our minds are full of thought-chatter. We feel an impulse to immerse our attention in distractions or activities in order to escape the discord inside us.

These two metacharacteristics obviously connect with each other. Inner quietness is partly the result of the transcendence of separation, because ego-separateness *encourages* self-absorption and self-reflection. At the same time, the transcendence of separation is partly the result of inner quietness, because constant thought-chatter reinforces our sense of ego and self-boundaries.

Several characteristics of wakefulness are linked to *both* of these metacharacteristics, combining their effects. For example, well-being is largely the result of losing the anxiety and incompleteness generated by ego-separateness, as well as freeing ourselves from the inner disturbance of thought-chatter and from the negative states of mind produced by negative thought-patterns. Well-being is also the result of our connection to the spacious radiance of our deeper being, brought on by ego-transcendence. In a similar way, altruism stems partly from the strong sense of connection and empathy generated by ego-transcendence and partly from becoming liberated from the self-preoccupation of our constant thought-chatter.

Finally, the deautomatized perception of wakefulness is largely the result of inner quietness but is also related to the soft boundaries — and overall softness and slightness — of the wakeful self-system. In our sleep state, it takes a lot of energy to maintain the strong boundaries and structures of our normal self-system as well as fuel its constant thought-chatter. The wakeful self-system takes much less energy to maintain, which frees up more energy for perception.

The Perennial Psychology Revisited

It's significant that the major characteristics of wakefulness I've identified through my research are essentially the same as those I highlighted in chapter 2 as the main themes of wakefulness as described in the world's spiritual traditions. (If you remember, these included union, inner stillness or inner emptiness, self-sufficiency, compassion and altruism, relinquishing personal agency, heightened awareness, and well-being.) This synchronicity validates the insights of spiritual traditions and shows that wakefulness can exist *outside* spiritual traditions and is more fundamental than the traditions themselves. It suggests that wakefulness exists as a psychological or ontological state in itself. It may be interpreted in terms of spiritual traditions, but it doesn't have to be.

Theologians and transpersonal psychologists have long debated the existence of a "perennial philosophy," a common core to the world's religions and spiritual traditions. According to the perennial view, the same basic truths lie behind all spiritual teachings but they're expressed in slightly different ways. They're simply different paths leading toward the peak of the same mountain, though there are some superficial differences between them, of course.

On the other hand, some people dispute the existence of a perennial philosophy, believing instead that spiritual and mystical traditions are independent. There isn't a common mountain — all the paths are heading in different directions toward different peaks. Any similarities between different traditions are the result of contact or influence. For example, the teachings of the ancient Indian Upanishads are similar to those of the medieval Christian mystic Meister Eckhart. Meister Eckhart's concept of the Godhead is similar to the Upanishads' concept of *brahman*. His view that at the deepest part of the soul human beings are one with God is similar to the Upanishadic idea that *atman* is one with *brahman*. This might seem to suggest that the Upanishadic sages and Meister Eckhart explored the same essential depths (or heights) of the human soul and simply explained their experience in terms of their own cultural references. However, a nonperennialist would point to evidence that Upanishadic teachers had contact with Greek travelers, through which their teachings may have influenced Greek Neoplatonist philosophers (such as Plotinus, whose teachings also have similarities to those of the Upanishads). And in turn, Christian mystics like Meister Eckhart were influenced by the Neoplatonist philosophers.

This seems highly implausible to me. For one thing, even if there was a chain of influence in the way this argument suggests, surely the original teachings would have been altered beyond recognition over centuries of dissipation (similar to a game of telephone), rather than remaining essentially the same. But the best way of verifying perennialism is to look outside spiritual traditions, as we've done in this book. Most of the participants of my research had no familiarity with spiritual traditions or practices at the time of their awakenings, but still described them in similar terms to the mystics of many different traditions. (Some of them became familiar with traditions later — in some cases, *many* years later; in other cases, only to a limited degree.) This strongly suggests that there exists some form of underlying or perennial landscape of experience that precedes interpretation by spiritual traditions.

Nonperennialists usually see spiritual experiences as being constructed by the beliefs and concepts of different traditions, but this obviously can't be the case when they happen to people who have no knowledge of these traditions. The same argument applies to temporary awakening experiences, which often occur outside the context of spiritual traditions and practices, to people who have no knowledge of them. (According to my research, the most common triggers of awakening experiences are psychological turmoil, contact with nature, meditation, and watching or listening to an arts performance.[6]) It also applies to children's awakening experiences. Research shows that children can have awakening experiences as early as three years old, although they are most common between the ages of five and fifteen.[7] This obviously can't be explained in terms of cultural influence. Children can't construct awakening experiences before they're mentally capable of absorbing the concepts and beliefs of their culture.

Wakefulness has been real and accessible for all human beings at all times and in all cultures. People from all cultures have been able to touch into it and explore its rich and radiant experiential landscape. They have simply interpreted and conceptualized it in slightly different ways, due to the different beliefs and conventions of their cultures. In Buddhism, perhaps because of Indian culture's belief in rebirth, wakefulness is partly conceived as a state in which a person no longer generates karma and no longer needs to be reborn. But when expressed through the more dynamic and world-embracing attitudes of early Chinese culture, wakefulness is partly conceived as a process of becoming attuned to the Dao and living in harmony with it. On the other hand, people who live in monotheistic cultures — Jewish, Sufi, and Christian cultures — see wakefulness in more transcendent terms. To them, it's natural to interpret the all-pervading spirit-force (which the Chinese conceive as the Dao and the Indians as *brahman*) in terms of God. They see it as *divine* energy, the being of God, and they conceive the goal of their development to be union with God.

In some respects, modern-day spiritual seekers are in a better position. In our secular culture we're less obliged to interpret wakefulness through the prism of religious or metaphysical frameworks. It's naive to think that there's such a thing as pure experience — some degree of interpretation will always take place. No phenomenon exists outside the culture in which it develops, and no phenomenon is free from cultural influence. But there are degrees of interpretation. When we look at wakefulness outside spiritual traditions, we're surely looking at it in a purer form, before added layers of interpretation. You could say that we're looking at the raw materials, before they go through the filtering and manufacturing processes of spiritual and religious traditions.[8]

The Wakeful Vision of the World

The two previous chapters make clear that awakened individuals literally live in a different world from that of other people.

In our normal sleep state, we tend to assume that we're seeing the world as it is, and that our view of life is objective and true. This is the basic assumption that underpins modern materialistic science, which is basically a paradigm of reality derived from the sleep state. According to this paradigm, matter is the only reality, and all phenomena can be explained in terms of the actions and interactions of matter. Consciousness can be explained in terms of brain activity (or as a cognitive illusion), evolution can be explained in terms of random mutations and natural selection, and all human behavior can be explained in terms of genetics and neuroscience. The world is a fundamentally inanimate place, and we're nothing more than biological machines. It's impossible to conceive of any form of life after death because our seeming identity and consciousness are just products of brain activity. When the brain dies, our consciousness disappears into nothingness, like the pictures on a television screen when the set is switched off. This worldview is a philosophical projection of the sleep state. And inevitably, when people make value judgments based on this worldview, these tend to be very bleak — for example, that the universe is fundamentally without purpose or direction, that life is fundamentally meaningless, that human beings are essentially selfish, and so on.

These value judgments are similar to those of existentialist philosophy, which was another projection of the sleep state. According to existentialism, there's no meaning to life except that which we create through our own choices and actions. In itself, life is meaningless and absurd, and the world — and all other human beings — exists in otherness to us. The world is fundamentally empty and indifferent to us, but unfortunately we're stranded in it until death (the ultimate absurdity) returns us to nothingness.

In some ways existentialist philosophers such as Jean-Paul Sartre and Albert Camus — and some modern materialistic scientists and philosophers — were (and are) insightful and wise, so it's strange that they never questioned the objectivity of their vision of the world. It never seemed to occur to them that the worldview that they believed was self-evidently true was just a *perspective* on reality, produced by their own particular state of being. It didn't seem to occur to them that from a different perspective, and in a different state of being, the world would appear a completely different place.

But the wakeful state tells us that the world is *not* an inanimate place, that matter is not the only reality, that life is not meaningless or purposeless, and that the universe is not indifferent to us. It tells us that consciousness is not just produced by the brain but is a fundamental quality of the universe that channels into our own individual beings. It tells us that we are not isolated individuals but share the same spiritual essence as every other living being, every object, and the whole universe itself. It reveals to us that there *is* meaning to life — a meaning that can't necessarily be explained (at least not directly) but that can certainly be sensed. We can look above us at the sky and sense something benevolent in it, a harmonious atmosphere. We can walk outside and sense a kind of meaning filling the landscape around us, emanating from the trees and fields. We can sense it flowing between us and other people, as a radiant connectedness, a sense of warmth and love. We can sense it inside us, as the radiant, blissful nature of our deepest being. Wakefulness reveals to us that the fundamental nature of reality is harmony, meaning, and love.

But hold on, isn't the wakeful vision of the world just a different perspective, which has no more validity than the sleep perspective? How can one perspective be truer than another?

The important point here is that the worldview of wakefulness is based on a *more intense* awareness of reality. It comes from an opening and an expansion of awareness, and a falling away of the mechanisms that normally restrict or dilute our awareness. It stems from an intensification of perceptual awareness, in the sense that the world around us becomes more vivid and real, and an expansion of *conceptual* awareness, in the sense that our perspective becomes wider and more universal. The worldview of the wakeful state is therefore more valid in the same way that a detailed, panoramic view of a landscape is truer than a blurred view through a narrow perspective.

14. The Natural Wakefulness of Children

Throughout this book, I've portrayed wakefulness as a higher state that is becoming increasingly common but that is still fairly unusual. We've seen that some people shift into wakefulness after intense psychological turmoil and that others develop it gradually, over years of following spiritual practices and paths. But perhaps in a sense we've *all* known wakefulness, even if we spend our whole adult lives asleep.

Is it possible that as children we experience a form of natural wakefulness that we lose as we grow into adults? And when we attain wakefulness as adults — either accidentally or through spiritual practice — are we effectively regaining our natural childhood state? Is spiritual development a matter of turning full circle and regaining something that we've lost?

This suggests that childhood is a time of heightened spiritual sensibility, intense awareness, and natural joy. William Wordsworth certainly portrays childhood in this way in his poem "Intimations of Immortality," describing how "heaven lies about us in our infancy!" and how, as we grow into adulthood, "Shades of the prison-house begin to close" and the world begins to "fade into the light of common day."[1] Similarly, the seventeenth-century poet Thomas Traherne famously describes his childhood as a time when the world appeared "inexpressibly rare and delightful and beautiful.... The green trees when I saw them first through one of the gates transported and ravished me, their sweetness and unusual beauty made my heart to leap, and almost mad with ecstasy, they were such strange and wonderful things."[2]

Some spiritual traditions also associate childhood with wakefulness and see spiritual development as a matter of recovering qualities of our childhood state. As we saw in chapter 2, the Dao De Jing advises us to "return to the state of the infant," and says that the person who "has in himself abundantly the attributes (of the Dao) is like an infant."[3] In Daoism, one of the aims of spiritual development is to recapture a childlike spontaneity, curiosity, openness, and natural harmony with the Dao. One of Jesus's most famous sayings is "unless you change and become like little children, you will never enter the kingdom of heaven."[4] One interpretation of this passage is that the phrase "kingdom of heaven" refers to the wonder and well-being of spiritual wakefulness.

But perhaps we're idealizing the childhood state. The philosopher Ken Wilber, for example, believes that children can't experience genuine spiritual states because they're at a "pre-egoic" stage of development. We have to develop an ego before we can gain access to transpersonal or spiritual states, which is obviously only possible for adults. Wilber admits that there are some similarities between the infant state and the awakened state. For example, each lacks an ego-boundary, which means there's no sense of separation between the self and the environment. But, as he sees it, this is *not* equivalent to the state of union with the cosmos experienced by mystics. You can't transcend separation without first developing a separate self. Otherwise there's just "de-differentiation," an immersion in a foggy soup of unconscious experience, which is not the same as union.[5]

However, Wilber's model, in my view, is a little too linear and hierarchical. Wakefulness doesn't just lie *on the other side* of our normal adult state, like the higher ranges of a mountain. It can be accessed at earlier stages of development, too, although it might manifest itself in different ways.

The wakeful state is paradoxical. In some ways wakefulness *is* extraordinary, in that the world becomes awe-inspiringly real and beautiful, and life becomes a wonderful adventure. At the same time, wakefulness seems perfectly ordinary. It doesn't seem *out* of this world but rather *more* of this world. It seems natural and easy, as if we have returned home to a place where we feel completely comfortable. We think, "Of course, this is how things are meant to be!" Wakefulness means connecting to the most fundamental, intrinsic part of our being — our spirit-essence, which is also the essence of everything else that exists — which is one reason it feels so natural and ordinary. But perhaps another reason is because we *have* already touched into wakefulness in this lifetime, as young children. Wakefulness is the place where we began, which we slipped away from when our adult egos developed. And it's the place we return to when we wake up as adults, the place we return to in a deeper and more integrated way.

Childhood Awakening Experiences

Temporary awakening experiences are certainly common during childhood — probably more common than in adulthood. (As I noted toward the end of the previous chapter, this is one of the main arguments in favor of a "perennial philosophy.") One study found that experiences of the "numinous" were common in children under age seven (becoming less frequent in older children),[6] while another study found that about half of a group of teenagers could recall having experiences of "nature mysticism" similar to those described by Wordsworth.[7]

I've never specifically studied childhood awakening experiences, which is why in this chapter I mostly rely on other sources, but I have been sent some reports of them. For example, Nicky described an awakening experience that occurred at the age of eleven, when she was singing in a church choir. She entered a "euphoric blissful state, feeling merged with the universe.... The world appeared to have a golden hue and all colours were intense, vivid, jewel-like."

Similarly, Joe, now in his fifties, recalled a very intense awakening experience that occurred just after he started school, at around the age of four:

> I came bounding out of my front door into the street [and] said to myself, "I just don't believe that I'm really here! Where did I come from? How did I get here?" No sooner had I thought this when everything just melted. I looked at the telegraph pole outside of my friend's house, four doors up — it was just pulsating with life and energy. The road surface was the same. I looked to myself — I was made up of the same pulsating energy. Time just melted as well. What came to me was that everything was just unreal, an illusion. I just saw through everything....

I carried on my way up to the local field, lay down, looked up to the sky and then just felt the oneness of everything, felt the Earth spinning in its orbit. I knew the Earth. I melted into the ground, though [now] everything looked as it would through normal vision except for the aliveness and brightness and newness of everything. I seemed to understand or know that everything is freshly created in every moment. There was no me. I just started laughing — surely everyone must know this? Why was everyone pretending?

This state of consciousness lingered for a few days, but Joe made the mistake of telling his parents about it. Inevitably, they didn't understand and took him to see a doctor. The doctor referred him to a child psychologist, and, tragically, Joe ended up being put on medication. (A graphic illustration of how easily wakefulness can be pathologized!) Nevertheless, Joe experienced other strange states of consciousness as a teenager, including frequent out-of-body experiences, and by then he had "learned to keep quiet, of course."

But in addition to regularly having high-intensity awakening *experiences*, children experience a form of wakefulness as a stable, ongoing state.

The Perceptual Wakefulness of Children

The most obvious way in which children are awake is in a perceptual sense. The intense perception and heightened awareness of the wakeful state is normal for them — especially for young children. You might be able to remember this from your own early childhood — how bright and colorful the world around you seemed, and how even mundane objects seemed to be imbued with richness and strangeness.

I had an interesting experience a couple of years ago when my mother brought some of my old childhood toys down from the loft so that my own kids could play with them. She brought down a box of building blocks, a couple of my old cuddly toys, and some of my old books and football magazines. I had no idea she had kept them; I hadn't seen them for thirty years or more. As I examined them I was immediately plunged back into the miraculous world of early childhood. I was seven or eight years old again, experiencing these objects exactly as I did then.

It's almost impossible to convey how powerfully vivid and exciting they seemed to me. The magazines looked fairly tacky and slipshod by modern standards, but I felt exhilarated by them, by the richness, brightness, and contrast of the colors and graphics. And when I picked up my old building blocks I reexperienced exactly how fascinating and attractive they seemed when I was a child. They seemed amazing in their smooth shininess, the perfect regularity of their shapes, and the radiance of their colors. I remembered exactly how wonderfully exciting it was to put the pieces together and build houses, cars, and other structures.

I wasn't just experiencing a nostalgic reminiscence of my childhood; I was actually experiencing the toys as I did back then. I think I have some degree of perceptual wakefulness all the time — I'm often struck by the beauty, strangeness, and vividness of the phenomena around me. But it was quite a shock to realize *how much more* perceptually awake I was as a young child.

If you spend time around young children (and particularly if you have children of your own) you've probably noticed this intensity of perception in them, too. I remember being especially struck by this with our first child, Hugh (who is thirteen years old at the time of writing). He had a very poetic way of expressing his perceptions. Once we were walking to his nursery on a rainy day, and the rain was dripping down the drainpipes of the houses and then bouncing up off the ground. "Look, Daddy," he said, "the rain is dancing!" A few months later, in the summer, we were in the garden and there was a book on the grass with its pages blowing open in the wind. "Look, Daddy," he said, "the wind is reading your book!"

When Hugh started walking I was amazed at how long it took us to walk anywhere — not just because he walked slowly, but also because he continually stopped to examine everything around him. We would walk to the local post office, along a path by the edge of a golf course, and what should have been a ten-minute walk took about a half hour. He would stop to look at — or to pick up — trees, bushes, stones, leaves, puddles, even discarded crisp packets and soda cans. Everything was a source of fascination.

This is one of the great things about being around young children — if we've forgotten, they can remind us of the wonder of being, the joy of paying attention to small things, the joy of taking time to *stop and look* rather than just rushing like an arrow to our destinations with our minds immersed in thought-chatter. Young children can rekindle perceptual wakefulness in us. In effect, by spending time with children we can become children ourselves again. We see the world through their eyes.

As I note in *Waking from Sleep*, books such as Edward Robinson's *The Original Vision* and Edward Hoffman's *Visions of Innocence* contain many accounts of adults who describe their childhoods as times of intense, clear awareness, with a sense of wonder at the strangeness and aliveness of their surroundings and a sense that the world is a harmonious and benevolent place. Alison Gopnik, one of the world's leading developmental psychologists, suggests that babies are "actually aware of much more, much more intensely, than we are."[8] She draws a parallel between the child's intense perception and the "sense of wonder" that motivates poets and scientists and that we adults occasionally experience through travel or meditation. As she writes, "Travel, meditation, and Romantic poetry can give us an empathetic first-person taste of infant experience."[9] Gopnik uses the term *lantern consciousness* to describe babies' and young children's awareness — a "vivid panoramic illumination of the everyday," which she recognizes as similar to the "exultation and ecstasy" of some religious and aesthetic experiences.[10]

I've already suggested the reason for children's intense perception. Children are free of the automatized perception we experience as adults, which is necessary to redirect our powerful ego-driven self-system. That strong self-system hasn't developed yet, so young children's perception is always powerful and direct. They are continuously open to the is-ness and richness and strangeness of the world, which we adults only rarely glimpse (as Alison Gopnik suggests).

It's also significant that children aren't immersed in thought-chatter in the way that adults are. They don't have a sense of being separate; they don't talk to themselves inside their own mental space. As a result, they live *in the world* much more than adults, with a more direct and immediate relationship to their experiences. You could say that young children have a natural state of *presence*. Wherever they are and whatever they're doing, they're always intensely *there*, giving themselves wholly to the reality of their moment-to-moment experience.

Other Characteristics

Children are certainly awake in other ways as well, most obviously in terms of their natural sense of well-being. As every parent knows, children can be very turbulent emotionally. Particularly during what psychologists call the impulsive stage, children experience discontent frequently, when their needs aren't satisfied or their desires are frustrated. Tragically, some children may become traumatized by abuse from their caregivers and become withdrawn or disturbed as a result. But in general, children radiate a powerful *joie de vivre*, an infectious positivity, a sense of exhilaration at being alive.

This is partly because children are free of the discord and negativity created by thought-chatter, including the negative cognitive scripts that we develop as adults (which often generate feelings of depression, low self-esteem, and bitterness or resentment). But probably the main reason for children's well-being is that the slightness — and the weak boundaries — of their self-system means that they are always connected to the radiance of their entire being.

As I suggested earlier, our being in its essence is an influx of the spiritual energy of the universe. Our individual spirit is one with the spirit of the universe in the same way that an inlet or estuary is one with the sea. In adulthood, our self-system (with the ego at its center) becomes so strong and boundaried that we become alienated from this spirit source and so lose connection with that radiant energy. (In the analogy I used in chapter 1, this is like a city becoming a separate entity from the landscape around it, and losing its connection to nature.) But young children haven't lost connection to their spirit source. Their spirit is not separated from their self. As a result, they exist in a state of pure being. They can always sense the energy of being — with its natural quality of well-being — flowing through them. The mature wakeful state brings exactly the same sense of radiant well-being. When our self-system becomes softer and more integrated with our whole being, we feel connected to spirit again.

A child's lack of a strong, boundaried self-system generates another important aspect of wakefulness: a strong sense of connection to the world around them. Young children don't have the sense of being "in here" — mental entities living inside our bodies — and looking "out there" at a world. They don't observe the world from a distance, but rather participate in it with no division between them and their experience. For example, in *The Original Vision*, Edward Robinson's study of childhood spiritual experiences, one person recalls how during their childhood, "Plants and animals radiated an aura of aliveness, and I often felt that I was simply part of a great Whole."[11] Another person describes how, at the age of around three, they felt "a euphoric unification with the space in front of me and all around."[12]

Children certainly also experience heightened energy, as any parent who tries to keep up with their play for any length of time will tell you. Children's amazing energy is one of the most striking things about them. An incredible vitality streams through them from the moment they bounce out of bed in the morning to the moment they go to bed. And they have a dynamic creativity that enables them to invent endless games and imaginary worlds of play. (Once when I was talking about this in a lecture, a member of the audience asked, "If children are so energetic, why do they have to sleep so much?" "That's probably an evolutionary adaptation," I joked. "Otherwise parents wouldn't be able to cope and there would be nobody to take care of them.") As we saw in chapter 8, this amazing vitality is referred to in Indian Tantric philosophy as *pranotthana*, a state of uplifted or intensified life-energy that we recapture through spiritual development.

The reason for this vitality is obvious: children haven't developed the adult self-system yet, which monopolizes so much of the energy of our being. And when in mature wakefulness a new, much less energy-intensive self-system is established, we recapture some of the amazing vitality and the dynamic creativity we had as children. This is one sense in which wakefulness means turning a full circle and recapturing what we've lost.

The childhood state includes some of the conceptual and behavioral characteristics of wakefulness, too. Most obviously, children don't have the need to *accumulate*, which is such a strong feature of our sleep state. Children love playing with toys and receiving presents, but they don't strive to accumulate possessions just for their own sake. They don't strive to accumulate wealth, just as they don't strive to gain power, status, or success. Neither do they attach themselves to their appearance and strive to gain significance through their achievements. They don't *need* to accumulate or attach themselves to anything because they don't experience the sense of separateness and incompleteness that gives rise to these impulses.

Their lack of ego-separateness also means that children don't have a need for group identity. Young children have no sense of religious or ethnic identity. I live in an ethnically diverse area in a big city (Manchester, in the UK). My kids have always had friends from different ethnic groups, without any notion that they were different from them in any way. They sometimes used their friends' different skin colors as a way of describing them ("Do you mean the boy with brown skin?") but   to paraphrase a Bob Marley song — this is of no more significance than the color of their friends' eyes.

As children grow up, adults try hard to inculcate a sense of group identity in them. They induct children into their religions, teach them the history of their "people," teach them to follow their conventions and codes of behavior, pass on their beliefs and perhaps a sense of prejudice or enmity toward other groups. Finally, children are convinced that they *are* Muslim, Jewish, Hindu, American, British, etc., and therefore distinct from other people who belong to different groups. (I describe this process of taking on identity in my poetic piece "The Primal Soul" in *The Calm Center*.)

Higher-Intensity Awakening Experiences

If children exist in a natural state of wakefulness, why do they have awakening *experiences*? Surely only people who are asleep can have temporary awakening experiences. If they are already awake, there's nothing for them to wake up from.

But it's a question of degrees. As we've seen, wakefulness has many gradations. People whose normal level of wakefulness is, say, a low or medium intensity can occasionally shift up to a *higher* intensity of wakefulness. Awakened individuals can still have awakening experiences, although it may be more accurate to refer to them as experiences of *more intense* wakefulness. Even if you're awake, you can still become *more* awake.

This is certainly the case with children. Children's awakening experiences appear to be generally *more intense* than adults' experiences. Children are beginning from a higher baseline, so to speak, and so have easier access to the highest intensities of wakefulness, just as climbers at the base camp of Mount Everest have easier access to its higher points than people at sea level. Like the two experiences from my own files above, childhood awakening experiences are often high-intensity experiences of union and fusion rather than, for example, low-intensity experiences of the vividness of one's surroundings, or a sense of harmony and well-being. Children already experience this vividness and harmony, so to them it's not a form of awakening.

The works of Edward Robinson and Edward Hoffman contain many examples of such experiences. At the age of three, one person had an experience in which they became "part of the flowers, and stones, and dusty earth. I could feel the dandelions pulsating in the sunlight, and experienced a timeless unity with all life."[13] Another person described a feeling of being "part of a world of meaning, unrestricted by space/time."[14] While at an even higher intensity of wakefulness, a person described a childhood experience of actually *becoming* everything: "A door opened, and I became the sun, the wind, and the sea. There was no 'I' anymore. 'I' had merged with everything else. All sensory perceptions had become one. Sound, smell, taste, touch, shape — all melted into a brilliant light. The pulsating energy went through me, and I was part of this energy."[15]

Differences between Mature and Immature Wakefulness

At the same time, there are clearly aspects of the mature wakeful state that children don't share.

Psychologists used to assume that young children couldn't be empathic or altruistic. The famous developmental psychologist Jean Piaget believed that children were unable to see the world from any point of view apart from their own and so were unable to empathize with other people. In a similar way, the psychologist Lawrence Kohlberg believed that children's sense of morality was "pre-conventional." That is, children have no concern for what is right or wrong, or for social rules or laws; their only motivation to behave morally is to avoid punishment or gain reward. In other words, both Piaget and Kohlberg saw children as *amoral*, in the sense that they are self-centered and unable to take the feelings of others into consideration or sense the effects of their actions on others.

But more recent research contradicts these views. Studies have shown that, almost from birth, children have the ability to identify with other people and take on other people's feelings. At the age of one, babies are able to tell the difference between actions that are done intentionally or unintentionally, and to view situations from the perspective of others. If a fourteen-month-old baby is encouraged to pick some food to offer to other people, they will assume that others like the same food they do and choose that. But by eighteen months old, a baby recognizes that other people may have different preferences and will pick different food for them. This certainly shows an ability to identify with other people.[16]

One-year-old babies are also capable of acting altruistically. Studies have shown that fourteen-month-old babies will go out of their way to pick up objects for other people, if they see them straining to reach them. If a person around them is in distress, they become upset themselves and try to comfort and console the person by kissing and petting.[17] As Alison Gopnik puts it, "Tiny babies recognize that their fear and sadness is your fear and sadness and that their joy is your joy. Even more profoundly, very young children feel that they should alleviate the fear and sadness of others, and help them get what they want."[18]

Nevertheless, although Piaget and Kohlberg were wrong, it would be misleading to suggest that children are empathic or altruistic to the same *high degree* as maturely awakened people. Because of their powerful impulses and desires, young children have a tendency to behave selfishly, and their ability to empathize is often *overridden* by their selfish impulses. To a young child who has decided they want an ice cream or feels aggrieved because they want to stay up and play instead of go to bed, nothing else matters apart from their desires. The strength of their impulses overrides any concern for others — including their stressed-out parents — or any rational notion of fairness.

Another important difference is that children aren't capable of the *all-embracing* compassion of mature wakefulness and the *active idealism* it often gives rise to. Children don't have a sense of identification with the whole human race, the urge to make the world a better place, or a general impulse to alleviate the sufferings of their fellow human beings. When they are altruistic, it's in response to specific situations, whereas the altruism of mature wakefulness is often spontaneous and unconditional.

This points to another way in which childhood wakefulness is different from mature wakefulness. Conceptually, children don't have the expansive outlook of the mature wakeful state. They don't have a sense of the whole world stretching around them, with an awareness of the predicaments of other human beings. They have little awareness of reality beyond their immediate, everyday worlds.

Another difference is that children don't — or at least, only rarely — experience the inner quietness of mature wakefulness. Children live in an almost constant state of extroversion, absorbed in their play, their interactions with other people, or in the events taking place around them. They rarely experience inner quietness, simply because they rarely experience *inwardness*.[19]

And finally, children don't experience the inner security and stability of the mature wakeful state. Their impulsive emotionality means that they can often be wildly unstable (especially if they are tired), swinging from elation to anger or upset at the drop of a hat. Children are certainly not "the same in pleasure and pain" (as the Bhagavad Gita advises us to be) or "never humiliated or upset by others" (as the Buddhist Heart Sutra suggests) — as anyone who has witnessed their child screaming because they don't like their dinner, or because their brother or sister has teased them, can attest.

Wakefulness, Before and After the Self-System

So what we see in children is a *different* kind of wakefulness, a kind of primal or immature wakefulness, which is mainly oriented toward perceptual and affective characteristics. Children are certainly awake but not in the same way as adults can be. Essentially, their wakefulness is one that comes *before* our self-system has developed or, more strictly speaking, *as* it's developing. Mature wakefulness comes *after* our self-system has developed. In fact, you could say that the reason why children experience *some* aspects of wakefulness is also the reason why they don't experience *other* aspects: they don't have a stable, well-developed self-system. They experience intense perception and energy and well-being because they lack a fully developed self-system; they don't have a sense of inner security and stability, and can't develop a wide perspective or a universal outlook for the same reason.

This illustrates that, although our normal self-system is the main obstacle to wakefulness (and the reason why we spend our lives asleep), we can't be awake, in a mature sense, without *some form* of self-system. We need some kind of self-system as an organizational center, to perform psychological functions and mediate between us and the world. Without any kind of self-system, we would be unable to function in the world and dependent on the care and guidance of others, as are babies and young children. We would be unable to perform the logical, intellectual, and practical tasks that adults take for granted; unable to make plans or decisions; unable to control our impulses; and so on. The wakeful self-system does all of these things for us.

This might remind you of the discussion on psychosis and wakefulness in chapter 10, where I suggested that the lack of a stable self-system is the main difference between psychosis and wakefulness. But this doesn't mean that the childhood state is equivalent to psychosis. In psychosis, our self-system has *broken down*; it's chaotic and disrupted. This is not the same as an *absence* of a self-system or one that is developing.

It's also important to realize that the immature wakefulness of childhood can be experienced by *adults*, too. If awakened adults lose the ability to control their impulses and become excessively self-centered, they may effectively regress to a childlike state. In fact, we've already encountered some examples of this in chapter 11: spiritual teachers who become narcissistic and megalomaniacal as a result of the power and temptations of their positions and the projections of their followers.

Sometimes, when I discuss childhood wakefulness in talks or lectures, I joke that children are a combination of enlightened beings and narcissistic monsters, then ask, "But isn't that a good description of some spiritual teachers?"

The Fall into Adulthood

Just as we went through a "fall" as a species, losing the natural wakefulness of earlier human beings, all of us go through a "fall" as individuals, when we lose the primal wakefulness of children. As we move toward later childhood and adolescence, the self-system of sleep gradually forms within our being. This is part of our developmental blueprint, our established pattern of mental development, that unfolds as we grow into adulthood. We gradually lose the heightened awareness of children as our ego becomes more powerful and energy-consuming and as, in response to this, our perception becomes automatized. As a result, the world that was once so full of wonder and beauty becomes a more mundane place. We gradually lose our sense of connection to the world — and our sense of *participating* in it — as the boundaries of our self-system become established. We gradually lose our sense of well-being as we become disconnected to the radiant life-energy of our essential being. As William Wordsworth describes it, the "shades of the prison-house begin to close" until eventually the divine vision of childhood disappears:

> The Man perceives it die away,
> And fade into the light of common day.[20]

The loss of childhood wakefulness is one of the reasons why adolescence can be such a difficult and turbulent time. Adolescence is the time of the individual "fall." After years of carefree well-being and wholeness, adolescents begin to experience themselves as separate entities, enclosed within their own mental space, with the discord of self-reflective thought-chatter constantly spinning through their consciousness. After years of feeling that they were part of the world, they have a new identity as an *ego*. And because of its separateness, this ego feels a tremendous sense of vulnerability and fragility.

This ego development is the reason why so many adolescents have identity crises and feel such a strong need to belong, to fit in — they join gangs, follow fashion trends and pop groups, or join organized religions (adolescence is a peak time for religious conversion). It's extremely important for adolescents to feel that they're accepted, part of a group, with an identity as a member of that group, to try to overcome their sense of vulnerability. Because of their weak inner security, adolescents can be devastated if they're not accepted by their peers, or if they feel they've been disrespected.

This state of ego separation and inner discord can be traumatic, especially after the ease and spontaneity of childhood. You could compare it to an agricultural worker who is used to the open air and the beauty of nature around him but is forced to head to the city to get a job, and now spends his days in a crowded, noisy, and stuffy factory.

But, of course, there are positive aspects to this as well, just as there are some positive aspects to the "fall" we underwent as a species. In both cases, the "fall" is also a "rise," to some extent. It would be impossible to remain in a childlike state for our whole lives. We have to be able to function in the world on a practical basis and develop the abilities to think conceptually and abstractly. The adult self-system enables us to do this. In addition to its negative aspects, the adult self-system gives us the benefits of conceptual knowledge, self-reflection, impulse control, exercise of our will, organizational skills, decision-making abilities, planning skills, and the capacity to manipulate our surroundings and live autonomously. It's precisely because they lack a fully developed self-system that children are unable to deal with the practical demands of life and need such intense nurturing.

The adult self-system is undoubtedly a massive developmental progression. It's just unfortunate that this self-system has such negative aspects; at the same time as being beneficial, it's also extremely aberrational.

However, this state of carefree wholeness and exhilarating aliveness isn't lost to us forever. Through gradual spiritual development, or sudden awakening, we regain the primal wakefulness of children in a more mature form. We regain children's heightened awareness and energy, and their sense of connection and well-being, but with a stable self-system that engenders other aspects of wakefulness. At the same time — crucially — this self-system allows us to retain the intellectual, volitional, self-reflective, and organizational abilities of the normal adult state.

Mature wakefulness is an integration of the childhood and the normal adult state, retaining the benefits of both.

15. Demythologizing Wakefulness

At the beginning of this book, I wrote that one of my aims was to clarify exactly what *wakefulness* means and dispel some of the confusion that surrounds it. This confusion has arisen partly because wakefulness has been interpreted in so many different ways, by different traditions and different teachers. Such variance makes it difficult to see the core truths that underlie the different interpretations. In this book, I've tried to uncover these core truths by taking wakefulness outside the context of spiritual traditions and examining the psychological or ontological landscape that *precedes* interpretation by the traditions.

Dispelling this confusion also involves examining some of the popular misunderstandings that have developed about wakefulness. Through my years of research, I've become aware of many common ideas and assumptions about the state — some of which I used to hold myself — that simply aren't true. It's these misunderstandings that I'd like to focus on in this chapter. This examination will also act as a summary of the book, bringing out the most salient points we've discussed over the previous fourteen chapters and the main points I'd like you to take away once you set the book down.

In what follows, I'll highlight some of the myths about wakefulness and then explain why I believe they're false.

Myth 1: Wakefulness is exceptional and extraordinary.

This is one of the biggest misconceptions about wakefulness — and one that I used to believe myself. When I first began my research, I was amazed at how easy it was to find cases of people who had woken up. And that's still true. I'm continually surprised at the large number of examples I come across — the awakened individuals I meet by chance or synchronicity and the people who write to me or come up to me after talks to tell me that they've read one of my articles and have been through (or are going through) the same experience. In most cases, they're people who don't have backgrounds in spiritual traditions and know very little about them. They're often ordinary people searching for an understanding of the remarkable shift they've been through. As a result, I'm certain there are thousands of other people out there who have experienced this shift (mostly triggered by intense psychological turmoil) and have yet to make sense of it — or even tell anyone about it, for fear of being misunderstood.

As I mentioned in the previous chapter, wakefulness is also unexceptional in the sense that the experience feels so *normal*. People who experience wakefulness are often surprised by how *ordinary* it seems, how natural and easy and right it appears. It feels utterly *familiar*, even if we have no recollection of experiencing it before. As the contemporary Christian mystic Bernadette Roberts puts it, "From the position of egoic consciousness, unitive consciousness always appears to be quite supernatural, mystical or nirvanic, but once we get there, it turns out to be utterly ordinary."[1]

In fact, when we wake up, it's our normal sleep state that seems peculiar and unnatural. Sleep seems aberrational in its discord, constrictedness, and shadowy, limited vision of reality. We realize that it's actually a pathological state that only appeared normal because it was all we knew. When we wake up there's a sense of returning home to the place where we were meant to be all along.

Myth 2: It's not possible to live in a continuous
state of wakefulness. It would make it impossible
for us to live in the world on a day-to-day basis.

Sometimes when I talk about wakefulness in lectures or public talks, people say, "This is all very well, but we can't actually *live* like this. We can't be in a state of ecstasy and union with the cosmos all the time. We've still got to cook meals, pay bills, and drive the car."

To be *able* to experience ecstasy and union doesn't necessarily mean that we *continuously* experience them. Awakened people still have powers of concentration; we can still exclude phenomena from our attention when necessary and narrow down our attention to specific tasks. In other words, when we need to focus on practical tasks (driving, cooking, paying bills) we're able to temporarily filter out our intensified awareness and sense of connection by using our concentrative abilities. The different aspects of wakefulness are always there potentially, but they sometimes recede into the background when we need to switch into an organizational or practical mode.

This is partly a question of integration. In the initial phase after awakening, many people find it difficult to function in everyday life. They may find it difficult to concentrate or interact with other people. They may even have difficulty speaking, understanding concepts like time, and retaining or remembering information. But these psychological abilities return as integration occurs.

Following integration, awakened people often remark that they find life *easier*, even on a practical basis. They actually find it easier to concentrate because their minds are clearer; there aren't streams of thought-chatter mingling with their conscious thought processes and pulling their attention away from what they want to think about. Their practical lives are also often less complex, because they don't fill their days with unnecessary activities. They keep their lives simple and do what needs to be done, efficiently and skillfully. As a result, they're less likely to become overwhelmed or exhausted by overactivity.

Overall, it's possible that awakened individuals actually get *better* at living in the world on a day-to-day basis.

Myth 3: You are either enlightened or not. There's no middle ground.

There's no clear dividing line between wakefulness and sleep. There are different degrees of sleep and different degrees of wakefulness, stretching across a wide continuum. Some people may be more deeply asleep than others; that is, they may have a stronger sense of separation, a more dulled perception of the phenomenal world, a greater identification with their thought-chatter, a more egocentric outlook, and a stronger sense of group identity. Some people may be more intensely awake than others; that is, they may have a stronger sense of union or connection, a more intense perception of the phenomenal world, a greater inner quietness and still-ness, a wider sense of perspective, and a deeper sense of identification with the human race as a whole. The characteristics of wakefulness can express themselves at different degrees of intensity.

The idea that there's a clear distinction between wakefulness and sleep — that either you're awakened or you're not — probably stems from the sudden nature of most awakenings. When the shift into wakefulness occurs suddenly, it may seem that there's a clear-cut distinction between the two states, as if they're different countries separated by a defined border. But as we've seen, wakefulness can also occur gradually. People move slowly through different gradations of wakefulness as they follow spiritual prac-tices and paths — or more spontaneously, as a result of living lives of ser-vice or mindfulness, or as a result of a long process of loss or failure. Even when awakening happens suddenly, a person can *shift up* to different de-grees of wakefulness, in the same way that, for example, an escalator can take people to higher or lower levels of a building.

Myth 4: Wakefulness is the end point, the culmination, of our development.

Wakefulness is sometimes depicted as the end of our journey, a destination and culmination. When we attain enlightenment we're surely safely home, on the other side of the river. We've reached a state of complete fulfillment and there's surely nowhere left to go. Why would we want to go anywhere else?

But in reality, awakening isn't the end of the journey but the begin-ning of a different one. It's not the end of the road but rather a switch to a different road. Awakened people continue to develop. They continue to find new resources inside themselves, uncover new potentials and energies, and evolve new aspects and depths of their relationships with themselves, with other human beings, and with the world in general. As one person described her shift to me, "It's raised me up a level....It's really a building block for me to move from."

Perhaps the best illustration of this is my friend Russel Williams, who — at the time of writing — is ninety-five years old and underwent his awakening sixty-six years ago. For him, wakefulness has always been a fluid state, which is still developing and changing after more than six decades. As Russel told me, "Over the years, new things have emerged, and I've begun to see in greater depth. One begins to look into more profound areas, to reach realms which one never knew were there, or to see the same thing but with more clarity. There's always something beyond. I'm beginning to wonder if there will ever be an end."[2]

Myth 5: Awakened people live in a state of continuous bliss and ease, free from all suffering and difficulty.

Despite their general sense of ease and the other aspects of well-being they experience (such as their sense of appreciation and their freedom from ego-isolation and thought-chatter), awakened individuals usually don't live lives of perfect, continuous bliss.

This is particularly true of the initial stages after sudden awakening. As we've seen, the early stages can be full of confusion and disturbance, which may take years to fade and settle. But difficulties may still arise even once a person's wakefulness becomes stable and integrated. The awakened person may not be entirely free of psychological discord. Negative personality traits such as a lack of self-confidence or a tendency to jealousy or guilt may be carried over from their previous state and take some time to fade away. Awakened people may also experience degrees of reactive negativity. For example, they may get irritated by other people's behavior, feel upset by family or relationship problems, or feel worried about health or financial issues. Awakening doesn't automatically eradicate personality traits, nor does it eradicate all problems.

"Degrees" is the important point, of course. Awakened individuals may not be completely free of negativity, but they're certainly *more free* of it. They're certainly *less likely* to be negatively affected by external events and *less prone* to reactive negativity. And this applies to different intensities of wakefulness. People who are more intensely awake will be correspondingly more free of negativity and correspondingly less prone to psychological discord and emotional upset. At the higher intensities of wakefulness, negativity *may* fade away completely.

Myth 6: Awakened individuals are incapable of behaving improperly.

This is closely linked to the previous myth concerning freedom from suffering. The notion of awakened individuals as perfect people who always behave with impeccable integrity and benevolence is as much of a romanticization as the notion that wakefulness is a state of perfect bliss. Again, awakened individuals undoubtedly tend to be less self-centered and more compassionate and altruistic than others due to their greater sense of empathy and their strong inner moral compass. But wakefulness doesn't completely eradicate the possibility of unethical behavior, as shown by many cases of narcissistic and exploitative spiritual teachers (many of whom were genuinely awakened, at least to begin with).

Myth 7: Awakened individuals are detached from the world. They become indifferent to worldly affairs and are content for the world to remain as it is, without interfering.

As I noted in chapter 13, this myth isn't completely without foundation, due to the otherworldly tendencies of some spiritual traditions. But in reality, most awakened individuals don't live like this. They likely feel *more* concerned about the sufferings of other people and the injustices of the world due to their empathy, their sense of morality, and their wide, global (rather than egocentric) perspective. They feel a strong impulse to help alleviate other people's sufferings, to encourage their development, and to make the world a better place.

Myth 8: Awakened individuals — or mystics — are passive and inactive. They just sit and meditate all day, immersed in their own blissfulness.

This myth is closely related to the myth about detachment and also isn't without foundation — again, largely due to Christian, Buddhist, and

Hindu traditions of monasticism and renunciation. (Interestingly, Jewish, Sufi, and Daoist spiritual traditions aren't monastic, which partly explains why they tend to be more worldly and communally oriented.) But again, although awakened individuals greatly enjoy *being* rather than *doing*, and may spend a lot more time "doing nothing" than other people, they may also be extremely active.

Increased activity usually expresses itself through creativity or altruism — sometimes both. Awakened individuals who are artists tend to be extremely prolific. D. H. Lawrence wrote over forty books during his short lifetime, while Walt Whitman and William Wordsworth both wrote thousands of poems, with almost inexhaustible creative energy. This prolific creativity is possible because there's little interference between the awakened artist's own mind and the transcendent source of their creativity. Other artists might struggle with writer's block or a lack of inspiration when their own thoughts and concepts obstruct the creative flow, but awakened artists are like channels that always remain wide open. The soft and subtle self-system of wakefulness ensures that inspiration and ideas continually flow through.

There are also many examples of awakened individuals who have pursued altruistic endeavors with incredible energy and determination. One of the best examples is Florence Nightingale, who effectively created the profession of modern nursing, founding many hospitals and training tens of thousands of nurses. She also initiated many other social reforms, completely revolutionizing approaches to health care and sanitation. A prolific writer, too, she was famous for her endless energy, which became known as "Nightingale power." But what is less well known about her is that she was a deeply spiritual person who wrote several books on Christian mysticism. Evelyn Underhill called her "one of the greatest and most balanced contemplatives of the nineteenth century."[3] As Nightingale herself writes, "Heaven is neither a place nor a time. There might be a Heaven not only here but now. Where shall I find God? In myself. That is the true Mystical Doctrine."[4]

Florence Nightingale's life of intense altruism is by no means unprecedented among female Christian mystics. The fourteenth-century Italian mystic Catherine of Siena spent three years living as a hermit and an ascetic before undergoing a permanent shift into wakefulness. At that point she abandoned her solitude and was active in society for the rest of her life, teaching, serving the poor and the sick, and trying to bring peace to the warring states of Italy. Similarly, her fifteenth-century compatriot (and namesake) Catherine of Genoa spent four years living as an ascetic, until she attained a stable state of awakening. From that point on, she was extremely active as a theologian and nurse, tending to the sick and the poor of Genoa and eventually becoming the manager and treasurer of the city hospital. Similarly, the sixteenth-century mystic Teresa of Avila lived a life of frenetic activity, including founding seventeen convents and writing several books.

Part of the reason why it's possible for awakened individuals to be so active and energetic is because their energy comes from a transcendent source. They don't have to *make an effort* — they simply allow action to flow through them. In Daoist terms, they engage in actionless activity (*wu wei*). They are in harmony with the Dao, which expresses itself purely through them. They are expressions of what I call *transpersonal purpose*. They don't have a purpose that they consciously try to fulfill, as other people might consciously aim to achieve goals or to gain status, success, or wealth. They may not even have a clear idea about what their purpose actually is. But their purpose flows through them, from a transcendent source, and they simply allow it to express itself without interference.[5]

Myth 9: In wakefulness, the world is revealed to be an illusion.

Here we move into some more subtle misconceptions of the wakeful state. The idea that the world becomes illusory when we wake up is related to the two previous myths. After all, if the world is an illusion, then we're entitled to be indifferent to it.

The Hindu concept of *maya* is sometimes translated as "illusion," but its actual meaning is closer to "deception." *Maya* is the force that deceives us into thinking of ourselves as separate entities and the world as consisting of separate, autonomous phenomena. In other words, *maya* prevents us from seeing the world as it really is. It blinds us to the unity that lies behind apparent diversity. It stops us from seeing the world as *brahman*, or spirit.

So it doesn't literally mean that the world is an illusion, but that it's not as it seems. It means that our vision of the world is not complete or objective, that there's more to reality than we superficially see.

The idea of the world as an illusion is sometimes specifically associated with Hindu Advaita Vedanta (or nonduality) philosophy, but this interpretation of Advaita stems from a similar misunderstanding. The most influential Advaita Vedanta philosopher was Sankara, who lived during the eighth and ninth centuries CE. Sankara famously made three statements (later reframed by Ramana Maharshi and others): "The universe is unreal. Brahman is real. The universe is Brahman." If the first two statements are taken alone and out of context — as they often are — then they suggest a duality between the world and spirit: the world is an illusion, and only spirit is real. But the third statement, which is often overlooked, completely reverses this. The third statement says that the universe is spirit, and so the universe actually *is* real. Sankara is not literally saying that the universe is unreal, only that it doesn't have an independent reality. It depends on *brahman* for its existence; it's pervaded with *brahman*, and can't exist without it.

Ramana Maharshi, perhaps the greatest Indian sage of the twentieth century, held a similar view. He explained that the world is not unreal in itself. It only becomes unreal when we perceive it purely in terms of its appearance and just see interacting separate objects rather than an underlying spirit. *That* world is unreal, in the same way that a dream is unreal, because it's based on delusion. But in itself the world is inseparable from spirit. It's a manifestation of spirit.[6]

This is exactly what wakefulness reveals — not that the world is an illusion but that the world as we normally see it is incomplete, a partial reality. In wakefulness, the world actually becomes *more* real, partly in the sense that it becomes more tangibly real and alive, more vivid and powerfully *there*, but also in the sense that it becomes infused with spirit. In wakefulness, we realize that there's no duality, no matter or spirit, no matter or mind. We realize that the physical world and the spiritual world are one, with no distinction. The world is gloriously infused with spirit and so gloriously real.

Nevertheless, the idea of the world as an illusion is appealing to many people, as it offers a way of circumventing problems. If you're facing difficulties in your own life, and if the world itself is full of the suffering of your fellow human beings, then it's comforting and convenient to tell yourself, "Oh well, it's all just an illusion, so there's no need to worry." In other words, it offers a means of spiritual bypassing, that is, using spiritual beliefs as a way of escaping issues that need addressing.[7] (The idea that the *self* is an illusion, which we'll address in a moment, is another example of this.)

A similar attitude is sometimes applied to the body. After all, the body is made of the same stuff as the world, so if the world is an illusion, the body must be too, or at least it can be seen as something different and inferior to the mind or spirit. There's a duality between the spirit and the body, just as there's a duality between the spirit and the physical world. This attitude can lead to a hostile, repressive attitude toward the body, an attitude of disgust toward its animalistic functions and impulses, including sex. This attitude is illustrated by early Christian Gnostic teachings, for example, which held that all matter is evil, and the body is a prison to escape from. But again, in wakefulness this duality is revealed to be false. The body is infused with spirit and is one with spirit. As Walt Whitman writes in "I Sing the Body Electric," after listing dozens of different parts of the body, "O I say these are not the parts and poems of the Body only, but of the soul, O I say now these are the soul!"[8]

Myth 10: In wakefulness, the self disappears.
There's literally "no one there."
Wakefulness is a state of selflessness.

This misconception is closely related to the last. According to this view, the self is an illusion, just as the world is. When we wake up, we become no one. Our sense of personal identity disappears. There's no longer a *doer* who performs actions; actions are just performed through us.

Some modern nonduality (or Neo-Advaita) teachers take this view, but again, it's based on a misunderstanding. One metaphor sometimes used to describe the awakening process is that of the wave and the ocean. In our sleep state, we see ourselves as individual waves, separate from the whole ocean. But when we wake up, we realize our oneness with the ocean, that we *are* the ocean, that we've emerged from it and are always part of it. However, this doesn't necessarily mean that we lose our identity *as* a wave. We can have an identity as a wave at the same time as being part of the ocean — at the same time as *being* the ocean. We can still function as individuals, with some degree of autonomy and identity, at the same time as being one with the whole universe.

One way to look at this is to see wakefulness not as a dissolution of self but as an *expansion* of self. In our sleep state, our identity is constricted, more or less confined to our own mind and body. But as we wake up, our identity opens up, expands outward. It incorporates and encompasses wider realities. It expands into other people, other living beings, the natural world, the earth itself, until eventually it encompasses the whole cosmos. In conceptual terms, this expresses itself as a movement beyond a narrow egocentric outlook (with a strong sense of group identity) toward a global, universal perspective, with a concern for overriding global issues and a sense of oneness with all human beings, irrespective of superficial differences of nationality or ethnicity.

Perhaps one reason why wakefulness is sometimes seen as a state of no-self is because the awakened self-system is so unobtrusive and well-integrated into the rest of our being that we may not actually *realize* that it's there, in the same way that if a person is sitting quietly in the corner of a dark room we may not notice that the room is occupied. The functioning of the self-system may be so subtle and quietly efficient that we may not realize that it's actually taking place. Its structure is so soft and labile that we may not realize that it's present.

Here we can return to the analogy of the city that I used in chapter 3. Our normal self-system is like a city with thick walls around it; it seems to exist as an entity in itself, in separation from the rest of the landscape. But in the wakeful state, our self-system is like a small unobtrusive settlement — an eco-village, perhaps — that is so well-integrated that you can hardly tell it apart from the landscape as a whole. It has clearly emerged from the landscape; it's made of the same materials as the landscape and merges into it without any sense of separation.

The important point, again, is that there *has* to be some kind of self-system within our being. There has to be some kind of organizational or administrative center within the landscape, even if it only plays a minimal, unobtrusive role. And a self-system implies some degree of identity, a sense of being someone who inhabits the landscape of our being.

You could say that awakening doesn't mean *no-self* so much as *new self*. Awakening means the emergence of a new self-system. After all, many of the shifters we've heard from throughout this book describe awakening in this way — as if an old self has dissolved away and a new one has emerged. They don't feel that they have no identity but as if they have a *new* identity. They don't feel that they have become nobody but that they have become somebody else. (In this sense, when traditions such as Buddhism speak of "no-self," it may be that they strictly mean "no separate self.")

You could think about this in terms of the concept of ego. Some spiritual teachers describe wakefulness in terms of having no ego, but this may not be strictly true. *Ego* is simply the Latin and ancient Greek word for "I." So strictly speaking, awakened people still have an ego, albeit a completely different one. Returning to our city metaphor, our normal ego is a powerful emperor who lives at the center of the city, in a giant castle that he keeps reinforcing and expanding. He believes he controls the whole city and even the whole landscape. But in the self-system of wakefulness, there's no emperor, just a simple administrator or executor whose authority is limited and who functions as a democratic, harmonious part of the whole system.

All too often, in spiritual circles, the concept of no-self is used as a form of spiritual bypass, a way of avoiding psychological problems. If you don't exist as a self, then all the problems associated with yourself no longer exist either. For example, you might suffer from anxiety and low self-esteem, or be frustrated because your job isn't suited to you, or distressed because your partner is abusive to you. But if you believe that the self is an illusion, you can disregard these problems, pretend that they're all just part of a "story" that has no significance.

This is why the idea of no-self is so appealing to some people, but also why it is so confusing to others. Many people have an intuitive sense that they have psychological issues that need to be resolved before they can undergo any real, stable spiritual development. They have a sense that they need to undergo some healing or integration as a way of preparing the ground for awakening. So to be told that this self, which they feel needs some healing or growth, doesn't exist doesn't seem to ring true to them. And indeed, in such cases, to see the self as an irrelevant illusion isn't just unhelpful but also counterproductive. It will actually intensify and extend the suffering of the separate self, not end it.

Myth 11: You can't make an effort to wake up.

According to this viewpoint, spiritual practices and paths aren't effective because to follow them implies *making an effort* to awaken and working toward a goal. After all, effort is *egoic* in nature. It means striving and so strengthens the ego, which takes you further away from wakefulness. To *seek* enlightenment is futile and self-defeating.

In a similar way, having enlightenment as a goal strengthens the illusion of time, which the ego thrives on. Goals invoke the future, which doesn't really exist. Enlightenment is timeless, so how can we reach it in time? You can only wake up right here, right now, by letting go of your striving.

There's certainly an element of truth to this. For some people, spiritual seeking *is* a form of egoic striving. They seek enlightenment in the same way that other people seek success or wealth — as a way of gaining something, of adding something to themselves. This is what Chogyam Trungpa calls "spiritual materialism," when the search for enlightenment becomes a way of compensating for a sense of lack, much like more overt kinds of materialism. To take an extreme example, such a person might say to themselves, "Okay, I'm going to read as many spiritual books as I can, visit as many spiritual teachers as I can, meditate for at least five hours a day, and make sure I'm enlightened by the age of thirty." They might force themselves to meditate even when they're feeling ill, tired, or depressed. They might spend endless hours trying to understand the most complex and esoteric spiritual teachings and eventually start to wonder when signs of awakening are going to appear. This kind of rigid ego effort *is* likely to be counterproductive and unlikely to lead to any real spiritual development.

However, not all spiritual seeking is egoic in this way. There's a much more deep-rooted and organic impulse to awaken, which doesn't stem from the ego but from the deepest part of our being. This impulse for growth and expansion completely transcends us as individuals; it's an *evolutionary* impulse that is actually hundreds of millions of years old. The urge that so many millions of people feel to explore spiritual teachings and follow spiritual practices and paths is, in most cases, an expression of the same dynamic impulse that has impelled living beings to become more complex and conscious ever since the beginnings of life on Earth. It's an impulse to expand and intensify consciousness, and progress to a higher-functioning, more integrated state, which is exactly what has been happening to life-forms for millions of years before us through the process of evolution.

In other words, for most people, spiritual development isn't about gaining something or striving for a goal but about allowing this evolutionary impulse to express itself through them. Ideally at least, spiritual seeking means that the process of evolution is acting through us, encouraging us to move toward a higher state of being on its behalf. It doesn't strengthen the ego but helps transcend it.

As with the myth that the self is a meaningless illusion, the idea that we can't *do* anything to wake up confuses many people. This is inevitable, because it contravenes their own deepest impulses and, in fact, contravenes one of the deepest drives of nature and the universe itself.

The blanket view of spiritual practices as counterproductive also stems from a misunderstanding of the nature of wakefulness and, in particular, the process of gradual awakening. As we've seen, gradual awakening involves a remolding of our self-system, a gradual shift from our old self-system to a new one. The whole purpose of spiritual practice and spiritual paths is to generate that shift. Following spiritual practices and paths slowly dismantles the old self-system, softens its boundaries and heals its discord, allowing a latent wakeful self-system to emerge slowly. This shift doesn't happen by accident, or through some kind of a realization or "seeing." There has to be some kind of inner structural change, which can happen suddenly and dramatically — usually following intense stress or turmoil — or gradually, through spiritual practice.

The view that we can't do anything to wake up is sometimes justified with the argument that we're *already* awake. How can we not already be one with the cosmos when our true nature is spirit? Surely, it's simply a question of accepting what we already are. And we can only do this by giving up striving and accepting our true nature.

This is true in an absolute sense but not in a relative one. That is, it's true that essentially we're one with spirit and therefore one with everything that exists. Wakefulness is therefore our deepest nature. But just because this is true doesn't mean that we actually *experience* it. It's actually normal for us to be alienated from our true nature, due to the structures and boundaries of the self-system of sleep. It's like saying to me — as an inhabitant of Manchester, one of the wettest cities in the United Kingdom — "Don't worry about the cloud cover because there's always blue sky beyond it; you just need to accept the essential blueness of the sky." The sky may always be blue, but unless the cloud cover actually clears, I won't be able to see it.

However, although it's a misconception, the idea that you can't do anything to awaken contains an element of truth. While we follow spiritual practices and paths, there's always a danger that our practice can become too rigid and goal oriented. It's possible that our deep impulse to awaken may become tainted with egoic striving. If this happens, then our conscious striving may block or obstruct the evolutionary impulse to awaken, in the same way that, for creative people, trying too hard or forcing themselves to compose or write may block the organic flow of creativity. In the same way that a writer may experience writer's block, a spiritual explorer may experience "spiritual block," when they become too self-conscious or goal-directed.

When this happens, letting go of the effort to wake up can actually be liberating. It *may* unblock our spiritual evolution and lead to a sudden flourishing, perhaps even to the sudden awakening we're hoping for. At that point, it might seem as if letting go of the effort was the *cause* of our awakening, but, of course, it wouldn't have happened without the years of development beforehand. (This can cause difficulties if we advise others to simply give up the spiritual search. Unless others have been through a similar developmental process to us, it's unlikely that giving up the spiritual search will be of any use to them.)

The above discussion of the evolutionary nature of our impulse to awaken reminds us that awakening isn't just an individual matter. It's not just something we choose to do or something that only has significance to us as individuals, or to the people around us. It's significant in that it can enable us to live much healthier, higher-functioning lives. But that's only a small part of its importance. Awakening has to be seen in a much vaster context, as vast as the whole universe itself. It has to be seen in the context of the evolution of life on our planet. And this is how we'll view it in the last chapter of this book.

16. The Evolutionary Leap: A Collective Awakening

On a physical level, evolution can be seen as a process by which living beings become increasingly complex and more intricately organized. According to the latest scientific research, the evolution of life on this planet began about four billion years ago — not long after the formation of the earth itself — with the emergence of the first simple single-celled bacteria. Over billions of years, these single-celled bacteria became more complex. They developed nuclei, gained the ability to photosynthesize, and eventually began to reproduce through sex. This led to much more complex multicelled creatures and then to the development of life-forms such as sponges, fungi, corals, and sea anemones, and then to insects, fish, land plants, forests, and mammals.

As evolution progressed, there was increased specialization and differentiation — more and more cells collected together and worked together more intricately, with different roles. This led to the development of the first brains (in flatworms). Over time, brains grew larger and larger, and their cells became more interconnected. After many millennia of gradually increasing complexity, the process led to the emergence of *Homo sapiens*, about two hundred thousand years ago. We're the most physically complex living beings evolution has yet produced, with a hundred *billion* cells in our brains, interconnected so intricately that even now neuroscientists barely understand how they work together.

But evolution has an *inner* dimension, too. The increasingly physical complexity is mirrored internally in the expansion of awareness and the intensification of consciousness. In these terms, we can see evolution as a process by which living beings become increasingly conscious and aware, both of the world and of themselves.

At the same time as being the most physically complex beings on this planet, human beings are probably also the most intensely *aware* and *conscious* living beings. Although we can't be certain, it seems likely that we have a more intricate and expansive awareness of reality and a higher degree of *self*-consciousness than any other animal.

Three Different Types of Awareness

Here it's useful to think in terms of three different types of awareness. In fact, I mentioned the first two of these in chapter 13: *perceptual* awareness, which means experiencing the phenomenal world around us, and *conceptual* awareness. Here my use of the term *conceptual awareness* is a little more general than in chapter 13. There I used it to describe how wakefulness expresses itself in conceptual terms, resulting in a wider sense of perspective, a lack of group identity, and so on. But in a more general sense — not just in terms of wakefulness — conceptual awareness means being aware of concepts such as time, the past and the future, death and — more subtly — morality and justice. It means being able to think in terms of categories and recognize the relationships, including the differences and similarities, between different phenomena. It's related to conceptual and symbolic developments such as alphabets and written languages, numbers and mathematics, and systems of laws.

The third type of awareness, which I haven't mentioned specifically before, is *subjective* awareness, which means awareness of our own selves and our own states of being. Even the simplest life-forms have perceptual awareness. For example, single-celled bacteria have the ability to move toward light or heat or sources of food, which shows that they have some form of rudimentary awareness. And some animals clearly have more acute perceptual awareness than human beings, at least in certain areas. For example, dogs have a much more acute sense of smell than we do, and they can hear sounds beyond our auditory range. But we human beings seem to possess the other two types of awareness — conceptual and subjective — to a more intense degree than other animals. Some animals show degrees of self-awareness — for example, magpies appear to be able to recognize themselves in mirrors — and some animals, such as apes, can be taught a rudimentary awareness of categories and numbers, showing some conceptual awareness. But the amazing intricacy and complexity of human language, compared to the apparently rudimentary languages of some animals, testifies to the unprecedented richness of our conceptual and subjective awareness. No other animals appear to be able to examine their own inner subjective world as deeply as human beings, or to have as rich and intricate an understanding of the world we inhabit.

However, we tend to forget that the human race as it presently is can't be the end point of the evolutionary process. It's completely illogical to assume that evolution is just behind us, rather than in front of us as well. The intensification and expansion of awareness will undoubtedly continue.

And in my view, the phenomenon of spiritual awakening shows that this process *is* continuing among us, right now.

Wakefulness represents an intensification of awareness in all three of the areas I've mentioned. It involves an intensified perceptual awareness, a broader conceptual awareness (with a wider sense of perspective, a transcendence of group identity, and a universal morality), and an intensification of subjective awareness, that is, an increased awareness of the richness and fullness of our inner lives. So to me it seems that evolution is working through human beings, moving us collectively toward a new stage of development that is more expansive than the present normal human state, in the same way that this normal state is more expansive than the consciousness of other animals. Although the state of wakefulness is relatively rare at the moment, one day — assuming we survive as a species — it will presumably become human beings' *normal* state. In this way, present-day awakened human beings are a kind of evolutionary throw-forward, a premature glimpse of our future as a species.[1]

Rethinking Evolution

I'm implying here that evolution isn't just a random process generated by genetic mutations and natural selection. In my view, there's an *impetus* behind evolution that encourages a movement toward both greater physical complexity and a more expansive awareness. In other words, living beings have an *innate tendency* to develop in the direction of more intense perceptual, conceptual, and subjective awareness.

This purposeful view might seem strange to anyone who has been taught the standard neo-Darwinist explanation of evolution, but there are, in fact, many problems with the standard view. It's beyond the scope of this book to address these fully (I'm hoping to write a book about it in the future), but one of the main arguments against the accidental view of evolution is that it seems implausible that such a staggeringly positive and creative process could be generated purely by a *negative* phenomenon such as random genetic mutations. According to the standard neo-Darwinist view, mutations almost always have negative effects, and the life-forms that have them don't reproduce and so the mutations quickly die out. But very occasionally they have a beneficial effect and give life-forms an advantage in survival. These beneficial mutations are selected and become established in the gene pool, creating variations in species and eventually generating distinct new species.

It's true that these mutations have had many millions of years to supposedly create new species, but many philosophers and scientists have doubted that such a negative accidental process could *ever* have had such creative consequences, no matter how much time it was allowed. This isn't just because positive mutations happen so rarely but also because, in order to create significant changes (including the generation of new species), a long series of beneficial mutations have to occur in sequence. Mutations have to be *cumulative*, matching perfectly to previous mutations and occurring at the right place and time.[2]

It seems more plausible that there's an impulse *in life itself* to move toward greater complexity and at the same time toward a more intense awareness. I sometimes compare evolution to the development of a human being from embryo to adulthood. Here development moves naturally and inevitably from the simplest state — when two cells meet and merge — through levels of increasing complexity, as cells split off and organize and start to form different parts of the body. The process unfolds along predetermined lines, following a kind of blueprint or mold specific to our species. I think evolution is similar to this but on an enormously extended time frame, unfolding over hundreds of millions of years. Perhaps the only difference is that the direction of evolution may not be as fixed as the development of individuals — perhaps there's a simple *tendency* to move toward greater complexity and awareness that is broadly directional without being completely predetermined.

So in my view, to believe that evolution is accidental is as illogical as trying to explain human development from an embryo to adulthood in terms of accidental factors. This process of *ontogenetic* (or individual) development closely parallels the course of evolution itself over the past four billion years, moving from simple cellular structures to increasing complexity and specialization. And this parallel includes the probability that both types of development aren't random but directional.

Evidence for an Evolutionary Leap

According to this view, there's something *inevitable* about awakening. It's the natural unfolding of a process that has been under way for millions of years. Wakefulness is latent inside us, waiting to emerge. You could say that, in a sense, it was *always* latent in living beings, even in the first single-celled bacteria. The Greek philosopher Aristotle originally put forward the idea (later taken up by other philosophers) that all higher evolutionary forms are latent in lower ones. He saw evolution as the unfolding of latent potential, leading to higher forms of life, all of which were inherent from the beginning.[3] At the present time, the latency of wakefulness has become so powerful that the state is ready to emerge. Indeed, wakefulness is *already* emerging within us collectively, gradually moving the whole human race to a higher-functioning state of being and a more expansive and intensive state of awareness. We are, I believe, on the threshold of an evolutionary leap.

There are a number of signs that this evolutionary leap is under way and that wakefulness is collectively emerging within the human race. The first four, which I will discuss now, relate to direct individual experiences of wakefulness.

Natural Wakefulness

First of all, as we've seen, wakefulness is natural for a small minority of people. These are evolutionary throw-forwards in whom wakefulness isn't latent but has already expressed itself. They seem to be the spearhead of collective transformation.

Of course, it could be that this is nothing new. Perhaps there have always been naturally wakeful people. We certainly know of many awakened individuals throughout history — for example, the Buddha, the Indian philosopher Sankara, the medieval Christian mystic Meister Eckhart, and the eighteenth-century Jewish mystic Ba'al Shem Tov. But in most cases we don't have enough biographical information to ascertain whether wakefulness was natural to them or developed gradually through spiritual paths, or through sudden transformation. At any rate, we *do* know that natural wakefulness is occurring now.

Temporary Awakening Experiences

The second sign of this evolutionary leap is that, among the great majority of people who are *not* born in a naturally wakeful state, awakening *experiences* are very common. Many people have temporary glimpses of the wakeful state, often when they're inactive and relaxed, and their minds become quiet and calm. For a few moments, the self-system of sleep slips away and the wakeful state emerges, like the sun from behind a wall of clouds. This suggests our normal sleep state has only a loose hold over us and can easily dissolve away, even if it usually manages to reestablish itself.

The Impulse to Awaken

The third sign is that so many people feel an *impulse* to awaken. More and more people seem to sense instinctively that something is wrong with their normal state of being, that it is limited and delusory. They're aware that they're asleep, and they want to wake up. As a result, they feel impelled to investigate methods of transcending their normal state such as following spiritual practices and traditions. Again, this suggests that our sleep state is losing its hold over us. It suggests that an evolutionary change is building momentum within our collective psyche. As I said in the last chapter, this individual impulse to awaken is an expression of the evolutionary impulse itself. It's the same urge toward an expansion and intensification of awareness expressing itself through us.

Awakening through Psychological Turmoil

The final sign, at least in terms of the individual experience of wakefulness, is the fact that awakening occurs so spontaneously and readily in response to psychological turmoil. This is probably the clearest sign of the increasing latency of wakefulness. For shifters who undergo awakening in this way, the wakeful self-system seems to emerge fully formed, as if it had been latent inside them, waiting for the possibility to unfold, like a butterfly inside a chrysalis. Although there are sometimes periods of confusion and disturbance as the old self-system fades away and the new one establishes itself, the process seems natural and inevitable.

As I've pointed out, this shift is much more common than is generally believed and is becoming more common. And again, this suggests that the wakeful self-system is ready to emerge within our collective psyche. It is already there, fully formed and integrated, but only able to emerge (at least for some people) when the old self-system dissolves away.

All of these are signs that the momentum of wakefulness is increasing, that it's beginning to unfold as the next stage in the evolution of life. As a result, it's manifesting itself in a variety of ways, in the same way that a rising water level manifests itself as overflowing rivers and lakes, and new streams, ponds, and tributaries. Wakefulness is also rising, and showing signs of its emergence everywhere.

A Cultural Shift

Wakefulness is showing signs of emergence in less direct ways, too — in *cultural* changes.

These changes, I believe, have been clearly visible for about 250 years. The second half of the eighteenth century was a very interesting time to be alive, particularly in Western Europe. For the previous few thousand years, Europe, like the rest of the world, had known little but brutality, oppression, and suffering. For the vast majority of people, life had been — in the words of the sixteenth-century philosopher Thomas Hobbes — "nasty, brutish and short." If you or I were able to travel back in time to, say, England in the early eighteenth century, we would be profoundly shocked by the cruelty and injustice we encountered, and the lack of compassion people showed to one another. We would be horrified by the brutality with which landlords and nobles treated peasants, by the cruel treatment of children, by the barbaric punishment of criminals (which often took place before crowds of cheering spectators), and the brutal treatment of animals. We would be shocked by the low status of women, who were unable to gain an education, take up any professions, or participate in any way in political or cultural life.

But in the second half of the eighteenth century, a shift started to occur. In *The Fall*, I refer to this as the Second Wave. The First Wave was the surge of spiritual exploration that began around three thousand years ago, when people in "fallen" cultures around the world began to realize that they were asleep and that it was possible to wake up; that is, they discovered that by following spiritual practices and paths they could transcend the limitations of normal awareness and experience a more expansive and harmonious state. For centuries, this spiritual exploration was confined to small groups of mystics and adepts, who were loosely — and often controversially — affiliated with mainstream religions, such as the Sufis of Islam, Christian mystics, the yogis of Hinduism, the monks of Buddhism, the followers of Kabbalah, and so on.

But the Second Wave brought more tangible and widespread signs of awakening. During this period, the second half of the eighteenth century, a new surge of compassion began to develop, together with a new awareness of the importance of justice and the rights of other human beings and other groups. This led to a whole host of social and cultural changes over the following decades, including the emergence of movements for women's rights, animal rights, and the abolition of slavery, and the development of concepts of democracy and egalitarianism, more lenient forms of punishment, and so on.

This was also the time of the French Revolution and the American constitution, both of which were responses to the gross injustices of the feudal system, and based on the principle that all human beings were born equal and entitled to the same opportunities and rights. And culturally, this was when the Romantic movement flourished, when poets, artists, and musicians developed a new relationship both to their own inner world and the natural world. The poets, painters, and musicians of the Romantic movement explored their inner beings in a way that artists had never done before and expressed a new ecstatic appreciation of the beauty and grandeur of nature. (In evolutionary terms, this suggests an expansion of both subjective and perceptual awareness.)

It was almost as if human beings were developing a new ability to transcend the separateness of the self-system of sleep. It was as if their identity was expanding beyond their own mind-space, bringing an ability to enter the mind-space of others and so to empathize with them and feel compassion for their sufferings. There was a new sense of connection — to other human beings, other living beings, and to the natural world in general.

At the same time, these changes suggest a different conceptual outlook, giving rise to new principles of justice and morality. There was a movement beyond egocentrism and self-centered morality toward a more universal perspective. There was a movement beyond group identity toward a sense of common humanity.

This process continued throughout the nineteenth century, expressing itself through new egalitarian political philosophies such as socialism and the spread of democracy. The women's rights movement gained increasing influence   women became able to own property independently of their husbands, go to university, and enter professions. (New Zealand became the first country to allow women to vote in 1897, with many others following over the next two or three decades.) In literature, novelists such as Charles Dickens, Emile Zola, and Fyodor Dostoyevsky documented the lives of their society's poorest and most downtrodden people, illustrating the increased sense of empathy and compassion that was developing.

During the twentieth century, the Second Wave intensified further and began to express itself in a wider variety of ways. The transcendence of ego-separation expressed itself as an increasing sense of connection to the body and an increasing openness to sex. A deepening connection to nature — and a wider conceptual outlook — gave rise to the ecological and environmental movements. Similarly, an increasing sense of empathy toward animals led to the popularity of vegetarianism and veganism (in addition to more awareness of animal rights).

Over the last few decades this psychological change has also — arguably — manifested itself in a decline in conflict and warfare throughout the world as a whole. It might not seem like it when we read the newspapers and watch television, but most historians agree that the last seventy years (since the end of the Second World War) have been the most peaceful period in recorded history, both in terms of conflicts between different countries and conflicts *within* countries (such as revolutions and civil wars). At the same time, over the past few decades, an increasing movement away from materialism toward simplicity has manifested itself in the downshifting and downsizing movements, based on an awareness that the consumerist lifestyle is an obstacle to well-being, rather than the source of it.

And finally, perhaps the biggest cultural change of the last few decades — and the strongest cultural sign of the occurrence of a collective movement toward wakefulness — is the massive (and still growing) upsurge in interest in spiritual philosophies and the spread of spiritual practices such as meditation, yoga, and other techniques of self-development. And it's significant that this increasing interest in spirituality has coincided with a decline in conventional religion. As we've seen, conventional religion can be seen as an attempt to compensate for the suffering generated by our sleep state. But now there seems to be growing movement to transcend our sleep state, rather than to simply escape its effects.

Everywhere there are signs of a growing sense of connection and empathy, a wider conceptual outlook, and a movement beyond both ego-isolation and egocentrism. At the same time, many of the behavioral traits linked to our sleep state, such as materialism and conventional theistic religion, have weakened — at least in some sections of society.

Particularly when coupled with the four direct individual signs of awakening I described above, these signs suggest that the human race is in the midst of a collective shift into a more expansive and higher-functioning state. Even if this process is a gradual and fitful one — and even if it may appear to be still in its nascent stages — we appear to be in the process of waking up.

The Trajectory of Human Evolution: Indigenous Wakefulness

But hold on, you might ask, didn't I suggest early on in this book that earlier human beings and indigenous peoples lived in a state of natural wakefulness? Didn't I say that our state of sleep occurred as a result of a "fall" out of this naturally wakeful state into separation and individuality? So how can wakefulness be an evolutionary advance when it was something that we already had but lost?

I do believe that earlier human beings and some of the world's indigenous peoples were naturally awake. The collective wakefulness that is developing now is, therefore, partly a return to that "unfallen" state. We are, in a sense, turning full circle.

But our collective awakening also means more than this. It means regaining what we lost at the same time as gaining something new. The wakefulness we're developing now is different from that of earlier human beings. At the same time as representing a return, it represents a progression. When our ancestors "fell" into a state of sleep, they lost earlier peoples' sense of connection to the world and their awareness of the sentience and sacredness of natural phenomena. But the Fall was also an advance, in that it enabled our ancestors to develop heightened intellectual and conceptual abilities.

It would be a mistake though to suggest that earlier human beings lived in an infant-like state. I think that the kind of wakefulness they experienced was more akin to our mature spiritual wakefulness than to the immature wakefulness we knew as children.[4] Unlike children, prehistoric and indigenous peoples clearly had (and have) some degree of individuality, practical and organizational ability, and ability to think abstractly and logically. (In fact, as I point out in *The Fall*, a great deal of evidence shows that prehistoric peoples were more technologically developed than is generally believed.) But when the Fall occurred, our ancestors became much more developed in these ways. We developed *increased* powers of abstraction, logic, and organization, which led to a more rational understanding of the world and significant technological and scientific advances. The Fall led to complex written languages and mathematics, and important inventions such as the wheel, metallurgy, and the plow. These were the positive sides of the highly individuated sense of ego that came with the Fall.

In fact, you could say that this was the very reason why the Fall occurred — these heightened intellectual powers became necessary. It's difficult to say what caused the Fall, but my suggestion (in the book of that name) is that it was due to an environmental change, a process of desertification that began around 4000 BCE and affected large parts of central Asia and central and southern Europe. It became much harder for the people who lived in these areas to survive, and in order to do so, they had to develop new practical and intellectual abilities, and a heightened sense of individuality. This entailed a reconstitution of the human psyche. A new, more individuated sense of ego formed, with heightened powers of abstraction and logic.

But because this new ego was so powerful, it required more energy, so the energy that human beings had previously always used *perceptually* was transferred to the ego. As I described in chapter 1, our ancestors' perception of the world became automatic as a way of conserving energy so that the new ego could have all the energy it needed to maintain its strong structure and its cognitive functioning. So our ancestors "fell" into a gray, shadowy world of familiarity and otherness, and became marooned in a meaningless inanimate world. (This is why we often have awakening experiences when our ego-minds become quiet and free of thoughts, because the energy that our ego-minds normally monopolize becomes freed up and is transferred back into perception. Our perceptions become deautomatized again.)

But what seems to be happening now — and the reason why we're undergoing an evolutionary advance rather than just a return — is that we're retaining the heightened intellectual and conceptual abilities we developed with the Fall, at the same time as *regaining* the heightened perceptual awareness and the sense of connection of earlier human beings. In fact, in conceptual terms, you could say that we're not just retaining conceptual abilities that our ancestors gained but also *extending* them by developing a much broader and deeper conceptual awareness. But far from becoming even more alienated from the world as a result of this, we're reconnecting with it. We're turning away from the shadows on the wall of the cave, back toward the radiant and vivid world that we lost sight of thousands of years ago.

In terms of the types of awareness we discussed earlier in this chapter, you could say that the Fall brought an increase in conceptual awareness (and intellectual ability) at the expense of a decrease in perceptual awareness. But in the Leap, this imbalance is corrected. Perceptual awareness increases to a similar level as before, without a decline in conceptual awareness (which actually increases, too).

Perhaps, most fundamentally, this is a matter of life-energy. The French philosopher Pierre Teilhard de Chardin believed that the process of evolution entails a progressive intensification of "spiritual energy" in living beings,[5] but I prefer to use the term *life-energy*. The increasing physical complexity of life-forms enables them to become more conscious and alive; that is, it facilitates an intensification of life-energy. As some contemporary philosophers have suggested, the purpose of the brain may not be to generate consciousness but to act as a receiver and a channel for it. According to this view, consciousness may be a fundamental force of the universe, which exists everywhere and in everything. The brain is like a radio set that receives consciousness and canalizes it into the individual being so that the person becomes individually conscious. It *localizes* consciousness in time and space so that we have the experience of being individual beings living through the moments of our lives. The more neurons a brain has, and the more intricately these are organized, the greater the intensity of consciousness it's able to receive.[6] But here, again, I'd use the term *life-energy* rather than *consciousness*. As cells become more numerous and more intricately organized, they enable living beings to become more imbued with life-energy, that is, more *alive*.

And this may be what is happening to us now. We're becoming more imbued with life-energy, more conscious and alive, which is precisely why we're able to regain heightened perceptual awareness without sac rificing our conceptual awareness and abilities. Fundamentally, it's the greater intensity of life-energy — or spiritual energy, using Teilhard de Chardin's term — that is generating this new wave of empathy and heightened awareness we're experiencing, together with our intensified conceptual awareness.

A possible problem with this argument, I'm aware, is that I've said that intensifying life-energy is linked to the increasing physical complexity, in particular of the brain. So am I saying that present-day human beings are more physically complex than our ancestors of, say, five hundred years ago, before this new influx of life-energy occurred?

Of course not. But the increasing complexity in this case may not lie in our brains or in us as individuals, but in us as a species. Over the last three hundred years, since the beginning of the industrial revolution, the human race has become increasingly interconnected in more and more complex ways. Distances have collapsed, borders and boundaries have faded away, populations have increased and merged, and new technologies have continually increased the communications and interactions between people. (Teilhard de Chardin believed this increasing interconnection was so significant that it was creating a whole new domain of reality — the *noosphere*, as he called it, which would unite the whole human race into a single inter-thinking group.) I admit that this is a very tentative idea, but it's conceivable that this increasing *global* interconnectivity is somehow facilitating (or at least is associated with) a collective intensification of life-energy.

The Time of Crisis — A Leap or a Collapse?

And this leads us to our present situation. Where are we now?

Despite the positive trends I've described above, we live in a time of crisis. It's true that we're living in a time of unprecedented spiritual awareness, unprecedented compassion and connection. But we're also living in a time of unprecedented danger. We live in a polarized world in which the trans-Fall movement I've described above is opposed by extremely negative trends. Although many people have begun to move beyond materialism, many others cling to materialist ideals more firmly. Obsession with celebrity and fashion and with the acquisition of material goods and status seems more entrenched than ever before, and it's spreading around the world. Although there's greater general concern for the environment than ever before, together with a greater sense of connection to the natural world, the destruction of the earth's life-support systems is continuing apace, with governments and global corporations still seeing the earth as little more than a supply of resources to be exploited. Although there's probably greater concern for the welfare of other species than ever before, some scientists estimate that between 150 and 200 plant or animal species are becoming extinct each day, due to human activities. Although many people are moving beyond group identity and conventional religion to an all-embracing spirituality, many others are clinging to their religious and national identity more firmly (as witnessed by the rise of Islamist terrorism, for example, the desire of many regions for independence, and the popularity of nationalist anti-immigrant political movements).

Perhaps we shouldn't be surprised that some of these opposing traits seem to be getting stronger. When a new phase begins, the characteristics of the previous one often become stronger and more entrenched, in response to the threat of their demise. You could compare it to how immigrant communities sometimes feel that their cultural values are threatened by the wider culture that surrounds them. In response, they cling to their values more firmly and become even more tradition-bound and resistant to change than members of their original culture. Essentially, the cultural conflict taking place now is between the old values and traits associated with our sleep state and the new values and traits associated with wakefulness. The old traits are threatened and so seem to be asserting themselves more strongly. It's almost as if, within our collective psyche, the self-system of sleep senses that it's being superseded and is trying to tighten its grip.

At the same time, the crisis we're going through could itself be having an awakening effect. The turmoil we're experiencing — ecological breakdown, economic instability, rampant materialism, the mass movement of populations due to poverty and warfare — isn't dissimilar to the kind of psychological turmoil that, for individuals, often precedes sudden awakening. You could even draw a parallel with encounters with death — which, as we saw in chapter 7, are the most powerful trigger of transformation. At the moment, we're *collectively* encountering mortality, facing our potential demise as a species. So this threat may be serving as a spur to collective transformation. The evolutionary leap was already under way before these problems became so serious, but perhaps it has become — and is becoming — more powerful as a result of them.

Waking Up in Time

The big question: Can we wake up collectively *in time?* Can the positive traits associated with wakefulness transcend the negative traits associated with sleep before our present crisis leads to catastrophe?

In relation to this, it's important to remember that our own individual psyche is connected to — and influences — our species as a whole. When we undergo awakening as individuals, we contribute to the awakening of our whole species. Our own Leap is part of the Leap of our whole species. As more and more of us move toward wakefulness, the easier it becomes for others to do the same. The blueprint of the wakeful self-system builds up within our collective psyche until eventually it may replace the self-system of sleep as the normal state that all human beings naturally develop in adulthood.

This is part of the reason why understanding wakefulness is so important, to help ensure that the people who undergo a sudden shift into awakening don't feel confused and repress their state (and aren't diagnosed as psychotic by psychiatrists). It's imperative that wakefulness is allowed to express itself so that its positive effects — both for the individual and our whole species — can manifest themselves in the world.

This is also why it's imperative for us as individuals to follow our own individual impulse to awaken. It's important for us not to suppress this impulse (perhaps under the misconception that making an effort to awaken is counterproductive) but to allow it to guide us toward spiritual practices and paths and consequently toward wakefulness. So long as we don't become too self-conscious and too rigid in our spiritual practice — in which case, it *may* become counterproductive — we, in our gradual awakening, contribute to the awakening of our whole species. When we follow this impulse to awaken in an organic way we act as agents of evolution, helping to intensify the shift that is already under way. Our own self-evolution contributes to the process of evolution itself.

Gradual awakening means practicing meditation and mindfulness, service and altruism. It means embracing quietness, simplicity, and inactivity so that we become comfortable within our inner space and learn to *be*. It means learning to quiet and disidentify with our random thought-chatter so that we know the peace of inner stillness and connect with our deepest nature. It means softening the strong boundaries of the ego so that we connect with other human beings, with nature, and with the whole cosmos. It means letting go of our psychological attachments to uncover the essence that they obscure and to allow our latent higher selves to emerge. And perhaps most fundamentally, as we saw in chapter 6, gradual awakening means remolding our psyche, transforming the self-system of sleep into the self-system of wakefulness.

There's no reason why this should involve any individual effort. It's not a question of pushing or striving, but rather of aligning ourselves with a process that is already under way, like allowing ourselves to float along with the fast-flowing current of a river. We don't need to swim, just let the river carry us. And at the same time, in a symbiotic way, our own momentum will intensify the momentum of the whole process itself. The universe wants us to wake up and will happily guide us toward wakefulness, if we create the right conditions.

The New World of Wakefulness

The discordant and disconnected "fallen" psyche has been creating ever more conflict and chaos in the world for thousands of years, and the process surely can't continue much longer. At the moment it's not clear whether the process is spiraling to a chaotic and cataclysmic end or leading to a new beginning. But if we do undergo collective transformation in time, and so survive as a species, we'll find ourselves in a different world. The dark and desperate world of sleep, which has blighted human life with so much psychological and social suffering over the last few thousand years, will give way to a bright, new world of wakefulness. The human race will move beyond rampant materialism and status seeking, beyond group identity, and beyond war and oppression. The whole human race will know a new radiant vision of reality, a new inner well-being and wholeness, a new all-embracing empathy and common sense of humanity, a new sense of connection to the natural world and the whole cosmos, and a new peace, both inwardly and outwardly. Our nightmare of discord and suffering will finally end. With a massive sense of relief, we will wake up to a new era of harmony and ease. And we will know that this isn't a delusion but actually the transcendence of a delusion, the uncovering of a deeper and truer reality.

Even if we don't survive, the earth will recover eventually. Evolution will continue. Its trajectory can't be reversed, only slowed down or frustrated temporarily. Eventually new living beings will emerge who will experience the expansiveness and clarity of wakefulness as their normal state. And evolution will continue even beyond that point, leading to new expanses and intensities of awareness that we can't conceive of. After all, there's no reason to assume that what we know as wakefulness is the end point of the evolutionary process, just as there's no reason to assume that our present state is.

But since we're so close to this collective awakening ourselves, right now, there's every reason for us to ensure that this process expresses itself fully — to ensure that we rise just a little higher, so that the Leap can complete itself.

The Human Race Will Rise Again

by Steve Taylor

The human race will rise again.
This chaos isn't inevitable; this discord won't last forever.
The evil that flows from us so easily isn't innate.
Our disorders are distortions, not permanent conditions,
symptoms of a disease which will one day be cured.

We weren't born for constant conflict,
to spend our lives fighting for survival, competing for recognition,
defending ourselves against oppression
with our minds infected with anxiety
and our souls corrupted with bitterness.
We were born for joy, and one day joy will return to us
as spring always returns, bursting with life and light
after the freezing winter.

The human race will rise again
as the cold hard masculine mind opens up
to the soft warm spirit of the feminine
as our solid frozen selves begin to melt
and merge with nature again
and selfishness gives way to empathy, and hierarchy to equality
and the impulse to connect transcends the desire for control.

The human race will rise again
as our senses begin to wake from centuries of sleep
and nature shines with sacredness again
and we're dazzled by the world's pristine beauty
and awed by the depths of meaning which reveal themselves
beneath the old flat surface of reality.

The human race will rise again, and is slowly rising now.
The shift is slowly settling.

Balance is returning, a new structure is emerging,
a pattern of vibrant new colors and shapes
with a new kind of harmony, more complex and dynamic,
an order that's stronger because it incorporates chaos,
a sanity that's deeper because it arose out of madness.

The human race will rise again.
The war will end, and the world will heal
and life will no longer be a frenzied struggle, full of stress and fear
but a glorious adventure, full of grace and ease,
no longer a punishment to be endured, but a privilege to be savored.

We were born for wholeness, and we will be whole again.
We were born for joy, and we will return to joy.

The human race will rise again.

Acknowledgments

First and foremost, I would like to express my deep gratitude to all of the people who have contacted me to share their experiences of awakening. In particular, I'm indebted to the participants of my PhD research, who allowed me to interview them at length. I'm also very grateful to Professor Les Lancaster, who, in addition to supervising my PhD research, has given so much to the field of transpersonal psychology over the last few decades. Thanks also to my technical assistant, Amber Fallon, for her patience and kindness. And finally, heartfelt thanks also to the team at New World Library and Eckhart Tolle Editions, especially to my editor, Jason Gardner, as well as to Munro Magruder, Marc Allen, Kim Eng, and Eckhart himself.

Appendix: An Inventory of Spiritual/Secular Wakefulness

(Taylor and Kilrea, 2016)

This inventory was based on studies of people who have undergone awakening, conducted by me and my co-researcher Kelly Kilrea. It was carefully examined and modified by other leading researchers (our "expert witnesses"), then piloted and amended, until it satisfied the criteria of standard psychological research tools.

After reading statements 1–28, select:

Strongly Agree

Agree

Neutral / Not Sure (if you neither agree nor disagree with the statement or are unable to decide)

Disagree

Strongly Disagree

1. I have an ongoing sense of inner contentment and ease.
2. I derive profound pleasure from engaging in ordinary activities.
3. I sense and know deeply that I am not my thoughts.
4. When life brings unexpected changes, it is fairly easy for me to accept and move on.
5. I experience a deep sense of union with life itself.
6. The past and future do not disturb my present experience.
7. I feel a sense of awe at the "is-ness" of the world around me.
8. How I look does not have any bearing on my self-worth or sense of identity.
9. I experience regular periods of mental quietness, when my mind is free of thoughts.
10. I feel intensely alive in my sensual experiences.

11. I feel deeply present.
12. I am incapable of causing intentional harm to anyone or anything.
13. I find it difficult to establish deep and authentic relationships.
14. I don't feel the need to belong to a group, community, or society, or conform to its conventions.
15. I feel intense aliveness in all of my senses.
16. Becoming a successful or prominent person is important to me.
17. I have no sense of needing to do anything; I am content to just be.
18. I notice my emotions as they arise without getting immersed in them.
19. Death frightens me.
20. I sense that seemingly separate things (like household objects, trees, and people) are part of the same all-pervading consciousness.
21. I feel equally connected and compassionate toward all human beings, regardless of their culture or country, and no matter how closely related they are to me.
22. There is a larger purpose or mission that is expressing itself through me.
23. I judge other people's behavior in my mind.
24. When making decisions I trust my feelings and intuition to take me in the right direction.
25. The world around me is intensely vivid and alive.
26. My sense of self-worth isn't affected by success or failure.
27. I often have a sense of timelessness.
28. I feel pressured to act in certain ways to gain acceptance.
29. In a short passage, please describe the most significant aspects of your perspective of the world and your perception of reality.

Note: Twenty-three of the statements are scored from 1 to 5, with 1 for strongly disagree, 2 for disagree, 3 for neutral/not sure, 4 for agree, and 5 for strongly agree. This excludes statements 13, 16, 19, 23, and 28, where the scoring sequence is reversed (so that strongly disagree scores as 5 and strongly agree scores as 1, etc.). Scores to the 28 statements should be totaled. A higher score indicates a more intense degree of wakefulness. Item 29 is included as a way of validating the responses to the inventory — that is, of testing whether the participants' responses match the way they describe their experience.

Notes

Introduction

1. McGinn, 1999.
2. Matthew 18:3, New International Version.

1. Falling Asleep, Longing to Awaken

1. Taylor, 2012b, p. 74.

2. Wakefulness in Different Cultures

1. Suzuki, 2000, p. 34.
2. In Spenser, 1963, p. 101.
3. Matthew 18:3, New International Version.
4. Lao-tzu, Chapters 28 and 55.
5. Lenski, 1978.
6. In Spenser, 1963, p. 321.
7. Lancaster, 2005; Hoffman, 2007.
8. In Underhill, 1911/1960.
9. In Underhill, 1911/1960, p. 389.
10. In Spenser, 1963, p. 241.
11. In Happold, 1986, p. 86.
12. In Spenser, 1963, p. 254.
13. Bhagavad Gita, 1988, p. 53.
14. Carpenter, 1906.
15. Brunton, 1972, p. 141.
16. Meister Eckhart, 1996, p. 11.
17. Upanishads, 1990, p. 103.
18. In van de Weyer, 2000, p. 7.
19. Bhagavad Gita, 1988, p. 68.
20. In van de Weyer, 2000, p. 8.
21. In Spenser, 1963, p. 200.
22. In Scharfstein, 1973, p. 28.

23. Upanishads, 1990, p. 111.
24.   To be pedantic, it might be more accurate to use the term *perennial phenomenology*, because the similarities between different traditions are basically experiential, and the term *phenomenology* refers to the study of experience. See Taylor (in press).

3. Natural Wakefulness: Awakened Artists

1. Whitman, 1980, p. 52.
2. Bucke, 1901.
3. Ibid.
4. Ibid. Interestingly, in my PhD study of twenty-five people who reported having undergone spiritual awakening, the average age at which awakening occurred was thirty-five. However, there were sixteen women participants and only nine men, which suggests that Bucke's gender bias was probably simply due to women's lack of opportunity to record cases of cosmic consciousness in male-dominated societies.
5. Ibid.
6. Ibid.
7. "Leaves of grass," (1881). Some people have suggested that Whitman was being mischievous here, and playing down his knowledge of Eastern philosophy. But even if this is true, it is unlikely that Whitman had any deep or detailed knowledge of Buddhist or Hindu teachings.
8. Bucke, 1901.
9. Whitman, 1980, p. 68.
10. Ibid., p. 95.
11. Ibid., p. 51.
12. Ibid., p. 220.
13. Ibid., p. 53.
14. Maslow, 1970, p. 163.
15. Whitman, 1980, p. 68.
16. Ibid., p. 348.
17. Ibid., p. 95.
18. Lawrence, 1923.
19. In Zang, 2011, p. xix.
20. Huxley, 1962, p. 1256.
21. Lawrence, 1994, p. 651.
22. Ibid., p. 578.
23. Ibid., p. 652.
24. Ibid., p. 700.
25. Huxley, 1962, p. 1265.
26. Lawrence, 1994, p. 676.
27. Jefferies, 1883, p. 86.
28. Ibid., p. 25.
29. Wordsworth, 1994, p. 205.
30. Ibid., p. 587.

31. Ibid., p. 511.
32. Blake, 2002, p. 88.
33. Shelley, 1994, p. 12.

4. Natural Wakefulness: Confusion and Integration

1. Peace Pilgrim, 1994, p. 2.
2. Ibid., p. 4.
3. Ibid.
4. Ibid., p. 7.
5. Ibid.
6. See Piechowski, 2009. I first read about Peace Pilgrim in this article.
7. Peace Pilgrim, 1994, p. 21.
8. Ibid., pp. 22–23.
9. Ibid., p. 73.
10. Ibid., p. 83.
11. As we've seen, Richard M. Bucke suggests that the onset of cosmic consciousness is most likely to occur between the ages of thirty and forty, while in my PhD thesis the average age at which awakening occurred was thirty-five. So it's interesting that Peace Pilgrim's state of wakefulness stabilized around the age of thirty, as did my own. Eckhart Tolle's spiritual awakening occurred at the age of twenty-nine, as did the awakening of my friend Russel Williams.

5. Gradual Awakening in Spiritual Traditions

1. This relates to the point I made in *Waking from Sleep* about the difference between ongoing and permanent wakefulness. Ongoing wakefulness is when awakening experiences are continually stimulated and merge into one another. There are certain activities such as meditation, contact with nature, or periods of silence and solitude, that generate awakening experiences quite reliably. So if you practice these activities regularly (as a monk might do, for example), it's possible that you might maintain an ongoing awakening experience. But this is different from an actual state of wakefulness. In terms of the metaphor I use here, ongoing wakefulness is like managing to keep outside of the house while it's still standing; in the wakeful state, the house is no longer there. Having said that, it's very likely that ongoing wakefulness will lead to permanent wakefulness by bringing about a gradual remolding of the self-system.
2. *Udana sutta*, 1998.
3. *Dhammapada*, 2005.
4. Yoga Kundalini Upanishad, 2013.
5. *Kundalini* can also be raised in a gradual and controlled way through the practice of *brahmacarya* (usually translated as "chastity" or "celibacy"). In *kundalini* yoga, *brahmacarya* isn't treated as a technique of suppression of sexuality based on a hostile attitude toward the body (as tends to be the case with celibacy in Christian

traditions), but as a dynamic process of transformation. In the practice of *urdhva-retas*, the instinctive energies associated with the lower chakras move upward and are transformed into the higher spiritual energy of *ojas*. This is a process of inner alchemy, in which energies are transmuted into a purer and higher form. There's a similar idea in Daoism, where spiritual development (or "cultivation," as it is more usually referred to) is also seen as an inner alchemy.

6. *Metta sutta*, 2004.

7. Deikman, 1980.

8. See, for example, Moore and Malinowski, 2009; Sauer, Walach, Offenbächer, Lynch, and Kohls, 2011; Tang, et al., 2007; Valentine and Sweet, 1999.

6. Gradual Awakening outside Spiritual Traditions

1. Williams, 2015, p. 76.

2. In Taylor, 2011, p. 25.

3. Ibid., p. 24.

7. Sudden Awakening: Transformation through Turmoil

1. Taylor, 2012a, p. 36.

2. Grof, 2000.

3. Ibid., p. 137.

4. Stanton, Bower, and Low, 2006.

5. Posttraumatic growth has been identified following life-threatening experiences such as combat (Maguen, Vogt, King, King, and Litz, 2006); natural disasters (Cryder, Kilmer, Tedeschi, and Calhoun, 2006); accidents (Snape, 1997); and other chronic illness besides cancer (Abraído-Lanza, Guier, and Colón, 1998).

6. Bray, 2011; Calhoun, Tedeschi, Cann, and Hanks, 2010.

7. van Lommel, 2004, p. 118.

8. Sabom, 1998.

9. In Taylor, 2011, p. 145.

10. Ibid., pp. 143–44.

11. "Wilko Johnson: 'Terminal cancer has made me feel alive.'" (2013, January 25).

12. Graham has published a book. See "Resources."

13. Reading spiritual literature can sometimes function as a kind of therapy, too, creating an opening for transformation. In chapter 6, we saw that it can sometimes be a factor in gradual awakening, and it can occasionally trigger sudden transformation during a period of psychological turmoil. For example, Moira, who was exhausted and depressed due to the demands of looking after a young baby, told me how she experienced a sudden awakening while "I was reading *The Power of Now* and looking at the space in the room when I suddenly felt my mind clear and I felt lighter as though all my problems had gone."

   Interestingly, I didn't find that spiritual practice was a major factor in transformation through turmoil. In theory, spiritual practice should make people more likely to undergo transformation by creating the same kind of opening as therapy. But perhaps this doesn't often occur simply because people who are caught up in intense turmoil are unlikely to be following spiritual practices. Spiritual practices and paths are more likely to be followed in times of stability and relative quietness. It's very difficult to meditate when your mind is full of stress and anxiety.

14. Sometimes it's difficult to distinguish posttraumatic transformation from cases where a person's natural wakefulness is being obstructed. A wakeful self-system that is ready to emerge but is being blocked often causes frustration. It's one of the basic laws of existence that the suppression or obstruction of natural processes creates tension and unease. This frustration can be powerful because the impulse to awaken is evolutionary and so has the whole force of evolution behind it. So in some cases, when a person experiences psychological turmoil prior to awakening, it's difficult to tell whether the turmoil is due to negative life events or the frustration of being unable to express their natural wakefulness. (Of course, it's highly likely that there will be turmoil from *both* sources.)

Eckhart Tolle is a possible example of this. He underwent a sudden spiritual awakening at the age of twenty-nine, after living for many years in what he describes as "a high state of anxiety, a state of depression, existential despair and anguish. There was a sense of great fear of life: fear of the future, fear of the meaninglessness underneath it all, but not wanting to fully face that meaninglessness and find out what underlies it." (Taylor, 2011, p. 105) There were some external factors that may have contributed to this state, such as the rootlessness of his family life, his parents' divorce, and his sense of isolation. However, it's also possible that Eckhart's depression and frustration stemmed from an innate wakefulness that wasn't able to express itself but which did eventually emerge, with great intensity, in his sudden awakening.

15. Williams, 2015, pp. 76–77.

8. Sudden Awakening: *Kundalini* and Energetic Awakening

1. Greyson, 1993.
2. Greenwell, 1995; Ring and Rosing, 1990.
3. Jnaneshvar, 1986, p. 130.
4. In Silburn, 1988, p. 42.
5. In my research, very few people located the source of this explosive energy specifically at (or close to) the bottom of the spine or described it as rising up through the spine. Most people gave more general descriptions of energy rising through their bodies or intensifying inside them. As two people whose experiences I didn't describe above put it, there was "a feeling of an energy rushing through my body" and "a tremendous amount of energy coursing through my body." A few other people reported experiences with similar characteristics to *kundalini* awakening but didn't actually describe them in terms of energy rising inside them. They spoke in terms of heat or light. For example, one person described a "huge golden bright light, circular" rising from her solar plexus, spinning and growing brighter until

it "moved through my body and filled my body. There was a flood of joy right through me." This suggests that the traditional concept of *kundalini* energy being coiled near the base of the spine and moving upward through a channel close to the spine may not be literally true.

6. Greenwell, 1995.
7. In Taylor, 2010, pp. 145–46.
8. In Taylor, 2012c.
9. Wade, 2004, p. 27.
10. Ibid. It is interesting, by the way, that all of the sexual awakening experiences I collected were from women. Jenny Wade also notes that the experiences appear to be more common among women. Perhaps this highlights a fundamental difference between male and female orgasms. According to Daoist teaching, because men and women are expressions of the archetypal forces of yin and yang, they experience sex differently and have different types of orgasm. The male orgasm is externalized and associated with expelling and dispersing energy, and reducing the life force. The female orgasm is internalized and has an intensifying and energizing effect (de Souza, 2011). From this point of view, it doesn't seem so surprising that sexual awakening experiences are more common in women.
11. Washburn, 1995, p. 82.

9. Other Types of Sudden Awakening: Is It Possible to Awaken through Psychedelics or Technology?

1. Stan Grof (2000) also notes that while spiritual emergencies are most commonly associated with intense psychological and emotional turmoil, they can also occur in response to spiritual practice, powerful sexual experiences, psychedelic experiences, or extreme physical exertion.
2. In Wong, 1998, p. 108.
3. Suzuki, 1964, p. 65.
4. Parsons, 1995, p. 20.
5. Ibid., pp. 20–21.
6. See, for example, Zaehner, 1972.
7. In Shaw, 2015, p. 301.
8. Grof, 2000.
9. A secondary shift sometimes follows from temporary awakening experiences. They often bring a new sense of optimism, trust, comfort, or confidence. For example, one person I spoke to had an intense awakening experience following a period of intense psychological turmoil and "felt the most intense love and peace and knew that all was well" (Taylor, 2011, p. 4). The experience probably only lasted for a few minutes, but in its aftermath she gained a new sense of appreciation and perspective, and a more positive outlook. As she told me, "I looked around and thought about all the good things in my life and the future. I felt more positive and resilient" (ibid.).

Awakening experiences bring an awareness of a new spiritual dimension of reality. The person was unaware of this dimension before, but now that they have glimpsed it they feel a strong desire to return to it. They often become interested in spiritual traditions and practices as a way of getting back there. For example, in an awakening experience apparently triggered by psychological turmoil, Emma described "a moment of enlightenment" in which "all my 'problems' and my suffering suddenly seemed meaningless, ridiculous, simply a misunderstanding of my true nature and everything around me" (Taylor, 2011, p. 8). The experience gave her a new spiritual awareness and awakened a lifelong interest in self-development. "In some ways," Emma told me, "I have spent the last 25 years since exploring what it meant and how I could perhaps go back there" (ibid.).

10. Huxley, 1988, p. 64.
11. Doblin, 1991. A similar 2006 study into the effects of psilocybin found that 60 percent of the volunteers described characteristics of mystical experiences, with just over one-third describing it as the most important spiritual experience of their lives, as significant as the birth of their first child. A follow-up study two months later found that most participants reported that their moods, attitudes, and behavior had become more positive, while psychological tests showed that they had a significantly higher level of well-being compared to other volunteers who were given a placebo at the same session (Griffiths et al., 2006).
12. McKenna, 2004, p. 122.
13. Hoffer, 1966.
14. See Chalmers (1996), Nagel (2012), and Kastrup (2014).
15. See Healy, 2015. Also Taylor, 2016a.

10. The Aftermath of Awakening: Spiritual Crisis

1. Upanishads, 1990, p. 86.
2. Roberts, 1993, p. 13.
3. Williams, 2015, pp. 114–15.
4. Ibid., p. 115.
5. Ibid., p. 116.
6. In Taylor, 2011, p. 170.
7. Spiritual Crisis Network, n. d.
8. Ibid.
9. Clarke, 2010, pp. 110–11.
10. Grof, 2000.
11. Phillips, Lukoff, & Stone, 2009, p. 8.

11. After the Storm: Lingering Traits and Questionable Teachers

1. Forman, 2011, p. 13.
2. Forman, 2012, p. 12.
3. Ibid.
4. Burkeman, 2009.
5. Cohen, 1992, p. 128.
6. In Benjamin, 2016.

12. What It Means to Be Awake: A New World and a New Self

1. Huxley, 1988. p. 121.
2. Williams, 2015, p. 94.
3. Ibid., p. 76.
4. In Taylor, 2011, p. 110.
5. Bhagavad Gita, 1988, p. 68.

13. What It Means to Be Awake: A New Mind and a New Life

1. This is what Ken Wilber calls the "worldcentric" or "universal" outlook, as opposed to the "egocentric" and "sociocentric" outlooks. At the egocentric stage, we're only concerned for our own well-being; at the sociocentric stage, we're identified with our group and our compassion and extend concern to members of the group but no further. But at the universal stage, as Wilber writes, "Awareness is no longer trapped and limited to my group or my tribe or my nation, but opens to a universal, global, worldcentric awareness, where all people are treated with justice and fairness, regardless of race, sex religion or creed" (Wilber, 2000, p. 158).
2. Adiswarananda, n. d.
3. The psychologist Lawrence Kohlberg (1981) describes this as a "post-conventional" morality. In sleep, people are much more likely to experience what Kohlberg calls "pre-conventional" or "conventional" levels of morality. At the pre-conventional level, morality means simply following your own desires, without considering how your behavior affects others. Your only real guiding principles are to avoid punishment and to gain reward. "Good" is simply what is good for you. At the conventional level, morality means obeying social rules, abiding by laws and moral codes, and doing what is right for your country, or what the majority of your fellow citizens would expect you to do. But at the post-conventional level, morality stems from an overriding sense of right and wrong.
4. Lawrence, 1994, p. 610.
5. Abraham Maslow recognized this autonomy as a characteristic of "self-actualizers." In his words, they were characterized by "independence of culture and environment" and "resistance to enculturation; the transcendence of any particular culture" (Maslow, 1971, p. 129).
6. See Taylor, 2012b.
7. Robinson, 1977; Hoffman, 1992.
8. Maslow makes a similar point about "peak experiences" in relation to traditional spiritual and mystical experiences. He likens peak experiences to "raw materials which can be used for different styles of structures, as the same bricks and mortar and lumber would be built into different kinds of houses by a Frenchman, a Japanese, or a Tahitian" (Maslow, 1994, p. 73).

14. The Natural Wakefulness of Children

1. Wordsworth, 1994, p. 587.
2. In Happold, 1986, p. 368.

3. Lao-tzu, Chapters 28 and 55.

4. Matthew 18:3, New International Version.

5. Wilber, 1997. This is an example of what Wilber calls the "pre/trans fallacy," which explains that it's easy to confuse "pre-rational" states of development with "trans-rational" ones, and vice versa. It's also an example of what he calls "retro-romanticism," our tendency to romanticize earlier phases of development. In Wilber's view, this applies to cultural development, too, so that we tend to romanticize earlier human cultures, when they were in fact much less advanced than ours.

6. Bindl, 1965.

7. Pafford, 1973.

8. Gopnik, 2009, p. 125.

9. Ibid., p. 131.

10. Ibid., p. 129.

11. Robinson, 1977, p. 53.

12. Ibid., p. 96.

13. Ibid., p. 49.

14. Ibid., p. 55.

15. Hoffman, 1992, pp. 38–39. One potential issue here is that reports of childhood spiritual experiences could be seen as questionable because they are retrospective — for example, sometimes elderly people describe experiences they had when they were four years old — and are conveyed in language that children couldn't possibly use. However, as Michael Piechowski (2001) points out, spiritual experiences are so powerful and unusual that they're remembered much more vividly and with less distortion than other experiences. In addition, the memories of children are more reliable than is generally believed. For example, research by Sheingold and Tenney (1982) found that three- and four-year-olds can recall the events of a year ago with a great deal of accuracy, and no less accurately than eight year olds. And in relation to language, spiritual experiences are by their nature translingual. Even as adults we struggle to describe them, with the subject/object duality of language, the different tenses, and the paucity of vocabulary for refined and intense states of awareness. An adult will certainly be able to explain the experience more clearly than a child, but only because of their wider vocabulary and ability to use metaphor. But that has no bearing on the experience itself, which exists prior to and beyond language.

16. Gopnik, 2009.

17. Warneken, 2013, 2015.

18. Gopnik, 2009, p. 212.

19. This is probably why childhood awakening experiences are rarely, in the terminology used by the scholar of mysticism Walter Stace (1964), "introvertive" experiences. That is, they're rarely experiences of withdrawing from the external world and attaining a state of inner well-being and spaciousness, or, at a higher intensity, a state of inner emptiness or pure consciousness in which we touch into the spiritual essence of all reality. They are almost always "extravertive"; that is, they are mainly experiences of heightened awareness and connection or union.

20. Wordsworth, 1994, p. 587.

15. Demythologizing Wakefulness

1. In Caplan, 1999, p. 517.
2. Williams, 2015, p. 149.
3. In Dossey, 2010, p. 10.
4. Ibid, p. 11.
5. See Taylor, 2016b.
6. Ramana Maharshi, 1991.
7. This concept was originally developed by John Welwood in his 1983 book *Awakening the Heart*.
8. Whitman, 1980, p. 105.

16. The Evolutionary Leap: A Collective Awakening

1. I'm certainly not the first person to put forward such a spiritual view of evolution. Many philosophers have suggested that evolution is a purposeful process of the unfolding and intensification of consciousness, including the German philosophers Georg Wilhelm Freidrich Hegel and Johann Gottlieb Fichte, the French philosophers Henri Bergson and Pierre Teilhard de Chardin, and the American philosopher Ken Wilber. Hegel saw human history as a progressive unfolding of spirit, leading to a state of reason — the culmination of human development — in which there's no distinction between the objective and subjective, and all things merge into oneness. Teilhard de Chardin saw evolution as a process of the spiritualization of matter, which was progressing toward an "Omega Point." This is the culmination of the whole evolutionary process, when all matter is wholly infused with spiritual energy and all phenomena, including human beings, become one. In his book *Cosmic Consciousness*, which I referred to in chapter 3, Richard M. Bucke describes his conviction that cosmic consciousness is a stage of development that awaits the human species as a whole. Bucke distinguishes two other types of consciousness. First, there is the simple consciousness of animals (and early human beings), which means that they are aware of their surroundings and have the ability to respond to changes in their environment. Second, there is the self-consciousness of human beings, which probably developed, according to Bucke, just a few thousand years ago. This means that, for the first time, in addition to being aware of their surroundings, human beings are aware of themselves. And now we're witnessing the onset of cosmic consciousness. Although, according to Bucke, it is quite rare at the moment, cosmic consciousness is becoming increasingly common and will eventually spread to every member of the human race. In the future, it will become human beings' normal state, which we all naturally develop into in adulthood.
2. For a powerful critique of the limitations of neo-Darwinism, see the philosopher Thomas Nagel's book *Mind and Cosmos* (2012).
3. O'Rourke, 2004.
4. To be more specific, of all the characteristics we looked at in chapters 12 and 13, the only ones I feel that primal human beings didn't possess were the conceptual

characteristics of "lack of group identity" and "wide perspective / universal out-look." Most primal peoples had a strong sense of tribal identity, although this prob-ably wasn't prompted by a need for security and belonging (as it is for most modern humans) but simply the result of a lack of other cultural references. Similarly, their lack of a universal outlook was probably the simple result of their narrow experi-ence of the world and other cultures.

5. Teilhard de Chardin, 1961.
6. See Chalmers (1996), Forman (1998), and also Kastrup (2014).

Bibliography

Abraído-Lanza, A. F., Guier, C., and Colón, R. M. (1998). Psychological thriving among Latinas with chronic illness. *Journal of Social Issues*, 54(2), 405–24.

Adiswarananda, Swami. (n. d.). Sri Ramakrishna. Retrieved from http://www .ramakrishna.org/rmk.htm.

Benjamin, E. (2016). Andrew Cohen's apology. Retrieved from http://www.integral world.net/benjamin79.html.

Bhagavad Gita. (1988). (J. Mascaro, Trans.). London, England: Penguin.

Bindl, M. (1965). *Religious experience mirrored in pictures: A developmental psychological investigation*. Freiburg, Germany: Herder.

Blake, W. (2002). *Collected poems* (W. B. Yeats, Ed.). London, England: Routledge.

Bray, P. (2011). Bereavement and transformation: A psycho-spiritual and post-traumatic growth perspective. *Journal of Religion and Health*, 52(3), 890–903.

Brunton, P. (1972). *A search in secret India*. London, England: Rider.

Bucke, R. M. (1901). *Cosmic consciousness: A study in the evolution of the human mind*. Retrieved from http://www.sacred-texts.com/eso/cc/.

Burkeman, O. (2009). The bedsit epiphany. Retrieved from http://www.theguardian .com/books/2009/apr/11/eckhart-tolle-interview-spirituality.

Calhoun, L. G., Tedeschi, R. G., Cann, A., and Hanks, E. A. (2010). Positive outcomes following bereavement: Paths to posttraumatic growth. *Psychologica Belgica*, 50(1), 125–43.

Caplan, M. (1999). *Halfway up the mountain*. Chino Valley, AZ: Hohm Press.

Carpenter, E. (1906). *Days with Walt Whitman: With some notes on his life and work*. London, England: George Allen & Unwin. Retrieved from http://www.whitman archive.org/criticism/interviews/transcriptions/med.00571.html.

Chalmers. D. (1996). *The conscious mind: In search of a fundamental theory*. Oxford, England: Oxford University Press.

Clarke, I. (Ed.). (2010). *Psychosis and spirituality: Consolidating the new paradigm*. Chichester, England: Wiley-Blackwell.

Cohen, A. (1992). *Autobiography of an awakening*. Corte Madera, CA: Moksha Press.

Cryder, C. H, Kilmer, R. P., Tedeschi, R. G., and Calhoun, L. G. (2006). An exploratory study of posttraumatic growth in children following a natural disaster. *The American Journal of Orthopsychiatry*, 76(1), 65–69.

Deikman, A. (1980). Deautomatization and the mystic experience. In R. Woods (Ed.), Understanding mysticism (pp. 240–60). London, England: Athlone Press.

Dhammapada. (2005). Retrieved 14/4/16 from http://www.accesstoinsight.org/ptf/dhamma/sacca/sacca4/samma-samadhi/jhana.html.

Doblin, R. (1991). Pahnke's "Good Friday experiment": A long-term follow-up and methodological critique. The Journal of Transpersonal Psychology, 23(1), 1–28.

Dossey, B. M. (2010). Florence Nightingale: A 19th century mystic. Journal of Holistic Nursing, 28(1), 10–35.

Forman, R. (1998). What does mysticism have to teach us about consciousness? Journal of Consciousness Studies, 5(2), 185–201.

Forman, R. (2011). Enlightenment ain't what it's cracked up to be. Ropley, England: O-Books.

Forman, R. (2012). Enlightenment ain't what it's cracked up to be. The Network Review, 109, 12–14.

Gopnik, A. (2009). The philosophical baby. London: Bodley Head.

Greenwell, B. (1995). Energies of transformation: A guide to the kundalini process. Cupertino, CA: Shakti River Press.

Greyson, B. (1993). Near-death experiences and the physio-kundalini syndrome. Journal of Religion and Health, 32(4), 277–90.

Griffiths, R. R., Richards, W. A., McCann, U., and Jesse, R. (2006). Psilocybin can occasion mystical-type experiences having substantial and sustained personal meaning and spiritual significance. Psychopharmacology, 187, 268–83. doi: 10.1007/s00213-006-0457-5.

Grof. S. (2000). The psychology of the future. Albany, NY: New York Press.

Happold, F. C. (1986). Mysticism: A study and anthology. London, England: Pelican.

Healy, D. (2015). Serotonin and depression: The marketing of a myth. Retrieved from http://2spl8q29vbqd3lm23j2qv8ck.wpengine.netdna-cdn.com/wp-content/uploads/2015/07/2015-Serotonin-and-Depression-bmj.h1771.pdf.

Hoffer, A. (1966). New hope for alcoholics. New York, NY: University Books.

Hoffman, E. (1992). Visions of innocence. Boston, MA: Shambhala.

Hoffman, E. (2007). The way of splendour: Jewish mysticism and modern psychology. New York, NY: Rowman and Littlefield.

Huxley, A. (1962). Introduction by Aldous Huxley to the letters of D. H. Lawrence. In H. T. Moore (Ed.), The letters of D. H. Lawrence (pp. 1247–68). London, England: Heinemann.

Huxley, A. (1988). The doors of perception and Heaven and hell. London, England: Penguin.

Jefferies, R. (1883). The story of my heart: An autobiography. Retrieved from http://richardjefferiessociety.co.uk/Story%20of%20My%20Heart.pdf.

Jnaneshvar, Sri. (1986). Jnaneshvari. Albany, NY: State University of New York Press.

Kastrup, B. (2014). Why materialism is baloney. Southampton, England: Iff Books.

Kohlberg, L. (1981). Essays on moral development, Vol. I: The philosophy of moral development. San Francisco, CA: Harper.

Lancaster, L. (2005). The essence of Kabbalah. London, England: Arcturus.

Lao-tzu. (n. d.). *Tao teh king*. (J. Legge, Trans.). Retrieved from http://www.thetao.info /english/english.htm.

Lawrence, D. H. (1923). Chapter 12: Whitman. *Studies in American literature*. Retrieved from http://xroads.virginia.edu/~hyper/lawrence/dhlch12.htm.

Lawrence, D. H. (1994). *Complete poems*. London, England: Penguin.

"Leaves of grass." (1881). (Commentary on the book *Leaves of grass*). *The Boston Globe*. Retrieved from http://www.whitmanarchive.org/criticism/reviews/leaves1881 /anc.00209.html.

Lenski, G. (1978). *Human societies* (2nd ed.). New York, NY: McGraw-Hill.

van Lommel, P. (2004). About the continuity of our consciousness. In C. Machado and D. A. Shewmon (Eds.), *Brain death and disorders of consciousness* (pp. 115–32). New York, NY: Kluwer Academic/Plenum Publishers.

Lukoff, D., Lu, F., and Turner, R. (1998). From spiritual emergency to spiritual problem: The transpersonal roots of the new DSM-IV Category. *Journal of Humanistic Psychology*, 38(2), 21–50.

Maguen, S., Vogt, D. S., King, L. A., King, D. W., and Litz, B. T. (2006). Posttraumatic growth among Gulf War I veterans: The predictive role of deployment-related experiences and background characteristics. *Journal of Loss and Trauma*, 11(5), 373–88.

Maslow, A. (1970). *Motivation and personality* (2nd ed.). New York, NY: Harper and Row.

Maslow, A.(1971). *The further reaches of human nature*. New York, NY: Viking.

Maslow, A. (1994). *Religious, values and peak experiences*. New York, NY: Arkana.

McGinn, C. (1999). *The mysterious flame: Conscious minds in a material world*. New York, NY: Basic Books.

McKenna, D. J. (2004). Clinical investigations of the therapeutic potential of ayahuasca: Rationale and regulatory challenges. *Pharmacology & Therapeutics*, 102(2), 111–29.

Meister Eckhart. (1996). *Meister Eckhart: From whom God hid nothing*. (D. O'Neal, Ed.). Boston, MA: Shambhala.

Metta sutta. (2004). (Amaravati Sangha, Trans.). Retrieved 13/2/16 from http://www .accesstoinsight.org/tipitaka/kn/snp/snp.1.08.amar.html.

Moore, A., and Malinowski, P. (2009). Meditation, mindfulness and cognitive flexibility. *Consciousness & Cognition*, 18(1), 176–86.

Nagel, T. (2012). *Mind and cosmos*. Oxford, England: Oxford University Press.

O'Rourke, F. (2004). Aristotle and the metaphysics of evolution. *The Review of Metaphysics*, 58(1), 3–59.

Pafford, M. (1973). *Inglorious Wordsworths: A study of some transcendental experiences in childhood and adolescence*. London, England: Hodder & Stoughton.

Parsons, T. (1995). *The open secret*. Shaftesbury, England: Open Secret Publishing.

Peace Pilgrim. (1994). *Her life and work in her own words*. Santa Fe, NM: Ocean Tree Books.

Phillips, R., Lukoff, D., and Stone, M. K. (2009). Integrating the spirit within psychosis: Alternative conceptualization of psychotic disorders. *Journal of Transpersonal Psychology*, 41, 61–80.

Piechowski, M. (2001). Childhood spirituality. *Journal of Transpersonal Psychology*, 33, 1–15.

Piechowski, M. (2009). Peace Pilgrim, exemplar of level V. *Roeper Review*, 31(2), 103–12.

Ramana Maharshi. (1991). *Be as you are: The teachings of Ramana Maharshi*. (D. Godman, Ed.). London, England: Arkana.

Ring, K., and Rosing, C. (1990). The omega project: An empirical study of the NDE-prone personality. *Journal of Near-Death Studies*, 8(4), 211–39.

Roberts, B. (1993). *The experience of no-self*. Albany, NY: SUNY.

Robinson, E. (1977). *The original vision: A study of religious experience of childhood*. Oxford, England: Religious Experience Research Unit.

Sabom, M. (1998). *Light and death: One doctor's fascinating account of near-death experiences*. Grand Rapids, MI: Zondervan.

Sauer, S., Walach, H., Offenbächer, M., Lynch, S., and Kohls, N. (2011). Measuring mindfulness: A Rasch analysis of the Freiburg Mindfulness Inventory. *Religions*, 2(4), 693–706.

Scharfstein, B. (1973). *Mystical experience*. Oxford, England: Basil Blackwell.

Shaw, G. (2015). Platonic siddhas: Supernatural philosophers of Neoplatonism. In E. F. Kelly, A. Crabtree, and P. Marshall (Eds.), *Beyond physicalism: Toward reconciliation of science and spirituality* (pp. 275–314). Lanham, MD: Rowman & Littlefield.

Sheingold, K., and Tenney, Y. (1982). Memory from a salient childhood. In U. Neisser (Ed.), *Memory observed*. New York, NY: W. H. Freeman.

Shelley, P. B. (1994). *The selected poems and prose of P. B. Shelley*. Ware, England: Wordsworth Editions.

Silburn, L. (1988). *The energy of the depths: A comprehensive study based on the scriptures of nondualistic Kashmir Shivaism* (V. J. Pradhan, Trans.). Albany, NY: State University of New York Press.

Snape, M. C. (1997). Reactions to a traumatic event: The good, the bad and the ugly? *Psychology, Health & Medicine*, 2(3), 237–42.

de Souza, E. (2011). Health and sexuality: Daoist practice and Reichian therapy. In L. Kohn (Ed.), *Living authentically: Daoist contributions to modern psychology*. St. Petersburg, FL: Three Pines Press.

Spenser, S. (1963). *Mysticism*. London, England: Pelican Books.

Spiritual Crisis Network. (n. d.). Our Description. Retrieved from http://spiritualcrisis network.org.uk/what-is-sc/our-description.

Stace, W. (1964). *Mysticism and philosophy*. Los Angeles, CA: J. P. Tarcher.

Stanton, A. L., Bower, J. E., and Low, C. A. (2006). Posttraumatic growth after cancer. In L. G. Calhoun and R. Tedeschi (Eds.), *Handbook of posttraumatic growth: Research and practice* (pp. 138–75). Mahwah, NJ: Lawrence Erlbaum Associate Publishers.

Suzuki, D. T. (1964). *An introduction to Zen Buddhism*. New York, NY: Grove Press.

Suzuki, D. T. (2000). *The awakening of Zen*. Boston, MA: Shambhala.

Tang, Y. Y., Ma, Y., Wang, J., Fan, Y., Feng, S., Lu, Q., and Posner, M. I. (2007). Short-term meditation training improves attention and self-regulation. *Proceedings of the National Academy of Sciences*, 104(43), 17152–56.

Taylor, S. (2009). Beyond the pre/prans fallacy: The validity of pre-egoic spiritual experience. *The Journal of Transpersonal Psychology*, 41(1), 22–43.

Taylor, S. (2010). *Waking from sleep: The sources of awakening experiences and how to make them permanent.* London, England: Hay House.

Taylor, S. (2011). *Out of the darkness: From turmoil to transformation.* London, England: Hay House.

Taylor, S. (2012a). Transformation through suffering: A study of individuals who have experienced positive psychological transformation following periods of intense turmoil and trauma. *The Journal of Humanistic Psychology*, 52(1), 30–52.

Taylor, S. (2012b). Spontaneous awakening experiences: Exploring the phenomenon beyond religion and spirituality. *The Journal of Transpersonal Psychology*, 44(1), 73–91.

Taylor, S. (2012c). Transcendent sex: How sex can generate higher states of consciousness. Retrieved from https://www.psychologytoday.com/blog/out-the-darkness/201201/transcendent-sex.

Taylor, S. (2016a). Chemical lobotomy: The madness of the mass prescription of psychotropic drugs. Retrieved from https://www.psychologytoday.com/blog/out-the-darkness/201603/chemical-lobotomy.

Taylor, S. (2016b). A model of purpose: From survival to transpersonal purpose. *Transpersonal Psychology Review*, 18(1), 12–25.

Taylor, S. (in press). From philosophy to phenomenology: The argument for a "soft" perennialism. *The International Journal of Transpersonal Studies.*

Teilhard de Chardin, P. (1961). *The phenomenon of man.* New York, NY: Harper.

Udana sutta. (1998). (J. D. Ireland, Trans.). Retrieved from http://www.accesstoinsight.org/tipitaka/kn/ud/ud.5.05.irel.html.

Underhill, E. (1960). *Mysticism.* London, England: Methuen. (Original work published in 1911.)

Upanishads. (1990). (J. Mascaro, Ed. and Trans.). London, England: Penguin.

Valentine, E. R., and Sweet, P. L. G. (1999). Meditation and attention: A comparison of the effects of concentrative and mindfulness meditation on sustained attention. *Mental Health, Religion & Culture*, 2(1), 59–70.

Wade, J. (2000). Mapping the course of heavenly bodies: The varieties of transcendent sexual experiences. *Journal of Transpersonal Psychology*, 32(2), 103–22.

Wade, J. (2004). *Transcendent sex: When lovemaking opens the veil.* New York, NY: Paraview Pocket Books.

Warneken, F. (2013). Young children proactively remedy unnoticed accidents. *Cognition*, 126(1), 101–8.

Warneken, F. (2015). Precocious prosociality: Why do young children help? *Child Development Perspectives*, 9(1), 1–6.

Washburn, M. (1995). *The ego and the dynamic ground.* Albany, NY: SUNY Press. (Originally published in 1980.)

Welwood, J. (1983). *Awakening of the Heart.* Boston: Shambhala.

van de Weyer, R. (Ed.). (2000). *366 readings from Buddhism.* Cleveland, OH: Pilgrim Press.

Whitman, W. (1980). *Leaves of grass.* New York, NY: Signet Books.

Wilber, K. (1997). *The eye of spirit: An integral vision for a world gone slightly mad.* Boston, MA: Shambhala.

Wilber, K. (2000). *Integral psychology.* Boston, MA: Shambhala.

"Wilko Johnson: 'Terminal cancer has made me feel alive.'" (2013, January 25). Retrieved from http://www.bbc.co.uk/news/entertainment-arts-21187740.

Williams, R. (2015). *Not I, not other than I: The life and teachings of Russel Williams.* Ropley, England: O-Books.

Wong, K. K. (1998). *The complete book of Zen.* London, England: Vermillion.

Wordsworth, W. (1994). *The works of William Wordsworth.* Ware, England: Wordsworth Editions.

Yoga Kundalini Upanishad. (2013). Retrieved from http://www.purna-yoga.ru/en/library/text/ancent/Yoga-Kundalini_Upanishad.pdf.

Zaehner, R. C. (1972). *Drugs, mysticism and make-believe.* London, England: Collins.

Zang, T. (2011). *D. H. Lawrence's philosophy of nature: An Eastern view.* Bloomington, IN: Trafford Publishing.

Resources

If you are undergoing a disruptive sudden spiritual awakening (or spiritual crisis), the following websites will help:

Spiritual Crisis Network
http://spiritualcrisisnetwork.uk

Spiritual Emergence Network
http://spiritualemergence.info

EmmaBragdon.com
http://emmabragdon.com

Some of the people I interviewed have their own websites — and have published books — as a way of sharing their experience of awakening:

Gavin Whyte (chapter 4)
Gavin has published a number of books, including *The Girl with the Green-Tinted Hair* (Huddersfield, UK: Being Books, 2015).

Cheryl Smith (chapter 6)
Being Mrs. Smith: A Very Unorthodox Love Story (Ropley, UK: O-Books, 2016)

JC Mac (chapter 7)
The Anatomy of a Spiritual Meltdown (jcmacsbook.blogspot.co.uk)

Graham Stew (chapter 7)
Too Simple for Words: Reflections on Non-Duality (Ropley, UK: O-Books, 2016)

Kimberley Jones (chapter 8)
www.kimberleyjones.com

William Murtha (chapter 10)
Dying for a Change: Survival, Hope, and the Miracle of Choice (Bloomington, IN: Transformation Media Books, 2009)

If you would like to share your own experience of wakefulness, you can do so through my website: www.stevenmtaylor.com.

Index

Abhisamayalamkara, 80
abiding in God (*baqa*), 3, 36, 38
absorption, 15, 16
abstinence, 62
abstraction, state of, 15–16
acceptance, power of, 117
accidents, 113. *See also* death
accumulation, beyond (nonmaterialism), 206–7
actionless activity (*wu wei*), 40
active idealism, 230
ADHD (attention deficit hyperactivity disorder), 155
adulthood, fall into (children), 232–34
alcoholism, sudden awakening because of, 106
Al-Ghazali, 40
Al-Hallaj, Mansur, 32
aliveness, 188
aloneness, feeling of, 19
Alpert, Richard, 152, 153
altruism, 23, 39, 84–85, 106, 204–5; Kabbalah, 33
animals, self-awareness of, 252
anticipation as thought-chatter, 15
anxiety, 16, 23
appreciation, 203–4
arahant (fully realized being), 28
artists, 43–59. *See also specific artists*
ascetic self-discipline, 76
atman (individual self), 27, 195, 214
attachments: beyond (nonmaterialism), 206–7; and involuntary gradual awakening, 98–101
attention deficit hyperactivity disorder, 155
Aurobindo, Sri, 79
authenticity, living with, 207–8; in relationships, 209–10

authoritarianism, 181
autonomy, 207–8
awakening, 1, 3; after (lingering traits), 175–82; in artists, 43–59; behavioral characteristics of, 204–10; characteristics of, 183–98; children and, 221–22, 225–27; Christian mystics, 34; cognitive characteristics of, 200–204; collective, 251–68; and concept of evolution, 253–54; conceptual characteristics of, 18–19, 200–204; crises, 264–65; definition of, 10, 11; deintensified perception, 17–18; differentiating psychosis and, 171–74; discovery of experiences, xi; evidence for evolutionary leaps, 255–57; gradual, 75–88, 158 (*see also* gradual awakening); higher-intensity experiences (children), 227–28; impulse to awaken, 256; indigenous wakefulness, 260–64; *kundalini*, 129–39, 165; mature and immature wakefulness, 228–30; meaningfulness of, 199–218; new self, 189–98; new world of wakefulness, 267–68; paths and practices of, 77–81; and Peace Pilgrim, 62–65; perceptual characteristics of, 184–88; perennial psychology, 213–16; process of, 8, 28; psychedelic substances and, 75, 76; *savikalpa*, 26; sexual awakening experiences, 136–37; shifts in, 150–53; sleep, 13–17, 19–20; spiritual crises, 157–74; spiritual literature as practice, 95; state of waking up, 13–24; sudden, 24, 157, 158 (*see also* sudden awakening); Taylor, Steve, 67–73; temporary, 6, 20–24; through psychological turmoil, 257; transformation

awakening (*continued*)
  through turmoil, 105–27; types of aware-
    ness, 252–53; wakeful vision of the world,
    216–18; and Whyte, Gavin, 65–67; and
    Williams, Russel, 163
awareness, 16, 252; conceptual, 218, 252–53;
    perceptual, 252–53; of presence, 187–88; of
    reality, 40, 218; subjective, 252–53
ayahuasca, 146, 147, 151. *See also* psychedelics

Ba'al Shem Tov, 256
Back to Sanity (Taylor), 15, 16
baqa (abiding in God), 3, 36, 38
being-consciousness-bliss (*satchitananda*), 37
bereavement: examples of sudden awakening
    due to, 116–19, 119–22; sudden awakening
    because of, 106, 115–22. *See also* death
Bhagavad Gita, 26, 37, 39, 47; inner security,
    198
bliss, 138–39, 188; examples of sudden awak-
    ening, 110–12; spiritual crises and, 157; and
    wakefulness, 239–40
bodhi (enlightenment), 3, 10
boredom, 205–6
brahman (spirit-force), 27, 29, 36, 37, 44, 51,
    80, 188; and Lawrence, D. H., 55; Meister
    Eckhart's Godhead concept of, 214; and
    Taylor, Steve, 71, 72; and well-being, 195;
    and Whitman, Walt, 53; and Wordsworth,
    William, 57
brain, study of activity, 4
Brunton, Paul, 37
Bucke, Richard M., 48, 49, 50, 199
Buddha, 47, 48, 256
Buddhaghosa, 80
Buddhism, 1, 3, 25, 30, 121; Ch'an (Chinese
    Buddhist), 141, 142, 144; Eightfold Path, 78,
    141; ethical behavior, 82; gradual awakening
    in, 76, 80; meditation, 85–87; *metta bhavana*,
    85; monastic lifestyles, 81; purgation and
    purification, 83; reincarnation, 28; spiritual
    energy, all-pervading, 187; temporary
    confusion, 162; unwholesome mental states
    (*kleshas*), 175; wakefulness (concepts of),
    27–28; Whyte, Gavin, 66; Zen, 141, 142, 144
Buddhist Heart Sutra, 39

Camus, Albert, 217
cancer and sudden awakening, 114–15

capitalism, 73
Carpenter, Edward, 37
Catherine of Genoa, 35, 242
Catherine of Siena, 241
celibacy, 83
chakras, 129–39
challenges, xi
Chalmers, David, 154
Ch'an (Chinese Buddhist), 141, 142, 144
children, 219; characteristics of awakening,
    225–27; childhood awakening experiences,
    221–22; creativity as, 226; energy and
    development, 138–39; fall into adulthood,
    232–34; higher-intensity awakening experi-
    ences and, 227–28; lack of ego-separateness
    in, 227; mature and immature wakefulness
    in, 228–30; natural wakefulness of, 219–34;
    perceptions as, 46; perceptual wakefulness
    of, 222–25; and self-system, 231–32; and
    spiritual traditions, 219–20; temporary
    awakening during, 221–22
China, spiritual practices in, 29
chi (vital energy), 81
Christianity, 1, 3, 30, 121; as conceptual reli-
    gion, 31; monastic lifestyles, 89; mystical,
    25; mystics, 34, 187; perennial psychology,
    216; wakefulness in, 31, 34–35
chronic fatigue syndrome, 167
Chuang-tzu, 29
clarity, 127. *See also* awakening
cleaving to the divine (*devekut*), 33, 38
cognition, 43
Cohen, Andrew, 180
Cole, Thomas, 59
collective awakening, 251–68; concept of
    evolution, 253–54; crises, 264–65; cultural
    shifts, 257–60; evidence for evolutionary
    leaps, 255–57;
    impulse to awaken, 256; indigenous wake-
    fulness, 260–64; new world of wakefulness,
    267–68; types of awareness, 252–53; waking
    up in time, 265–67
collective spiritual awakening, 7
commonality of religions, 41–42
compassion, 39, 84–85, 193, 230
concentration, 43; Eightfold Path (Buddhism),
    78
conceptual awareness, 218, 252–53

confusion, 61–74, 158–63; misunderstanding of wakefulness, 162; and Peace Pilgrim, 159; temporary, 162; and Williams, Russel, 159, 160, 161

connectedness, 188, 192–93; to spirit source (children), 225

consciousness, 216, 252, x; localization of, 263

Constable, John, 59

contemporary spirituality, sudden awakening in, 142–45

Cordovero, Moses, 40

Cosmic Consciousness (Bucke), 48

creativity, 168; as children, 226

crises, spiritual, 157–74; and confusion, 158–63; differentiating psychosis and awakening, 171–74; difficult relationships, 163–64; health problems, 166–67; importance of understanding, 167–70, psychological disturbances, 164–66; Spiritual Crisis Network, 168; sudden awakening and psychosis, 170–71

cruel behavior, 181

cultural shifts, 257–60

cultures, wakefulness in different, 25–42

Cummings, E. E., 58

curiosity, 203–4

Dalai Lama, 170

Dante, 48

Dao De Jing, 30, 47; childlike qualities, 220; and Whitman, Walt, 53

Daoism, 25, 29; gradual awakening in, 81; meditation, 85–87; perennial psychology, 216; sexual energy (xing), 136, 137; spiritual energy, all-pervading, 187; temporary confusion, 162; wakefulness in, 29–30; Whyte, Gavin, 66; wu wei (actionless activity), 40

Darwin, Charles, 254. See also evolution

Dass, Ram, 152, 153

death, 16; fear of, 195–97; near-death experiences, 154; sudden awakening because of encounters with, 106, 112–22

deception (maya), 40

de-differentiation, 220

deification, 3

Deikman, Arthur, 86

deintensified perception, 17–18

demythologizing wakefulness, 235–50

depression, 99, 155; examples of sudden awakening during, 108–10; sudden awakening because of, 106

deprivation, sleep, 25

de Suso, Henry, 83

devekut (cleaving to the divine), 33, 38

development, wakefulness as end of, 238–39

dharmakaya, 28, 29

Dickens, Charles, 259

Dickinson, Emily, 58

difficult relationships, 163–64

disability, sudden awakening because of, 106

disconnection, sense of, 13–17

disruptions to psychological functioning, 130. See also turmoil

disturbance, sense of, 16

divine reading (lectio divina), 95

divinity, 31, devekut (cleaving to the divine), 33, 38; union of, 32

DMT (N,N-Dimethyltryptamine), 146, 153. See also psychedelics

Doblin, Rick, 152

dogs, 252

The Doors of Perception (Huxley), 151, 185

Dostoyevsky, Fyodor, 259

doubt, 159. See also spiritual crises

Dr. Feelgood (band), 114

duality, 40, 111

ecstasy, 148; "tied to a particular form" (savi-kalpa samadhi), 26

ego: -boundaries, shifts in, 151; -centrism, 260; children and, 225; definition of, 246; effort to wake up, 247; -identity, 189; -isolation, 14, 15, 31, 260; pre-egoic stage of development, 220; -separateness, lack of (in children), 227; sleep state as egocentric, 18. See also self-system

Eightfold Path (Buddhism), 78, 82, 141

eight-limbed path (Yoga Sutras), 79, 141

elsewhereness, state of, 15

Emerson, Ralph Waldo, 58, 177

empathy, 193

emptiness: inner, 38; state of (ming), 29, 38

energetic awakening, 129–39; energy and development, 138–39; examples of, 130–35; integration, 135; through sexual experiences, 136–37 energy: heightened, from awakening, 198; intensification and stilling of life-energy (ISLE), 198, 263

engagement, 204–5

enlightenment, 1, 3, 142; chemical, 146 (see also psychedelics); definition of, 10; middle ground of, 237–38

Enlightenment Ain't What It's Cracked Up to Be (Forman), 176

enlightenment (bodhi), 3, 10

En Sof (without end), 32, 36, 40

ethical behavior, 78, 82

evidence for evolutionary leaps, 255–57

evolution, x; concept of, 253–54; process of, 251

evolutionary leaps, 74, xi; collective awakening, 251–68; crises and, 264–65; cultural shifts and, 257–60; evidence for, 255–57; indigenous wakefulness, 260–64; new world of wakefulness, 267–68; types of awareness, 252–53; waking up in time, 265–67

exercise (physical), 168

exercises, Tantric, 180

experiential states, 158

The Fall (Taylor), 6; First Wave in, 36, 258; monotheistic religions in, 30; Second Wave in, 258; technological development of prehistoric peoples in, 261

fasting, 25

fatigue, 167

fear, 16; of death, 195–97

fibromyalgia, 167

First Wave, 258

Forman, Robert, 176, 177

fragilities, 20; need for belonging as, 19

fragmentedness, 14

freedom (moksha), 3

French Revolution, 258

Friedrich, Caspar David, 59, 185

fully realized being (arahant), 28

Gandhi, Mahatma, 51, 203

Garrie, John, 160

"Gladness of Death," 56

global interconnectivity, 264

goals, 247

God, 36, 48, 121; abiding in (baqa), 36; mystics' view of, 32; Peace Pilgrim and, 62;

perennial psychology, 216; presence of, 33, 34; spiritual energy, all-pervading, 187; union with, 34; as Universal Source of all life, ix. See also divinity

gods, concepts of, 30

Gopnik, Alison, 224

gradual awakening, 75–88, 158; common themes of, 82–87; ethical behavior and, 82; examples of, 90–93, 93–94; involuntary, 96–98; meditation and, 85–87; outside spiritual traditions, 87–88, 89–104; paths and practices of, 77–81; psychological attachments and, 98–101; purgation, 82–83; purification, 82–83; renunciation, 83–84; service, 84–85; spiritual crises, 158; spiritual literature as practice, 94–96; understanding, 101–4

Greek Neoplatonist philosophers, 214

Greenwell, Bonnie, 136

Greyson, Bruce, 130

Grof, Stanislav, 108, 149

group identities, 23, 200–201; sleep, 18–19

growth, posttraumatic, 105

Happold, F. C., 71, 95

harmony, 188

Harvard University, 152

Hasidism, 33, 34. See also Judaism

healing of the world (tikkun olam), 65

health problems, 166–67

heaven, 220

Heraclitus, 29

Hindu Advaita Vedanta (or nonduality) philosophy, 243

Hinduism, 1, 3, 27, 30; ethical behavior in, 82; gradual awakening in, 80; Krishna, 42; monastic lifestyles, 81; samskaras, 177

Hobbes, Thomas, 257

Hoffman, Edward, 224, 228

homeostasis disruption, 167

Homo sapiens, 251

Hood, Glyn, 116

Hui-Neng, 142

"The Human Race Will Rise Again" (Taylor), 269–70

Huxley, Aldous, 51, 54, 56, 151, 185

"Hymn to Intellectual Beauty" (Shelley), 58

Iamblichus, 148

identity: essential, x; group, 23; need for belonging, 18–19; sense of, 112; shifts, 86

illness, 106

immature wakefulness, 228–30

inactivity, enjoyment of, 205–6

Inarticulate Speech of the Heart (album; Morrison), 71

incomprehension, 161. *See also* confusion

India, 73; Dass, Ram, and, 152, 153; example of gradual awakening in, 90–93; wakefulness traditions in, 26–27, 78

indigenous peoples: deintensified perception, 17–18; sense of separation of, 14

indigenous wakefulness, 260–64

individuality, 46

individual self (*atman*), 27

influenza epidemic (1919), 56

information processing, 43

inner emptiness, 38

inner life, changes to, 189. *See also* new self (characteristics of awakening)

inner light, 37

inner quietness, 189–91

inner security, 198

inner stillness, 38

Inness, George, 59

insecurities, 16, 20

insomnia, 167

inspiration, 71

integration, 61–74, 111, 112; of energetic awakening, 135

intensification and stilling of life-energy (ISLE), 198

intensified perception, 184–86

interconnectivity, global, 264

"Intimations of Immortality" (Wordsworth), 58

involuntary gradual awakening, 96–98; psychological attachments and, 98–101. *See also* gradual awakening

inwardness, 230

irritation, 178

"I Sing the Body Electric" (Whitman), 244

Islam, 30; as conceptual religion, 31; wakefulness in, 31

James, William, 51

Jefferies, Richard, 57

Jeffers, Robinson, 58

Jesus Christ, 9, 30, 42, 48, 49, 220. *See also* Christianity

Jewish tradition. *See* Judaism

John of the Cross, 35

Johnson, Wilko, 114, 115

Judaism, 30; Ba'al Shem Tov, 256; as conceptual religion, 31; mystics, 187; perennial psychology, 216; service in, 85; wakefulness in, 31, 32–34

Kabbalah, 25, 32; and altruism, 33; concept of wakefulness, 40; gradual awakening in, 76; lifestyle guidelines, 81; and meditation, 33, 85–87; purgation and purification, 83; *tikkun olam* (the healing of the world), 65; union with God, 34; Zohar, 32, 33 (*see also* Kabbalah). *See also* Judaism

Kashmiri Shaivism, 54

Katie, Byron, 96

kensho (seeing into one's true nature), 142

Kilrea, Kelly, 182

kindness, 106

King, Martin Luther, Jr., 203

kleshas (unwholesome mental states), 175

Kohlberg, Lawrence, 229

Krishna, 42

kundalini awakening, 129–39, 165; energy and development, 138–39; integration, 135; sexual awakening experiences, 136–37

Lamartine, Alphonse de, 59

lantern consciousness, 224

Lawrence, D. H., 53–56, 57, 71, 73, 177, 242; boredom and, 205–6; intensified perception in, 185; natural wakefulness of, 61

laws, 229

Leary, Timothy, 146

Leaves of Grass (Whitman), 49

lectio divina (divine reading), 95

Lenski, Gerhard, 30

libido, 136, 137

life-energy, 198, 263

lifestyle guidelines, 77–81

life-threatening experiences, 113. *See also* death

"Lines Written a Few Miles above Tintern Abbey" (Wordsworth), 57–58

LSD, 75, 146, 147. *See also* psychedelics

Mac, JC, 110–12, 133, 139, 165, 166
Mahayana Buddhism, 28, 187. *See also* Buddhism
maintaining wakefulness, 236–37
Making Time (Taylor), 187
Marie de l'Incarnation, 35
Martin, Hugh, 114
Maslow, Abraham, 51, 52
materialism, 217, 260
mature wakefulness, 228–30, 234
maya (deception), 40
McKenna, Dennis, 152
The Meaning (Taylor), 47
meditation, 8, 25; beyond traditions, 87–88; Dass, Ram, 152, 153; gradual awakening, 85–87; Kabbalah, 33; Taylor, Steve, 70; temporary confusion, 162; transcending separateness of ego, 101; *Vipassana*, 86, 92
Meister Eckhart, 34, 35, 214, 256
memories: memory problems, 166; as thought-chatter, 15
mental illness, 8, 9, 164–66
metta bhavana (Buddhism), 85
Miller, Henry, 58
mind, 43. *See also* self-systems
ming (state of emptiness), 29, 38
miracles, 52
moksha (freedom), 3
monastic lifestyles, 76, 81, 83–84, 89
Monet, Claude, 59
monotheistic religions, wakefulness in, 30–42
morality, sense of, 202–3
Morrison, Van, 71
Moses, 48
Murry, John Middleton, 54
Murtha, William, 160, 161
mutations, 254
mystical Christianity, 25
mysticism, 199; nature, 221
Mysticism: A Study and Anthology (Happold), 71, 95
mystics, 35; Christian, 34; Christianity, 187; Jewish, 187; passive behavior, 240–42; Sufism, 187; view of God, 32. *See also specific mystics*
myths of wakefulness, 235–50

Nagel, Thomas, 154
"Name the Gods" (Lawrence), 55
narcissism, 181
National Secular Society, 151
natural disasters, 113
natural wakefulness: of artists, 43–59; of children, 219–34; confusion and integration, 61–74; evidence for evolutionary leaps, 255–56; Peace Pilgrim, 62–65; Taylor, Steve, 67–73; understanding, 73–74; Whyte, Gavin, 65–67
nature: attitudes toward, 14; deintensified perception, 17–18; mysticism, 221
near-death experiences, 41, 113, 154
negative thoughts, 178, 179
negativity: cruel behavior, 181; reactive, 177
new self (characteristics of awakening), 189–98
Nightingale, Florence, 241
nirvana (blowing out), 27
nirvikalpa samadhi (world of form disappears), 26, 36, 80
No Guru, No Method, No Teacher (album; Morrison), 71
nonmaterialism, 206–7
noosphere, 264
Norman, Mildred (Peace Pilgrim), 62–65, 73; confusion of, 159; renunciation by, 84
Not I, Not Other Than I (Williams), 125, 159–60

objects as sentient beings, 17, 18
On Cleaving to God, 34
oneness, 188, 192; *dharmakaya*, 28, 29; permanent/ongoing (*sahaja samadhi*), 3, 22, 27, 36, 38; sense of, 26
"On the Beach at Night, Alone" (Whitman), 51
ontogenetic development, 255
The Original Vision (Robinson), 226
Out of the Darkness (Taylor), 54, 56; awakening through bereavement, 116, 117; Murtha, William, 160, 161; posttraumatic transformation in, 114; psychological attachments, 98; transformation shifts, 105, 106, 107
The Outsider (Wilson), 71, 76

Pahnke, Walter, 152
pains (physical), 167
Parsons, Tony, 144

Patanjali, 29, 79
"Pax" (Lawrence), 55
Peace Pilgrim, 62–65, 73; confusion of, 159; renunciation by, 84
"peek experiences," 76
perception, deintensified, 17–18
perceptual awareness, 252–53
perennial psychology, 41–42, 213–16
permanent wakefulness, 6, 22, 23
physical problems, 166–67
Piaget, Jean, 229
Pissarro, Camille, 59
Plato, 29
Plotinus, 214
posttraumatic growth, 105
posttraumatic stress disorder (PTSD), 99
posttraumatic transformation, 114, 122–23
Practicing the Power of Now (Tolle), 96
pranotthana (Tantra), 226
pre-egoic stage of development, 220
prehistoric human beings: intensified perception of, 17–18; sense of separation of, 14
presence: awareness of, 187–88; children and, 225
primary shift, 150–53
psychedelics, 25, 75; examples of, 149–50, 151; and primary and secondary shifts, 150–53; sudden awakening through, 141–56, 146–50
psychological attachments, 98–101
psychological disturbances, 164–66
psychological turmoil, 8, 257. *See also* turmoil
psychosis, 170–74
purgation, 82–83
purification, 82–83

quietness, inner, 189–91

The Rainbow (Lawrence), 55
Ramakrishna, 181, 201
Ramana Maharshi, 37, 181, 243
reactive negativity, 177
reality, awareness of, 40, 218
reflections as thought-chatter, 15
Reiki, 167
reincarnation, 28
relationships: authenticity, living with, 209–10; difficult, 163–64

religions: commonality of, 41–42; group identities and, 18, 19; influence of, 90; wakefulness in monotheistic, 30–42. *See also specific religions*
Renoir, Pierre-Auguste, 59
renunciation, 83–84, 96
right conduct (*sila*), 180
Rilke, Rainer Maria, 59
Roberts, Bernadette, 157, 236
Robinson, Edward, 226, 228
Romantic movement, 258
Royal College of Psychiatry, 170
Rumi, 95

Sabom, Michael, 113
sacredness, 30, 31
sahaja samadhi (permanent or ongoing oneness), 3, 22, 27, 36, 38
sahasrara (crown chakra), 80
samskaras, 177
Sankara, 243, 256
Sartre, Jean-Paul, 217
satchitananda (being-consciousness-bliss), 37
savikalpa samadhi (ecstasy tied to a particular form), 26
savikalpa (temporary awakening), 26
secondary shift, 150–53
Second Wave (*The Fall*), 258
security, inner, 198
Selected Poems (Lawrence), 71
self-acceptance, 61
self-awareness, 61, 252
self-confidence, 72
self-discipline, 76, 82–83
selfishness, 217
self-loathing, 34
self-sacrifice, 23
self-sufficiency, 39
self-system, 21, 101; boundaries of, 147; lack of (in children), 226; meditation and, 86; myths of wakefulness and, 245; wakefulness and, 43–45; wakefulness before and after, 231–32
sentient beings, objects as, 17, 18
separation: sense of, 13–17, 23, 28, 40, 46; transcendence of, 192–93
service, 84–85

sexual awakening experiences, 136–37
sexual energy (*xing*), 136, 137
Shantideva, 40
Shelley, Percy, 58
shifts: cultural, 257–60; due to near-death ex-
    periences, 113; primary, 150–53; secondary,
    150–53; into state of wakefulness, 105, 106
    (*see also* turmoil); and Williams, Russel,
    159, 160, 161. *See also* transformation
shifts, identity, 86
sila (right conduct), 180
sleep, 236; abstraction, 15–16; anxiety, 16; char-
    acteristics of, 13–17, 18–20; deprivation,
    25; discontentment, 16; egocentric outlook
    of, 18; as escape from suffering, 25; group
    identities and, 18–19; and temporary wake-
    fulness, 20–24; thought-chatter, 15
sleeplessness, 167
"Snake-Simile Discourse" (Buddhism), 28
social rules, 229
"Song of Myself" (Whitman), 50–51, 52, 53, 71
Source, ix
spirit-force (*brahman*), 27, 29, 36, 37, 44, 51,
    80, 188; Lawrence, D. H., 55; Taylor, Steve,
    71, 72; well-being, 195; Whitman, Walt, 53;
    Wordsworth, William, 57
spiritual awakening: collective, 7; Peace Pil-
    grim, 62–65; Taylor, Steve, 67–73; types of,
    1–3; Whyte, Gavin, 65–67
spiritual crises, 157–74; confusion, 158–63;
    difficult relationships, 163–64; health prob-
    lems, 166–67; importance of understanding,
    167–70; psychological disturbances, 164–66;
    sudden awakening and psychosis, 170–74
Spiritual Crisis Network, 168, 169
spiritual emergence, 108. *See also* sudden
    awakening
Spiritual Emergence Network, 168
spiritual emergencies, 121; examples of, 108–12
spiritual energy, all-pervading, 187–88
spirituality: contemporary, 142–45; reasons to
    adopt, 76; traditional, 141–42
Spirituality and Psychiatry Special Interest
    Group, 170
spiritual literature as practice, 94–96
spiritual paths: Eightfold Path (Buddhism), 78;
    eight-limbed path (Yoga Sutras), 79, 141;
    gradual awakening, 77–81

spiritual practices: of gradual awakening,
    77–81; meditation, 85–87; spiritual literature
    as, 94–96
spiritual teachers, 175–82
spiritual traditions, 26; children and, 219–20;
    gradual awakening in, 75–88, 76; gradual
    awakening outside, 87–88, 89–104; sudden
    awakening in, 141–42. *See also specific
    religions*
Stace, Walter, 199
Steps Toward Inner Peace (Peace Pilgrim), 63,
    64
Stew, Graham, 116, 117
The Story of My Heart (Jefferies), 57
stress, awakening because of, 106, 130–35
subjective awareness, 252–53
sudden awakening, 24, 157; because of bereave-
    ment, 106, 115–22; because of encounters
    with death, 106, 112–22; and cancer, 114–15;
    in contemporary spirituality, 142–45; energy
    and development, 138–39; examples of,
    108–12, 126, 130–35; integration of, 135;
    kundalini awakening, 129–39; posttraumatic
    transformation, 122–23; primary and sec-
    ondary shifts, 150–53; and psychosis, 170–71;
    sexual awakening experiences, 136–37; spiri-
    tual crises, 158; spiritual emergencies, 107–12;
    through psychedelics, 146–50; in traditional
    spirituality, 141–42; transformation through
    turmoil, 105–27; who it happens to, 123–25
suffering: Buddhist concept of, 28; sleep as
    escape from, 25
Sufism, 3, 25; Al-Ghazali, 40; Al-Hallaj,
    Mansur, 32; gradual awakening in, 76;
    meditation, 85–87; mystics, 187; perennial
    psychology, 216; service, 85; wakefulness in,
    35–36. *See also* Islam
support, importance of, 167–70
Supreme Spirit, 37
Sutras (Yoga), 79
Suzuki, D. T., 28, 142

Tantra, 26; exercises, 180; *kundalini* awakening,
    129–39; *pranotthana*, 226; *Vijnanabhairav-
    atantra*, 130
Tao Te Ching, 30, 47; childlike qualities, 220;
    Whitman, Walt, 53
Taylor, Steve, 67–73, xi, xii

technology: sudden awakening through, 141–56; technological wakefulness, 153–56

Teilhard de Chardin, Pierre, 264

temporary awakening, 20–24, 136; during childhood, 221–22; evidence for evolutionary leaps, 256; experiences, 6; with psychedelics, 146; *savikalpa*, 26

temporary confusion, 162

Teresa of Avila, 35

Thailand, 73

Theravada Buddhism, 27, 36. *See also* Buddhism

Thoreau, Henry David, 49, 58, 177

thought-chatter: children and, 224–25; sleep, 15

thought-mind, 190

timelessness, 186–87

Tolle, Eckhart, 96, 121, 133, 170; and inner quietness, 189; irritation in, 178

"To One Shortly to Die" (Whitman), 52

traditional spirituality, sudden awakening in, 141–42

Traherne, Thomas, 219

transcendence of separation, 192–93

Transcendental Meditation (TM), 70, 87, 176

transformation, 177, difficult relationships because of, 163–64; posttraumatic, 114, 122–23; spiritual emergencies, 107–12; sudden awakening, 125–27; through turmoil, 105–27

trauma, 106; posttraumatic transformation, 114, 122–23; spiritual awakening as cause of, 2. *See also* turmoil

Trungpa, Chogyam, 247

turmoil, x; awakening through psychological, 257; examples of energetic awakening, 130–35; spiritual awakening as cause of, 2, 8; spiritual emergencies, 107–12; transformation through, 105–27

Turner, William, 59; intensified perception, 185

Tutu, Desmond, 203

Udana, 78. *See also* Buddhism

Underhill, Evelyn, 34, 35, 48, 199

understanding, importance of, 167–70

union, 38

unity, 24

universal outlooks, 202

Universal Source, ix

unwholesome mental states (*kleshas*), 175

Upanishads, 26, 39, 47; and spiritual crises, 157; and Whitman, Walt, 53. *See also brahman* (spirit-force)

van Gogh, Vincent, 59

van Lommel, Pim, 113

Vedanta, 25, 41

Vijnanabhairavatantra (Tantric text), 130

Vipassana meditation, 86, 92

vital energy (*chi*), 81

Vivekananda, 181

von Hocheim, Eckhart, 34, 35, 214, 256

vulnerabilities, 16, 20; need for belonging as, 19

Wade, Jenny, 137

wakefulness, 5; before and after the self-system, 231–32; bliss and, 239–40; Buddhist concepts of, 27–28; characteristics of, 18–19, 36–41, 183–98; in Christianity, 31, 34–35; in Daoism, 29–30; definition of, 10, 11; deintensified perception, 17–18; demythologizing, 235–50; detachment/indifference to world affairs, 240; in different cultures, 25–42; different intensities of, 210–11; doubt, 159; efforts toward, 247–49; as end of development, 238–39; evidence for evolutionary leaps, 255–56; gradual awakening, 75–88; immature, 228–30; improper behavior and, 240; in Indian traditions, 26–27; indigenous, 260–64; inventory of, 273–74; in Islam, 31; in Judaism, 31, 32–34; maintaining, 236–37; mature, 228–30, 234; meaningfulness of, 199–218; metacharacteristics of, 211–13; middle ground of enlightenment, 237–38; misunderstanding of, 162; in monotheistic religions, 30–42; natural, 43–59 (*see also* natural wakefulness); new self, 189–98; new world of, 267–68; passive behavior, 240–42; perceptual characteristics of, 184–88; perceptual, of children, 222–25; perennial psychology, 213–16; permanent, 6, 22, 23; self-systems, 43–45; shifts into state of, 105, 106 (*see also* turmoil); spiritual crises, 157–74; state of waking up, 13–24; in Sufism, 35–36; technology, 153–56; temporary, 20–24, 136; traditions in India, 78; wakeful vision of the world, 216–18; world as an illusion, 242–44

Waking from Sleep (Taylor), 6, 10, 70; homeostasis disruption, 167; perceptual wakefulness of children, 224; psychedelics, 146;
temporary wakefulness, 21, 136
warfare, 7
well-being, 194–95
"Whispers of Heavenly Death" (Whitman) 58
Whitman, Walt, 37, 48–53, 57, 58, 59, 71, 73,
95, 244; intensified perception, 185; natural
wakefulness, 61
Whyte, Gavin, 65–67
wide perspectives (universal outlooks), 202
Wilber, Ken, 76, 79, 220
Williams, Russel, 97, 125, 145; awakening
of, 163; confusion of, 159, 160, 161; inner
quietness of, 189
Wilson, Colin, 71, 76
wisdom, Eightfold Path (Buddhism), 78
women, oppression of, 7
Women in Love (Lawrence), 55
Women's International League for Peace and
Freedom, 63

Wordsworth, William, 52, 57, 59, 241; childhood of, 219; intensified perception of, 185;
nature mysticism, 221
World War I, 56
World War II, 63, 126, 260
wu wei (actionless activity), 40

xing (sexual energy), 136, 137

Yoga, 26; eight-limbed path, 141; *kundalini*
awakening, 129–39; meditation, 85–87;
Patanjali, 29; purgation and purification, 83;
Sutras, 79
Yogi, Maharishi Mahesh, 87

Zen Buddhism, 28, 66, 141, 142, 144. *See also*
Buddhism
Zohar, 32, 33, 34, 37
Zola, Emile, 259

About the Author

S teve Taylor, PhD, is the author of several books on spirituality and psychology, including *The Fall* and *Waking from Sleep*. He has also published two books of poetic spiritual reflections, including *The Calm Center*. He is a senior lecturer in psychology at Leeds Beckett University in the United Kingdom. Since 2011, he has appeared annually in *Mind, Body, Spirit* magazine's list of "the world's 100 most spiritually influential living people." Visit his website at www.stevenmtaylor.com.

About Eckhart Tolle Editions

Eckhart Tolle Editions was launched in 2015 to publish life-changing works, both old and new, that have been personally selected by Eckhart Tolle. This imprint of New World Library presents books that can powerfully aid in transforming consciousness and awakening readers to a life of purpose and presence.

Learn more about Eckhart Tolle at

www.eckharttolle.com

NEW WORLD LIBRARY is dedicated to publishing books and other media that inspire and challenge us to improve the quality of our lives and the world.

We are a socially and environmentally aware company. We recognize that we have an ethical responsibility to our customers, our staff members, and our planet.

We serve our customers by creating the finest publications possible on personal growth, creativity, spirituality, wellness, and other areas of emerging importance. We serve New World Library employees with generous benefits, significant profit sharing, and constant encouragement to pursue their most expansive dreams.

As a member of the Green Press Initiative, we print an increasing number of books with soy-based ink on 100 percent postconsumer-waste recycled paper. Also, we power our offices with solar energy and contribute to non-profit organizations working to make the world a better place for us all.

Our products are available in bookstores everywhere.

www.newworldlibrary.co

At NewWorldLibrary.com you can downlo
subscribe to our e-newsletter, read
and link to authors' websites, videos, ar

Find us on Facebook, follow us on Twitter, and w

Send your questions and comments
You make it possible for us to do what w

Phone: 415-884-2100 or 800-972-6657
Catalog requests: Ext. 10 | Orders: Ext. 10 | Fax: 415-884-2199
escort@newworldlibrary.com

NEW WORLD LIBRARY
publishing books that change lives   14 Pamaron Way, Novato, CA 94949